Stating the Family

Stating the Family

New Directions in the Study
of American Politics

Edited by

Julie Novkov

and

Carol Nackenoff

University Press of Kansas

Published by the University Press of Kansas (Lawrence, Kansas 66045),
which was organized by the Kansas Board of Regents and is operated and
funded by Emporia State University, Fort Hays State University, Kansas State
University, Pittsburg State University, the University of Kansas, and Wichita
State University

Library of Congress Cataloging-in-Publication Data

Names: Novkov, Julie, 1966– editor. | Nackenoff, Carol, editor.
Title: Stating the family : new directions in the study of American politics /
edited by Julie Novkov and Carol Nackenoff.
Description: Lawrence, Kansas : University Press of Kansas, [2020] | Includes
bibliographical references and index.
Identifiers: LCCN 2019038625 (print) | LCCN 2019038626 (ebook)
  ISBN 9780700629220 (cloth)
  ISBN 9780700629237 (paperback)
  ISBN 9780700629244 (epub)
Subjects: LCSH: Families—Political aspects—United States. | Marriage—
Political aspects—United States. | Family policy—United States. |
Neoliberalism—United States. | United States—Social policy. | United
States—Politics and government.
Classification: LCC HQ536 .S7245 2020 (print) | LCC HQ536 (ebook) |
DDC 306.850973—dc23
LC record available at https://lccn.loc.gov/2019038625.
LC ebook record available at https://lccn.loc.gov/2019038626.

British Library Cataloguing-in-Publication Data is available.

Printed in the United States of America

10 9 8 7 6 5 4 3 2 1

The paper used in this publication is recycled and contains 30 percent
postconsumer waste. It is acid free and meets the minimum requirements
of the American National Standard for Permanence of Paper for Printed
Library Materials Z39.48-1992.

Contents

Foreword
Responsibility for the Well-Being of Families

Joan C. Tronto

Imagine a democratic political order that was fully committed to the well-being of its citizens. In such a democracy, citizens would feel that, despite their differences, they trusted that the governments they elected functioned well and were responsive to the needs of the people. They would live lives in which they understood their roles as citizens and participated in public life. Citizens would also feel free: they would live according to their own ideals of what made life most meaningful. In such a democracy, many institutions in addition to a proper political constitution would need to contribute to citizens' well-being. This book helps us to explore this question: What roles should *families* play to help achieve such well-being?

Family seems to be of fundamental importance to Americans. In a recent open-ended survey, the Pew Research Center asked Americans to name what gave meaning to their lives. The single response that garnered the most support was "family"; 63 percent believed that family gave their lives meaning.[1] But what does that response mean? Is it not surprising that slightly more than one-third of Americans did *not* say that family gave their lives meaning? Perhaps this is just a demographic matter. Around 28 percent of households in the United States consist of a single person; perhaps they are the ones who overlooked the importance of family in the Pew survey.[2] Or, perhaps some of the people who did not say "family" have had difficult family experiences: abuse, conflict, unmet expectations. Or, perhaps, given the ways in which we associate freedom with "choice," their families created necessities (for example, to help care for a disabled sibling or aging parent, or to contribute their income to other family members) that they associated with a loss of choice. Whether families provide meaning or thwart attempts to achieve it, they have a profound influence on people's lives and on the lives of people as citizens.

As Julie Novkov and Carol Nackenoff make clear in the Introduction, American political scientists do not spend much time thinking about the family. But its political significance is hiding in plain sight. It is true that the United States has a much less coherent family policy than do other high-income countries, and that political scientists' focus on individual behavior makes family less visible. But there are very high stakes if we avoid studying the family politically. In the first place, the family is one of the most basic institutions among human communities; indeed, it is found as a fundamental form in virtually all cultures and is named a human right in the Universal Declaration of Human Rights.[3] It is so fundamental that for many, it appears to be natural. And while it is true that all human communities seem to have some form of family, even historical changes in recent decades in the United States make clear that no single form of family is entirely natural, and that political life has an impact on what shape families take and what functions they perform in society. Families, in turn, play a large part in politics, whether this influence is acknowledged or not.

Families are institutions that play political, social, economic, cultural, and religious roles in human societies. From a theoretical perspective, then, one of the more interesting questions to ask is: how well does this institution fulfill its purpose? Of course, this question also relies upon highly contested ideas about the family's purpose and whether economic, social, political, religious, or other purposes are more or less important. As if those issues were not complicated enough, a related question we can ask of any institution is whether and how it might become corrupt, using "corruption" in its original sense of being taken away from its purposes.[4] One way to read the chapters in this book is to see them as taking on that question, in multiple ways.

Another and more specific kind of reading is also possible. In a democratic society in which the terms of democracy are increasingly contested, what does it mean to think of the family as a *democratic* institution? In Chapter 1 in this volume, June Carbone and Naomi Cahn demonstrate how "the family" is a source of disagreement between "red" and "blue" ways of thinking in contemporary American ideologies. But the place of family in democracies is as old as discussions of democracies themselves. To take the Western tradition, both Plato and Aristotle recognized that familial dissatisfaction could wreak havoc on political order (consider, e.g., the role of family members in the decline of the state in the *Republic*), or provide the basis of social stability.

As one of the great observers of democratic life, Alexis de Tocqueville had a sophisticated understanding of the positive and potentially harmful effects of the family on political life.[5] On the one hand, he saw the family as the proper container of women's activities and he followed the long-standing tradition of republican motherhood in emphasizing how children raised properly were necessarily better citizens.[6] On the other hand, he was deeply concerned about the disappearance of public space[7] and the growth of "individualism," which he defined as "a reflective and tranquil sentiment that disposes each citizen to cut himself [*sic*] off from the mass of his fellow men and withdraw into the circle of family and friends, so that, having created a little society for his own use, he gladly leaves the larger society to take care of itself."[8] When family becomes all, when it becomes, in Christopher Lasch's famous phrase, a "haven in a heartless world," then Tocqueville feared that the conditions of democratic equality could be undermined.[9] The family's success, ironically, could become the source of its corruption as an institution linked to democratic life. If people (for Tocqueville, male heads of households) became too attached to family, then their interest in the political life of their community could weaken. Thus, not only should we raise the question about the well-being of families for the sake of families, but also for the sake of democratic political life.

Since the time when Tocqueville observed family life almost two centuries ago, many more institutions have emerged in modern life. Most importantly, economic productivity now occurs outside the household. Already by the time Tocqueville was writing, the household was ceasing to be the main unit of economic production.[10] As the means for economic survival became more deeply intertwined with the fate of other institutions, such as factories, markets, commercial and later industrial farms, and schools, so too the regulation of those institutions began to affect family life. While most care had been provided in families, by the turn of the twentieth century new institutions, including hospitals and nursing homes, schools and police departments, corporations, and complex financial institutions, began to employ social workers, schoolteachers, clerks, typewriters, police, among many others. Gradually, these institutions shaped an economy where people mostly came to rely on sources outside the family to meet the basic needs of birth, death, and the activities of life between them.[11]

That families are deeply affected by changes in the political economy over time seems an obvious point. But the nature of those changes is neither simple nor driven only by economic considerations. Some families are always doing better than other families. As Mignon Duffy observes, as forms of care became outsourced from the family, nurturant caring roles were most often taken up by white female professionals, while women and men of color and migrants were stuck with non-nurturant, "dirty work" care.

Obviously, both conscious political actions, such as struggles for a "family wage" at the turn of the twentieth century, and less consciously directed structural factors, such as de-industrialization in the last quarter of the twentieth century, have influenced how the family has fared. Much of the postwar economic boom in the United States depended upon increased consumer spending: families went from being units of economic production to also being units of economic consumption. The enormous growth of consumption became an engine of economic growth. As manufacturing jobs dwindled, families continued to support economic activity through consumption. Yet with higher standards of living, it also became more expensive for families to raise children. Families shrank. Demographic changes occurred, but political scientists did not think how these changes affected other institutions and how society functions. Who will take up caring for the elderly as the population ages? Such questions come to the fore only when society considers the centrality of the family as an institution, and not just in moralistic and sentimental ways.

Another serious change is also occurring at present. As work becomes more precarious, the idea that a job will provide the financial stability necessary to keep a family together also is sinking. As a result, the numbers of children born outside traditional marriages, as well as more diverse and less stable family forms, are on the increase. Current realities about which families flourish and which ones do not, can be summarized this way: well-financed families are stable while other families are not. As June Carbone and Naomi Cahn put it, "Marriage, once universal, once the subject of rebellion, has emerged as a marker of the new class lines remaking American society. Stable unions have become a hallmark of privilege."[12]

Discursively, the focus on the family as a financial institution requires that people think of their relationships, and their relationships with their children, as investments.[13] What becomes of the family under such conditions? In *Affective Equality*, Kathleen Lynch offers the simple proposition that the real basis of family policy should be to support families to allow them, in their plurality, to care for their members.[14] Everyone deserves, she argues, to be able to care adequately for their loved ones and to receive such care. But if families become the site of investment, understood in financial terms, this is a dismaying development. After all, no one would argue that care offers a good "return on investment" in monetary terms.

Perhaps this situation will provide the basis for a rethinking of who is responsible for the well-being of families. What is clear from the current economic recovery is that while formal unemployment rates are dropping, many families are still struggling; in Minnesota, for example, though the unemployment rate is below 3 percent, roughly one-fifth of people qualify for subsidized health care.[15] For a long time, state support has focused on providing opportunities for household heads to obtain good jobs. What has become clear now is that the state is going to have to support families more directly in their caring functions. Such a focus will require new ways of thinking politically. As many of the chapters in this volume suggest, the United States has not always been so welcoming to diverse forms of family, often using the policing of families as a way to accomplish other political ends. Political scientists who want to think ahead about the nature of democratic life will do well to consider these issues now.

To return to the original question of this foreword, then, who is responsible for the well-being of families in the United States? We will know that we are living up to the promise of supporting democratic citizens when we can answer that question.

Notes

1. Pew Research Center, "Where Americans Find Meaning in Life," November 20, 2018, https://www.pewforum.org/2018/11/20/where-americans -find-meaning-in-life/.

2. U.S. Census Bureau, "U.S. Census Bureau Releases 2018 Families and Living Arrangements Tables," Press release no. CB18-TPS.54, November 14, 2018, https://www.census.gov/newsroom/press-releases/2018/families.html.

3. Article 16 of the *Universal Declaration of Human Rights:*

(1) Men and women of full age, without any limitation due to race, nationality or religion, have the right to marry and to found a family. They are entitled to equal rights as to marriage, during marriage and at its dissolution.

(2) Marriage shall be entered into only with the free and full consent of the intending spouses.

(3) The family is the natural and fundamental group unit of society and is entitled to protection by society and the State.

4. I draw upon Peter Levine, *We Are the Ones We Have Been Waiting For: The Promise of Civic Renewal in America* (New York: Oxford University Press, 2015), for this account of corruption.

5. Alexis de Tocqueville, *Democracy in America,* translated by Arthur Goldhammer (New York: Library of America, 2004).

6. Leonie Huddy, "The Group Foundations of Democratic Political Behavior," *Critical Review* 30, nos. 1–2: 71–86, doi: 10.1080/08913811.2018.1466857.

7. Sheldon S. Wolin, *Tocqueville Between Two Worlds: The Making of a Political and Theoretical Life* (Princeton, NJ: Princeton University Press, 2003).

8. Tocqueville, *Democracy in America,* 585.

9. Christopher Lasch, *Haven in a Heartless World: The Family Besieged* (New York: W. W. Norton, 1995).

10. Stephen Leonard and Joan C. Tronto, "The Genders of Citizenship," *American Political Science Review* 101, no. 1 (2007): 33–46.

11. Mignon Duffy, *Making Care Count: A Century of Gender, Race, and Paid Care Work* (New Brunswick, NJ: Rutgers University Press, 2011), chaps. 2–3.

12. June Carbone and Naomi Cahn, *Marriage Markets: How Inequality Is Remaking the American Family* (New York: Oxford University Press, 2014), 19.

13. Shelly Lundberg and Robert A. Pollak, "The Evolving Role of Marriage: 1950–2010," *The Future of Children* 25, no. 2 (2015): 29–50.

14. Kathleen Lynch, *Affective Equality: Love, Care and Injustice* (London: Palgrave, 2009). Similar arguments are made in this volume, drawing upon the work of Maxine Eichner, *The Supportive State: Families, Government, and America's Political Ideals* (New York: Oxford University Press, 2010), and Martha Albertson Fineman, *The Autonomy Myth: A Theory of Dependency* (New York: New Press, 2004).

15. Glenn Howatt, "Minnesota Has Plenty of Jobs, But Health Insurance? No." *Star Tribune,* December 17, 2018.

Introduction

Stated Families, Family Stakes: The Family, the American State, and Political Development

Julie Novkov and Carol Nackenoff

The family plays a key role in politics, public policy, and political development in the United States. It also figures centrally in public rhetoric. The 2016 Democratic Party platform made no fewer than sixty-eight mentions of family or families—even more than the Republican Party platform's forty-eight.[1] The family is also an evolving partisan institution; there is evidence of the emergence of distinct family ideologies in each of the two major parties.[2] Views about families map onto liberal and conservative views about the role of government in society more generally, and sometimes help cement the loyalties of some groups to particular parties.[3] In its interactions with the state, the family functions as a status, an ordering mechanism, a distributor of goods and services, a site of citizen-making, and an object of regulation and management. As a focus of law, politics, and policy, the family mobilizes civic action and provokes sharp disagreements in both normative and practical registers. Its state-associated functions are of public importance and warrant public intervention and ordering, but the family also operates to render certain kinds of actions and relationships as private or autonomous, shielding them from state scrutiny and the reach of policy.

This volume contributes to a deeper understanding of politics and institutions by placing family centrally in the analysis. As a focus of political struggle, a site for the implementation of policy, a mechanism for distributing governmental goods, a fundamental unit of the state, and a means of defining individuals' relationships with the state and with each other, family does a great deal of political work. Considering this work in a sustained fashion across several of its dimensions strengthens both understandings of politics and policy and of family itself. It also helps to elucidate the role of family as both a state institution and an institution that stands to some degree independent from, and even in contention with, state actors and state policies.

The authors in this volume span disciplinary boundaries, reflecting political and legal theory as well as political science and historically inclined analysis, but reinforce related themes. A conversation across common themes is already underway, and we hope to deepen it here. A panel we put together at the Western Political Science Association (WPSA) meetings in 2015 on this theme was invited to develop a symposium issue of *Polity*,[4] and we organized a follow up conference-within-a-conference on the same subject at the WPSA meetings in spring 2016. The chapters we have invited reflect the fruits of ongoing conversations about family and the work it does, as well as its significance in state-building. This collection also reflects our growing concern about how the contemporary regulation of family reinforces and reproduces neo-liberal agendas, along with our recognition of the work that family may do at the margins to press state policies and actors to adopt more inclusive and egalitarian agendas.

Bringing together a group of leading scholars who have engaged this work in different areas, the volume contributes a broad and multifaceted account of the work that family does to structure politics. This account illustrates the relationship between family and politics, but it does more. Tracing the understanding of family as a political institution raises questions about political matters that affect topics and people often left outside the mainstream of political science. The family, it turns out, is crucially important for discussions of migration, sexual and gendered identity, inequality, how status conditions citizenship, and the boundary between private and public. Ambitions to regulate family ties and to use family as a tool for policy often coalesce around critical questions of belonging in American politics.

What Is Family, and Why Is Its Relationship to Politics Important?

The concept of family itself has multiple dimensions that demand different tools and frameworks for analysis. Most closely related to politics is family as a legally defined set of relationships that imply duties of care and responsibility within its boundaries, state support for these duties and relationships in some regard, and state forbearance in other regard to protect intimacy and privacy. The political analysis of family also requires recognition of its functional aspects, acknowledging both the tasks that family performs for civil society and the state, and the extraction of recognition of relationships as familial when the individuals involved are behaving as a family. Social definitions of family rely on broader acknowledgments of family within a community, which may be based in the perceived natural character of the relationships. Finally, we encourage more attention to the institutional aspects of family— how it operates as a mechanism for ordering work and benefits. While feminist historians, legal scholars, political theorists, and sociologists have touched on many of these themes, this volume links these questions directly to political institutions, structures, and processes, delving deeply into how the politics of family translates into policy, and how policies around families shape other critical political decisions and institutions.

We do not mean to imply that scholars have ignored the many formal policies in the United States that define, regulate, and implicate family. Since the colonies became states, common law and statutory law have defined and regulated marriage, divorce, parenthood, permissible sexual intimacy, and the duties and privileges associated with these relationships. Historians have traced how family law has changed on the state level over time.[5] While federal law initially had few points of direct tangency with families, Congress, the federal courts, and the executive branch have increasingly become involved in determining family status for the provision of benefits, setting constitutional minima for state regulation of familial relationships, and actively conditioning eligibility for government largesse on family status.[6]

Because of the policy-based implications, definitions of family have high stakes, and thus have invited state interest and debate. To the extent that an individual is understood as a family member, status, benefits, and responsibilities may flow from this understanding. As several of the chapters in this volume illustrate, following the insights of historian Peggy Pascoe, definitions of family, while institutionally, legally, and socially constructed, are often presented in state institutional contexts as natural. When family is understood as a natural set of relationships that the state merely confirms and recognizes, law intervenes only to confirm that some constructed relationships can fulfill the same purposes as natural, pre-political ones or to identify those relationships that go against or threaten nature.

The chapters in this volume reject the concept of family as natural and pre-political, instead exploring it as an entity that is constructed and reconstructed, and examining its relationship to liberal and neoliberal political institutions. Some authors analyze the work that arguments about nature perform in reinforcing ideological constructs. Some of the authors also highlight how policy changes may have unintended consequences that disrupt families or create new kinds of political constituencies connected to familial identities or roles, constituencies that may come to understand themselves as bound by natural roles. All of our authors, though, recognize that family definition, family forms, public and private dimensions of family, and the rights and responsibilities of family members have varied with changes in the state and in state agendas. The purposes for which the state has regulated and supported the family are important objects of inquiry. One agenda of this volume is to illustrate that individuals seeking to mobilize state regulation of families often incorporate normative and naturalized understandings of family and its work.[7]

Despite the political implications of all these aspects of family, political science and mainstream scholarship in associated disciplines have often shunted it, and the institutions and policy areas it shapes most directly, to the side as of only parochial or partial interest. Patricia Strach asks: "If politics is truly separate from family, why has family played such a prominent role in political practice?"[8] Only women (and tenured ones at that, often feminist theorists) are left to examine its importance. We claim that the absence of the family as a recognized institution, and as an object of investigation in political science, is related to unexamined but all-too-common assumptions that the family exists only in the private sphere and therefore is not political, is not a means through which the state acts and achieves policy goals, is not a target of state action, and is not shaped by the state—or if it is, its interactions with the state are intrinsically uninteresting and sealed off from other policy problems. Even when it is acknowledged to have some political salience, it is often reduced to a mere variable like marital or parental status, not directly confronted as a structuring and structured political institution.

Its absence as a focus of analysis has created blind spots that distort our understanding of politics and policy. A 2019 keyword search in the *American Political Science Review*, the leading journal for the discipline of political science, produces 124 results for "family." "Mothers" produces thirty-two.[9] Important issues routinely discussed without any consideration of families include tax policy, the politics of American entitlement and welfare programs, immigration policy, partisanship, and politics. If Americans are unaware of the government benefits they receive because of the way policies are designed in "the submerged state,"[10] political scientists seem unaware of the way families are enlisted in delivery of numerous policy goals.

However, since the early 2000s, a group of scholars have developed projects that speak to the relationship among the family, the state, and American political development, showing how this relationship has shaped families, governmental policies, and the American state and how families are deployed in service to public purposes. Moving out of the realm of political theory, these writers consider how, in concrete terms, family affects the state and the state affects—and even constitutes—families.[11] The family does not exist in a protected realm that the state cannot enter.[12] And the state does not practice "family values" as a matter of course, political rhetoric to the contrary. At times, policy makers intervene in the family to produce particular outcomes, while at other times, the intersection of family with the world of law and policy produces unintended effects that nonetheless have political implications. State interventions furthermore bear differing relationships to the care work that family performs: defining and formalizing its allocation, supporting particular manifestations of it, supporting it for some families, and undercutting or denying it for others.[13]

This emerging literature builds on considerations of family from other disciplinary perspectives. Historians, sociologists, cultural anthropologists, and feminist philosophers have explored different facets of family's role in structuring legal, cultural, economic, and social interactions. These considerations have illuminated the multiple ways that family operates as an ordering institution, but they raise significant questions about how the political aspects of family interact with state institutions, and how the state-managed aspects of family perform political functions.

The Political Work That Family Does

The chapters in this volume all address aspects of the family's relationship to politics, providing exemplars for how this relationship can be analyzed and what can be gained by considering it. We contend that understanding this relationship reveals powerful aspects of politics and political development that have not received sufficient attention or analysis. The failure to recognize family as a driver or a target of political action and political development impoverishes our understanding of both politics and the family. Recognizing these connections and developing explanations for how they work on the ground both contributes to better understanding and enables criticism and positive theorizing about needed change.

The authors in this volume conduct concrete case studies to make normative claims about neoliberalism and the family's role in managing its implications, the provision and withholding of benefits on the basis of family status, ideological clashes over family that activate partisan and political interests, and the political and policy-oriented connections between migration and family. These studies bring into focus how orderings that appear natural and pre-political are actually politically constructed, embedded in the state, and subject to contestation. The structuring of political contestation around family complicates policy debate by shifting the ways that engagement occurs, rendering some elements of the contest less visible or naturalized. This has the effect of hiding some political choices or rendering them less vulnerable to criticism as political choices. Understanding the political nature of family itself and its role as a political institution opens all aspects of these debates to interpretive analysis. It also encourages more attention to the ways in which the state uses the institution of the family as an instrument through which to accomplish particular policy goals, including housing policy, welfare policy, and immigration policy.[14]

One major theme in this volume is the family's role in neoliberal projects, including how family structures and responsibilities are changing in response to neoliberal policies. As Margaret Somers observed in 2008, the rapid growth of market power has disrupted the balance of power among state, market, and citizens in civil society. This shift has caused "the risks and costs of managing human frailties under capitalism once shouldered by government and corporations [to] get displaced onto individual workers and vulnerable families."[15]

A number of scholars have contended that strong families offer deep benefits to society, and that policy makers therefore rely on families to do some kinds of state work for the benefit of the social order. Families care for members and develop bonds of empathy that are important to democratic citizenship.[16] In one formulation, families are vital for developing citizens capable of personal and democratic self-government (fostering capacity), for fostering equality, and for fostering responsibility.[17] Neoliberal policies and reform agendas not only expect families to be able to perform these roles but have shifted increasing burdens onto increasingly fragile families. Caregivers, most often female, are left vulnerable. This necessary labor is often at odds with state taxation and spending priorities, making care economically irrational.[18]

Neoliberalism depends on the deployment of the family as a support structure, performing vital public and private functions, and family structures and responsibilities are changing in response to neoliberal policies and agendas. It presumes, in Somer's terms, that citizenship functions contractually, with those able to perform civic actions competently and independently being rewarded by state recognition and protection.[19] "Neoliberalism is not only a description of economic life, it is also an ethical system that posits that only personal responsibility matters."[20] While state-family relations have varied over time, the shift toward neoliberalism marks a change in the nature of the relationship beyond just a reallocation of responsibilities. In the last several decades, the risks and responsibilities of raising and caring for families have shifted, with more of the burden falling on American family members. And middle-class families are less equipped than they were half a century ago to meet the demands of care, in part because in the idealized conception of the contemporary American family, women are expected both to continue to perform vital care work and contribute significantly to household incomes—a burden that poor and single women have often borne unaided. In the current political economy, care responsibilities place unsustainable stresses on families, contributing to inequalities faced by women and others who provide care.[21] The disappearance of the family wage; the rising costs of education, housing, and health care; and the provision of child care, care for the elderly, and care for family members with chronic illnesses falls upon family members at a time when two incomes are increasingly necessary to live middle-class lives and work is more precarious.[22] Women are expected to provide care at the very time when more women are participating in the paid labor force, by choice or necessity. For those who can afford to do so, care is also outsourced. Joan Tronto reminds us that non-familial care work in the United States is assigned according to race and class and is devalued.[23]

Kathy Thelen has pointed out the rise of the "gig" or "Turk" economy that now employs (depending on how one counts) 20 percent to perhaps 40 percent of the American workforce in casual, less stable, and less secure work with lower wages and fewer benefits than the more traditional economy; these workers are among those onto whom risks are shifted.[24] These changes heighten the stakes for considering the growth of economic inequality in the United States through the lens of family.

Family, Politics, and Institutions: This Volume's Agenda

Rather than attempting to provide a comprehensive account of family's relationship to politics, policy, and political development, the volume focuses on a selection of issues that intersect with each other in illuminating ways. Some of our authors consider the relationship of family to neoliberalism and the tensions associated with the state's employment of family to achieve formerly publicly supported agendas. This line of inquiry shows why studying the family, even in historical context, is important for understanding how neoliberal state agendas mobilize sufficient capacity to accomplish critically important state work. The volume also considers the regulation of marriage and the uses of marriage to structure rights, benefits, and political status, with different contemporary and historical considerations outlining the political projects that marriage undergirds and how individuals link marriage to their own demands on the state.

The questions that marriage raises imply a related set of questions about the legal boundaries and definitions of family itself. The volume presents contrasting takes on fathers and mothers, encouraging deeper consideration of how gendered parental roles may be either politically mobilized and constructed or, alternatively, may incorporate prepolitical and non-liberal identities and agendas into the political sphere. Various chapters raise questions about the impact of policy dysfunction and unintended consequences on families. Finally, the volume shows how state actors mobilize familial relations and familial status to draw boundaries around citizenship and belonging as well as to accomplish exclusionary agendas.

This volume begins with two chapters that address changes in family structure and the rise of neoliberalism. The family's long-standing association with care work and its historical location as the heart of privacy have contributed to its important operational significance in neoliberal policy work. June Carbone and Naomi Cahn open the volume by situating families as the fundamental unit in society, but considering how economic orders influence the relationship between family and state. They show how increasing distance between the rich and the poor is creating two kinds of families: those with the resources to step in and provide support, companionship, care, and enrichment to take advantage of a new range of private opportunities that increasingly supplant or replace formerly public goods, and the increasingly fragile and threatened poor families that struggle just to stay intact in the face of an increased onslaught of responsibility and pressure. As the authors have been documenting for some time, the emergence of a "marriage gap," with decline in marriage for all but the most well-educated and affluent segment of the American population, has staggering implications for different sorts of families.[25] This raises a puzzle about the state's role in creating—and apparent failure to respond to—this deepening class divide, a question complicated by American federalism.

Martha Fineman has noted that "the state is always actively involved in the allocation, preservation, or maintenance of privilege and disadvantage."[26] She contends that, accompanied by noninterventionist rhetoric, "the state . . . has withdrawn or been prevented by entrenched interests from fulfilling one of its traditional roles in the social compact: to act as the principal monitor or guarantor of an equal society."[27] In the trajectory traced by Carbone and Cahn in Chapter 1, is the state driving, asleep at the wheel, or pursuing a dysfunctional policy course?

The insights of Carbone and Cahn mesh effectively with Tamara Metz's observations in Chapter 2 about the path to *Obergefell v. Hodges*, the celebrated Supreme Court decision that legalized same-sex marriage nationally. Analyzing Justice Anthony Kennedy's opinion for the Court in *Obergefell*, Metz emphasizes that a civil rights gain for gay couples came through the equation of these couples with heterosexual families. The decision—a gain in terms of rights, but arguably a mixed gain—must be read in the context of the rise of neoliberal politics and its vision of marriage, which shifts responsibility onto individuals and their families and radically privatizes the risks and costs of intimate care. Gay unions can now participate in the benefits the state confers upon marriage, but they also take on the burdens assigned to families for providing care to their members. Furthermore, reading the extension of marriage to same-sex couples as an unqualified victory for liberalism ignores the ways that contemporary marriage underlines class divisions and augments the state's investment in wealthy, stable families. Metz's analysis shows that as marriage became detached from gender roles and the gendered responsibility of care, the family increasingly became a private institution expected to do work for the public good. Metz demonstrates that families are legal constructions, a theme pursued in a number of chapters in this volume.

As the recent interest in the politics of marriage suggests, marriage promotes and rewards desirable family forms by allocating benefits and recognition.[28] Some families are discouraged, stigmatized, destabilized, or penalized. Sometimes, unconventional families that function as families are recognized by the state, while others are not.[29] As Alison Gash and Priscilla Yamin have shown elsewhere, family formations capable of functioning independently of the state and not requiring welfare assistance are more likely to be recognized as families.[30] Long before neoliberalism, marriage has been a structuring and state-defined institution, and families have been used to serve the state's interests.[31] Marriage confers a number of state benefits that extend far beyond the tax code, determining access to adoption, health benefits, and retirement benefits. At the same time, however, marriage holds an important emotional place in Americans' thinking about citizenship and belonging. Ellen Andersen's work in Chapter 3 explains both the emotional and practical import of marriage through the lens of same-sex marriage, considering the marriage waves and the attitudes of individuals who participated in them. Each state's institutional context had a lot to do with why people opted for marriage and what kinds of significance they placed upon the marital relationship, highlighting the importance of thinking about marriage as more than just an equal right, and recognizing its public as well as its private significance.

States have traditionally been the first point of governmental regulation of family, working through marriage to regulate race, gender, ethnicity, and sexuality. When law and common understandings did not clearly determine racial statuses, Julie Novkov has shown that state courts decided the race of plaintiffs.[32] Where state infrastructure was available to transform marriage and families in the late nineteenth and early twentieth centuries, policy makers used it. In the same period, Yamin has shown that common law unions were increasingly discouraged by state licensing and registration requirements for marriage, and inheritance could hinge upon compliance.[33] On the West Coast, states frequently barred "Mongolians" from intermarriage with whites, adding to the delegitimation of families formed between African Americans, Latinos, Native Americans, and whites. Early in the twentieth century, eugenic marriage laws implemented on the state level sought to bar family formation by those thought unfit to produce children who would become good citizens.

The federal government has also played an important role in establishing family policies. When states could not regulate—as on Indian reservations or in the territories—Congress, the federal courts, and federal agencies filled the breach. In the second half of the nineteenth century, federal law delegitimized polygamous relationships among Latter-Day Saints in Utah Territory and, supported by an 1875 Supreme Court decision, coerced territorial acquiescence to this policy prior to statehood.[34] Novkov and Yamin have each pointed out that during Reconstruction, newly freed slaves in the South were pressured by federal agents to enter marriage contracts, sometimes to the point of having to select a single monogamous relationship to privilege above others.[35] Carol Nackenoff has shown that Native Americans were barred by Bureau of Indian Affairs policy from forming new polygamous unions upon pain of loss of rations, fines, or imprisonment, and were urged into male-headed, single-family dwellings so that they would cohabit as a monogamous family, spurred on by allotment policies and reformers in the field.[36] Families that performed their expected roles and identities secured title to lands and to children's inheritance of the same; those who failed to comply were often dispossessed.

The volume draws upon and extends this agenda. A number of chapters in this volume explain how federal courts and federal policies define and shape families (Chapters 1, 2, 5, 7, and 8). We also learn that gains for American women have tended to come when the liberal state is linked to and likened more to the caregiving family (Chapter 6).

The role of states and state courts in defining family is highlighted by Gwendoline Alphonso and Richard Bensel in Chapter 4. Familial roles, which social scientists often interpret primarily through sociological lenses, have significant political import, and Alphonso and Bensel (along with Sharrow and McDonagh in Chapters 5 and 6, discussed below) use the political import of familial roles as an axis of analysis. Alphonso and Bensel analyze how intimate relationships could sometimes privilege white men's decisions about how to allocate property to sexual partners and children, even if formal legal marriage was unavailable to mark the status of the individuals involved. In antebellum Louisiana, the authors demonstrate how messy, cross-racial family practices and affective ties complicated implementation of the laws of slavery, official acknowledgment of paternity, and rights of inheritance; an examination of court records highlights the tension between respect for family and the mandate to uphold slavery and the color line.[37] Their identification of the family as the fundamental unit of the state, an insight that is not limited to the antebellum era, shows how families and familial membership at times influenced and even shaped racial orders.

The authority of the father in these antebellum cases may seem antiquated, but Elizabeth Sharrow's work in Chapter 5 illustrates how fathers became empowered and unified as a political interest group in their relationship to Title IX of the Education Amendments of 1972. Few might have predicted that the broad anti-discrimination legislation might mobilize a political constituency with roots in the members' collective roles as fathers, but Sharrow shows that the legislation had the unintended effect of facilitating the rise of an activist group of fathers unified around a gendered vision of equal opportunity for access to sports.[38]

Social institutions and social policies, as Patricia Hill Collins has argued, are often constructed via rhetoric about the family, producing complex, intersectional outcomes and hierarchies of citizenship.[39] She also contends that "if the nation-state is conceptualized as a national family with the traditional family ideal providing ideas about family, then the standards used to assess the contributions of family members in heterosexual married-couple households with children become foundational for assessing group contributions to overall national well-being."[40] The public figure of a gendered parent—in Eileen McDonagh's case, the mother—can contribute to political mobilization and development. In Chapter 6, McDonagh makes the argument that familial care, when performed by monarchical families, offers a model for provision of social welfare that underpins a public sense that the state is responsible for providing robust social welfare services.[41] McDonagh insists that the family is not a *liberal* governing institution. It is, rather, based on feudal principles and is analogous to the monarchical state; in this view, the family cannot become liberal since it requires care and inequality. The relationship between parent and child is inherently unequal and cannot be made so.[42] Using the battle in Congress over suffrage as an illustration, McDonagh contends that women's political inclusion in the United States advanced when they were able to draw successful analogies between the family and the emerging public welfare state—a model that now seems to be collapsing under the advance of neoliberal restructuring of civil society and care work.

The family is a state-licensed status, bestowed or denied in the service of various policy goals (see Chapter 8). Immigration policies have been an important site where families are acknowledged, destabilized, or penalized in order to advance the state's agendas. Restrictive immigration policies and their enforcement are deeply raced and gendered, often having dramatic implications for women and children. Until recently, the relationship of immigration to the politics of family received little attention among mainstream political scientists, but as the controversy over the Trump administration's separation of parents and children who entered the United States without documentation illustrates, this intersection is and has been politically salient. The Trump administration also seeks to displace family unity provisions in current policy; deportations of parents or a parent of US-born children place many affective and biological families in crisis. While it may be comforting to assume that immigration policies favoring stable and economically secure families would further the work families do in raising and caring for future democratic citizens, immigration policy history reveals a different and more complex pattern with regard to some immigrants.

Two chapters in this volume explore struggles over immigration in light of intersections with race, gender, and family status.[43] Since the latter part of the nineteenth century, establishment of immigration policy has been claimed as a federal government prerogative. In Chapter 7, Nackenoff and Novkov's investigation of Chinese familial relationships in late-nineteenth-century and early-twentieth-century immigration struggles illustrates that federal courts at times scrutinized evidence purporting to establish family ties and allowed this evidence to ground the reversal of orders of deportation or exclusion. Chinese women and children's family status was vigorously challenged at the borders as exclusion laws proliferated. In addition to describing courts' struggles with evidence and administrative oversight, the chapter highlights the significance of family ties in structuring policy. The rights and privileges of Chinese wives rested upon their husbands' status; the wives of laborers were subject to exclusion and deportation, but merchants' wives could enter and stay, as long as they could establish their wifely status convincingly. If a male legitimately within the United States died or deserted his wife, his spouse could be deported.[44] Children faced a different challenge, that of ensuring that inspectors would accept their claims either of proper descent (from a Chinese man claiming citizenship) or of their own birth within the geographic boundaries of the United States.

This conditioning of immigration status on family status continues to play a role in American law and policy, as Alison Gash and Priscilla Yamin demonstrate in Chapter 8. However, in their analysis, US immigration policy mobilizes the emotional and affective qualities of the family as an institution to discourage certain kinds of immigration. Examining recent immigration policies, the authors find a pattern of destabilizing and disassembling some families and recognizing others. The state sometimes tailors family values to encompass the families that policymakers wish to foster and support. Gash and Yamin argue that, in the immigration context, practice has to be understood in the context of demand for and control over types of labor, and both granting and withholding family status are equally potent expressions of state power.

The Volume's Contributions

Extending throughout the volume is a concern with the dynamic function of the family in American political development. The family is not simply an institution that structures private life. Rather, it is both an institution and an idea that influences and shapes the state. At the same time, various state institutions and actions change what family is and how it works (sometimes not by intentional design). Further, the family is not just an end of policy but also a means used to effect policy, and in these cases, "the state relies on families as a fundamental part of state capacity."[45] Bringing in an American political development perspective shows "how political actors and states marshal family, how it changes over time, and what this says more broadly about the shifting lines between public and private."[46]

Another widely shared concern among authors in this volume is exploration of the relationship between state actors' efforts to define family roles and the definition of gender and race. State-recognized family statuses generate recognizable political identities; "family and state are constructed, fluid, raced, gendered, sexed, and classed in a manner that shapes political citizenship."[47] Several of the chapters address the flip side of the dynamic produced when the state reinforces or defines family status through gender and race, and explicitly or implicitly work through how these defined identities and roles contribute to development and change. However, when individuals' family roles are activated by policies, there can be unanticipated political results, as Sharrow shows us, and ideological frameworks employing family do not always produce politics and policies that map in conventionally recognized categories and ways, as we see in McDonagh's work as well as in Carbone and Cahn's.

This volume adds to a growing body of literature that emphasizes how state policy structures families and rewards and disciplines the kinds of families that fit and thwart its ends. The use of perceived natural, pre-political familial ties in the service of policy goals at times obscures the role of state interventions, a point driven home in different ways by Andersen and Metz in this volume. The normative policy work of familial recognition is submerged when family appears as a natural and pre-political institution, but scholars' focus on policies that recognize, regulate, or discourage family formations lays bare the state's normative agendas.[48] And, as Martha Fineman has argued, when the state engages with dependent and vulnerable families, often "the political and legal response to such [vulnerable] populations is surveillance and regulation . . . It can also be paternalistic and stigmatizing."[49] Policies can make families either more vulnerable or more resilient, and an important political question is whether—and for whom—institutions compensate for or mitigate vulnerability or contribute to resilience.[50] When families are made legally cognizable, the state can support, grant a degree of autonomy, or engage in insidious interventions.

Another important political question that our work raises is about the impact and dynamics of policy change—or indeed, of policy drift—in a changing political economy. Policies can produce unintended consequences, such as the creation of unenvisioned stakeholders, mobilizations, and counter-mobilizations. Policies can also be dysfunctional, undermining, for example, the creation and stability of the very families the state expects to provide nurture and support to the next generation (and to those in ill health or the elderly). Policy mismatches are hardly uncommon, and create sites where new ideas, new agendas, and new movements can emerge.[51]

The chapters in *Stating the Family* illustrate the tremendous amount of political work the family does in American politics, and we challenge political scientists to pay it the attention and professional respect it deserves. Otherwise, many blind spots and incomplete understandings of both politics and policy follow. The work must begin with the very definitions of family—high-stakes and politically contested—that create statuses, benefits, responsibilities, and citizenship. It includes incorporating family as a key variable in investigating a number of public policies; as a variable, family adapts and changes as an intended or unintended result of policy changes. As a variable, family can become the object of both qualitative and quantitative studies. Families are shaped, defined, and given recognition by law; the flip side of this process of recognition is that some unions are destabilized or excluded by these same processes. Families of varying sorts are also sites of political mobilization, and are deserving of political study for that very reason as well. As some commitments of the mid-twentieth-century welfare state are shucked off, more of the work, and more of the risk, falls on families. When political science fails to make the political nature of families visible, it helps mask some of the most important consequences of changes in the welfare state. There is much work to be done.

Notes

1. Democratic Party Platform, July 21, 2016, American Presidency Project, University of California, Santa Barbara, http://www.presidency.ucsb.edu/papers_pdf/117717.pdf. Republican Party Platform, 2016, http://www.presidency.ucsb.edu/papers_pdf/117718.pdf.

2. Gwendoline Alphonso, *Polarized Families, Polarized Parties: Contesting Values and Economics in American Politics* (Philadelphia: University of Pennsylvania Press, 2018). See also Naomi Cahn and June Carbone, *Red Families v. Blue Families: Legal Polarization and the Creation of Culture* (New York: Oxford University Press, 2010), for the argument that different regional economic differences have created class-based changes in marriage and divorce patterns.

3. See Patricia Strach, "The Family," in *Oxford Handbook of American Political Development*, ed. Richard M. Valelly, Suzanne Mettler, and Robert C. Lieberman (Oxford: Oxford University Press, 2016): 704, 715; and Robert O. Self, *All in the Family: The Realignment of American Democracy Since the 1960s* (New York: Hill and Wang, 2012). Cahn and Carbone, in *Red Families v. Blue Families*, have found that "red" families emphasize religion, and the unity of marriage, sex, and procreation; "blue" families focus on choice, education, and delayed childbearing.

4. *Polity* 48, no. 2 (April 2016): 137–242.

5. Amy Dru Stanley, *From Bondage to Contract: Wage Labor, Marriage, and the Market in the Era of Slave Emancipation* (New York: Cambridge University Press,

1998); Michael Grossberg, *Governing the Hearth: Law and the Family in Nineteenth-Century America* (Chapel Hill: University of North Carolina Press, 1985); Peggy Pascoe, *What Comes Naturally: Miscegenation Law and the Making of Race in America* (New York: Oxford University Press, 2009).

6. Patricia Strach, *All in the Family: The Private Roots of American Public Policy* (Stanford, CA: Stanford University Press, 2007); Priscilla Yamin, *American Marriage: A Political Institution* (Philadelphia: University of Pennsylvania Press, 2015); Theda Skocpol, *Protecting Soldiers and Mothers: The Political Origins of Social Policy in the United States* (Cambridge, MA: Harvard University Press, 1995).

7. Linda C. McClain, "The Family, the State, and American Political Development as a Big Tent: Asking Basic Questions about Basic Institutions," *Polity* 48, no. 2 (April 2016): see 224–225 for these points.

8. Patricia Strach, "The Family," 704.

9. Search conducted on May 13, 2019, in the University at Albany, SUNY's electronic catalog holdings for the *American Political Science Review* for its entire date range. "Fathers" does a little better, with forty-six results, but some of these references are to the founding fathers.

10. Suzanne Mettler, *The Submerged State: How Invisible Government Policies Undermine American Democracy* (Chicago: University of Chicago Press, 2011).

11. Eileen McDonagh, "The Family-State Nexus in American Political Development: Explaining Women's Political Citizenship," *Polity* 48, no. 2 (April 2016): 186–204.

12. See James E. Fleming and Linda C. McClain, *Ordered Liberty: Rights, Responsibilities, and Virtues* (Cambridge, MA: Harvard University Press, 2013), 249.

13. Martha Fineman, "The Vulnerable Subject: Anchoring Equality in the Human Condition," *Yale Journal of Law and Feminism* 20 (2008): 1–23; and Dorothy Roberts, *Killing the Black Body: Race, Reproduction, and the Meaning of Liberty* (New York: Penguin Random House, 1998).

14. See Strach, *All in the Family*. See also Yamin, *American Marriage*; Alison Gash and Priscilla Yamin, "'Illegalizing' Families: State, Status, and Deportability," *New Political Science* 41, no. 1 (2019): 1–16; Gash and Yamin, "State, Status, and the American Family," *Polity* 48, no. 2 (April 2016): 146–164; and Julie Novkov and Carol Nackenoff, "Civic Membership, Family Status, and the Chinese in America, 1870s–1920s," *Polity* 48, no. 2 (April 2016): 165–185.

15. Margaret Somer, *Genealogies of Citizenship: Markets, Statelessness, and the Right to Have Rights* (New York: Cambridge University Press, 2008), 2.

16. See Joan Tronto, *Moral Boundaries* (New York: Routledge, 1993).

17. Linda McClain, *The Place of Families* (Cambridge, MA: Harvard University Press, 2006), 4–5.

18. Nancy Folbre, *The Rise and Decline of Patriarchal Systems* (London: Verso Books, 2020); Folbre, *The Invisible Heart: Economics and Family Values* (New York:

New Press 2001). The author suggests that the state may tacitly encourage immigration, especially from those with high levels of human capital, to make up for declining birth rates resulting from the economic costs of providing care (which presumably includes education costs) for the young.

19. Somer, *Genealogies of Citizenship*, 71–73.

20. Tronto, *Caring Democracy: Markets, Equality, and Justice* (New York: New York University Press, 2013), 38.

21. Jennifer Nedelsky, "What Will It Take to Revalue Care?," presented at the 2018 Western Political Science Association meetings, San Francisco, with an appendix describing the forthcoming project, *A Care Manifesto*, co-authored with Tom Malleson, http://www.wpsanet.org/papers/docs/nedelsky2018.pdf.

22. Jacob S. Hacker, *The Great Risk Shift* (Oxford: Oxford University Press, 2006), 89–108.

23. Tronto, *Moral Boundaries*, ca. 103.

24. Kathleen Thelen, "The American Precariat: U.S. Capitalism in Comparative Perspective," *Perspectives on Politics* 17, no. 1 (March 2019): 5–27. A prominent example of the gig economy is Mechanical Turk, a crowdsourcing marketplace that Amazon runs, enabling individuals to volunteer to do small repetitive tasks over the internet at piece rates; other individuals and businesses post tasks and rates. See https://www.mturk.com/.

25. See June Carbone and Naomi Cahn, *Marriage Markets: How Inequality Is Remaking the American Family* (New York: Oxford University Press, 2014); and Carbone and Cahn, Chapter 1 in this volume. See also Linda C. McClain, "The Other Marriage Equality Problem," *Boston University Law Review* 93 (2013): 921–970.

26. Martha Fineman, "Understanding Vulnerability Theory," n.d.

27. Fineman, "The Vulnerable Subject," 6.

28. Yamin, *American Marriage*, 9.

29. Gash and Yamin, "State, Status, and the American Family"; Alison Gash, *Below the Radar: How Silence Can Save Civil Rights* (New York: Oxford University Press, 2015).

30. Lynch, *Affective Equality*; Eichner, *The Supportive State*; Fineman, *The Autonomy Myth*.

31. See Yamin, *American Marriage*.

32. Julie Novkov, *Racial Union: Law, Intimacy, and the White State in Alabama, 1865–1954* (Ann Arbor: University of Michigan Press, 2008); Strach, "The Family," 710–711; and Alphonso and Bensel, Chapter 4 in this volume.

33. Priscilla Yamin, "The Search for Marital Order: Civic Membership and the Politics of Marriage in the Progressive Era," *Polity* 41, no. 1 (January 2009): 93, 96.

34. *Reynolds v. United States*, 98 U.S. 145 (1879). See also Gretchen Ritter,

The Constitution as Social Design: Gender and Civic Membership in the American Constitutional Order (Palo Alto: Stanford University Press, 2006).

35. Julie Novkov, "Making Citizens of Freedmen and Polygamists," in *Statebuilding from the Margins*, ed. Carol Nackenoff and Julie Novkov (Philadelphia: University of Pennsylvania Press, 2014), 31–64; Yamin, *American Marriage.*

36. Carol Nackenoff, with Allison Hrabar, "Quaker Roles in Making and Implementing Federal Indian Policy: From Grant's Peace Policy through the Early Dawes Act Era (1869–1900)," in *Quakers and Native Americans*, ed. Ignacio Gallup-Diaz and Geoffrey Plank (Leiden: Brill Publishers, 2019).

37. Gwendolyn Alphonso and Richard Bensel, "The Legal Construction of Motherhood and Paternity: Interracial Unions and the Color Line in Antebellum Louisiana," in this volume.

38. We also note interesting new work by political scientist H. Howell Williams at Western Connecticut State University on how federal child support enforcement efforts mobilized middle-class men (speaking about victimization by the government), while obscuring the strong racial politics of this governmental venture. See "Intimate Narratives, State Anxieties, and Child Support in the United States," presented at the 2019 meetings of the Western Political Science Association, San Diego, CA.

39. Patricia Hill Collins, "It's All in the Family: Intersections of Gender, Race, and Nation," *Hypatia* 13, no. 3 (Part 2, Summer 1998): 63, 66.

40. Collins, "It's All in the Family," 64.

41. Eileen McDonagh, "Ripples from the First Wave: The Monarchical Origins of the Welfare State," *Perspectives on Politics* 13, no. 4 (December 2015): 992–1016.

42. This point is also made by Martha Fineman in "Understanding Vulnerability Theory," n.d. Fineman concludes that equality and antidiscrimination frameworks are inappropriate for thinking about justice in this and certain other contexts.

43. See Anna Sampaio, *Terrorizing Latina/o Immigrants: Race, Gender, and Immigration Politics in the Age of Security* (Philadelphia: Temple University Press, 2015).

44. Novkov and Nackenoff, "Civic Membership, Family Status, and the Chinese in America, 1870s–1920s."

45. Strach, "The Family," 708.

46. Strach, 706. See also Patricia Strach and Kathleen Sullivan, "The State's Relations: What the Institution of Family Tells Us about Governance," *Political Research Quarterly* 64 (2011): 94–106.

47. Susan Burgess, "Introduction: Family, State, and Difference in Political Time," *Polity* 48, no. 2 (2016): 141.

48. See, generally, Peggy Pascoe, *What Comes Naturally.*

49. Martha Albertson Fineman, "Equality, Autonomy, and the Vulnerable Subject in Law and Politics," in *Vulnerability: Reflections on a New Ethical Foundation for Law and Politics*, ed. Martha Albertson Fineman and Anna Grear (Farnham, England: Ashgate Publishers, 2013), 16.

50. For Fineman, vulnerability is part of the human condition and is universal, inevitable, and enduring. On vulnerability, see Fineman, "The Vulnerable Subject," 8.

51. While Karen Orren and Stephen Skowronek look at institutional and developmental mismatches as sites of innovation in American political development, Nackenoff and Novkov explored the interface of public and private actors and the role of non-state actors in institutional innovation, drawing on Elisabeth S. Clemens, William Novak, Brian Balogh, and other scholars. See Nackenoff and Novkov, "Introduction," in *Statebuilding from the Margins*; Elisabeth S. Clemens, "Lineages of the Rube Goldberg State: Building and Blurring Public Programs, 1900–1940," in *Rethinking Political Institutions*, ed. Ian Shapiro, Stephen Skowronek, and Daniel Galvin (New York: New York University Press, 2006), 187–215; William J. Novak, "The Myth of the 'Weak' American State," *American Historical Review* 113 (June 2008): 752–772; Brian Balogh, *A Government Out of Sight: The Mystery of National Authority in Nineteenth-Century America* (Cambridge: Cambridge University Press, 2009); and Karen Orren and Stephen Skowronek, *The Search for American Political Development* (Cambridge: Cambridge University Press, 2004).

1 | Democracy and Family

June Carbone and Naomi Cahn

The family, the economy, and the nature of the state are intrinsically connected. Each is shaped by the other in an iterative process, and the goals of the state in regulating and supporting the family are "important objects of inquiry," while the role of the economy in shaping the family is similarly critical—but less examined.[1] In the midst of an emerging information economy, Americans cannot agree on what state objectives for the family should be or what kind of families the state should promote. The changing economy has rendered the gendered nuclear family of the manufacturing age obsolete, producing broadly shared concerns about increasing family instability and the role of the family in exacerbating social divisions and economic insecurity. Despite this, the definition of a new family order, much less the role of the state in promoting it, is the subject of deep discord. Traditionalists, whom we term "red," tend to favor a minimal state and privatized families;[2] they advocate a return to age-old understandings about sexuality, reproduction, and marriage, which they associate with a private assumption of responsibility for the dependent.[3] Modernists, whom we term "blue," tend to favor a more robust state role; they advocate public support for all children irrespective of the circumstances of their birth and greater autonomy for individuals to forge families of choice. They see state support for families as essential to equality and to fostering the capacity for citizenship necessary for democracy.[4] The intensity of this debate has blocked an unequivocal state embrace of either approach.

This debate about the relationship between state and family goes to the heart of the political order, with Carol Nackenoff questioning how "deeply divisive issues in contemporary American politics . . . become subject of constitutional scrutiny."[5] It also challenges the foundation of democratic society, which depends on an informed and capable citizenry to sustain democratic institutions. Yet, today's society places marriage—

and stable family life inside or outside marriage—beyond the reach of many of its citizens. Consequently, "issues concerning both growing family and marriage inequality and equality show the importance of sustained study of the relationship between the family and the state."[6]

In this chapter, we examine the relationship between family and state, review the economic changes that have destabilized the family of the industrial age, identify the sources of division that prevent a new consensus-based approach, and sketch what we believe are the appropriate goals of state support that could once again bring stable family life within the reach of the vast majority of the population. We conclude that the relationship between democracy and families will depend on the redefinition of the connection between state and individual in the information age.

The Family and the State

A study of American political development examines "durable shifts in governing authority,"[7] considering how the nature of state power and the sources of legitimacy for state intervention change over time. Few topics have been more difficult than the family. Part of the reason is that the state role in regulating the family is complex, not monolithic, and subject to conflicting imperatives. This is true in part because the relationship between state and family often depends on the state's ability to inculcate shared norms about family formation and function;[8] when national consensus is impossible, whether on the appropriate grounds for divorce or whether same-sex couples can form legally recognized families, the nation's ability to rely on the family as foundational to state function suffers. Thus, the US Constitution left family law to the states.[9] Political theorist Anne Dailey adds that this theory of "localism" is associated with "the view that the law of domestic relations necessarily promotes a shared moral vision of the good family life."[10] The federal government has nevertheless intervened at times when it perceived the need to protect important state objectives such as constitutional rights to equality, establish national rules to settle interstate jurisdictional disputes, or set the terms for the provision of resources to the states.[11]As Carol Nackenoff observes, the Supreme Court has had to resolve some of the most intractable conflicts in family law, with the Court's decision in *Obergefell v. Hodges*, which recognized marriage equality as a constitutional right, simply the most recent example of the judicial role in overcoming political roadblocks to family redefinition.[12] Even then, some states continue to undermine the *Obergefell* holding, while others gradually integrate it into state family policies that nonetheless differ across numerous other dimensions, from spousal inheritance to determinations of legal parentage. This federalist system makes it difficult to speak of one monolithic state institutional role, and that complexity is an important theme in the rest of this chapter.

Despite these difficulties in forging shared values and maintaining them as circumstances change, the state and the family are deeply intertwined,[13] and the family has always reflected the state allocation of resources (just as the family has always been important to state institutions[14]). As Julie Novkov and Carol Nackenoff observe in the Introduction to this volume, the family, in its interactions with the state, "functions as a status, an ordering mechanism, a distributor of goods and services, a site of citizen-making, and an object of regulation and management."[15] Less directly, it also acts in important ways as a source of stability and security, cushioning family members from the full effects of a volatile market economy.[16] This role of the family as a buffer depends on the state's role in linking family formation to the economic resources necessary to serve as a foundation for secure family life. At the core of the current debate is not just the question of differing family values. It is also a question of whether in a period of growing economic inequality, the state can reforge the links between shared understandings of how, when, and with whom to create families and family stability at all. The task is a particularly fraught one in part because the changing economy has called into question the state's traditional methods for linking family regularity to greater security.

The state has historically sought to forge such links through three mutually reinforcing systems linked to the economy. The first involves policing family formation. The state has long acted to distinguish "legitimate" from "illegitimate" families, with marriage serving, for example, as a basic structure for securing the availability of private resources for children and for determining eligibility for public benefits.[17] Underlying this regulation, however, have often been assumptions about readiness to enter marriage. At the time of the country's founding, the United States differed from England in that young white men could acquire landownership for farming (and thus the ability to support a family) simply by moving farther west, with the state often acting to insure the broad distribution of landownership that facilitated higher rates of marriage at younger ages than in the Old World.[18] Today, in contrast, a significant portion of American households lack secure employment, even minimal savings, or realistic hopes of becoming more financially secure in the future. The ability to link marriage—or any other marker of family formation—to the resources necessary for family stability has accordingly been called into question.

The second system involves establishing private spheres in which the state will *not* intervene, and these spheres depend on understandings about gender. As Martha Fineman emphasizes, the historic purpose of such privacy was not state neutrality, but rather state sanction for the decision-making authority of privileged actors.[19] Within marriage, for example, the state reinforced patriarchal authority by refusing to police domestic violence or even recognize the possibility of marital rape.[20] Today, with the decline in marriage rates, the determination of legal parentage may be as important as marriage in creating zones in which the state will not interfere.[21] Moreover, given frequent divorce and the redefinition of marriage as an institution of shared authority, many adults may find that they enjoy greater freedom from state intervention outside marriage than within it. Primary caretakers may find it easier to enjoy sole custody rights if they do not marry,[22] and so, too, partners with higher incomes may find it easier to control their greater individual assets outside marriage.[23] The state's role in creating and policing zones of privacy has accordingly become more complex as families become more varied. And a more coherent allocation of family decision-making power falls along the fault lines of cultural divisions, with some favoring greater state intervention to secure fathers' inclusion in their children's lives,[24] while others favor greater autonomy for women's caretaking role—or dismantling gendered roles altogether.[25] As a result, while parents constitutionally enjoy greater rights over the care of their children than nonparents, many parents nonetheless lack secure authority over the children for whom they provide care. The state intervenes more readily to take children away than to assist struggling parents in providing care.

The third system involves state efforts to expand the circumstances in which a larger portion of the population can enjoy the benefits of state-sanctioned relationships. The United States, for example, during the twentieth century promoted a male "family wage" and more secure employment in an effort to establish the financial foundation for traditional families. Today, there is neither agreement on the components necessary to promote family stability nor the political will to implement the proposals that exist.[26] The debate over these issues often seems not to be about the family at all, but rather about the role of the state in promoting economic security of any kind. Yet, state promotion of economic security, whether through land distribution or unionization, has historically been mindful of the relationship between economic and family stability. Indeed, the Moynihan Report of 1965, in calling attention to declining marriage rates in the African American community, proposed improving male employment prospects as the primary state response.

These purposes for state regulation of the family have become particularly acute because a changing economy and the remaking of women's roles have destabilized earlier efforts to tie state oversight of the family almost exclusively to its role in overseeing and encouraging marriage. This oversight process has always been a delicate one. On the one hand, the state, as numerous political theorists have observed, relies less on direct commands than on the socialization of its citizens to embrace shared family norms,[27] and this socialization is typically more effective when the norms are seen as timeless and self-evident.[28] On the other hand, in times of wholesale shifts in the organization of the economy and the relationship between state and family, the state purpose becomes one of responding to and reinforcing new understandings of the institutions that order family life. The terms of any such shift become durable only when the new norms that underlie them become widely accepted. Yet, the process of inculcating such new family terms, which bridges historical and modern understandings and alters the power structure that underlay the older terms, is inevitably contested and often takes place across multiple dimensions whose relationship to each other is not always apparent. It is little wonder that feminist scholars of American political development acknowledge "the centrality and persistence of marriage politics in American political questions."[29]

The Supreme Court's embrace of marriage equality constitutes a step in the larger political struggle to redefine how the state addresses the relationship between economic and family security. The opinion in *Obergefell v. Hodges* itself embraced marriage as an institution of continuing social importance, but underlying the decision was an implicit question of whether marriage will retain its vitality for all social classes.[30] While class has historically been "invisible" in American society—most people think of themselves as middle class—class divergences in family form is a new locus for political polarization and state paralysis. Neoliberal state policies continue to exacerbate economic inequality though a dysfunctional approach in which some money is spent on enticing couples to attend marriage promotion classes, but not on creating the jobs that might make marriage more viable. These efforts are designed to reinforce the values of "red" or traditional theorists, for whom changing family form is a function of social and cultural disintegration, but such efforts, like the opposition to marriage equality, amount to no more than a symbolic dissent to the changing cultural understandings that have arisen as a result of economic change.[31] At the same time, the prominence of cultural issues helps deflect attention from the economic forces undermining employment—and family—stability. At a time when traditional marriage is beyond the reach of large portions of the population, state efforts to promote it without providing the economic support necessary for it to flourish become cruel, where they are not simply ineffectual. These conflicts point to a "nonlinear aspect of modernization processes," in which the state has grudgingly acknowledged new forms of family outside the traditional heterosexual nuclear unit, but still focuses on marriage as the preeminent socializing institution.[32] To "undo" further the connection between the traditional family and the state requires reckoning with the role of greater economic inequality in undermining marriage's ability to meet the needs of a postindustrial era, and to consider more directly the role of the state in securing the next generation of children's full participation in American society.

The Relationship among State Capacity, Individual Autonomy, and the Family

Over the course of American history, the economy has profoundly affected the role of the state in regulating the family. State efforts to promote marriage have historically been tied to marriage's role in securing male resources as the foundation for family life. Today, the source of family economic security has shifted from superior male resources to dual-earning arrangements that require greater flexibility and trust to endure. Yet, the state neither provides the stable employment that served as the foundation for marriage in the industrial era nor supports family ability to weather the economic shocks that destabilize more informal relationships. In this context, genuine commitment to a partner can threaten rather than strengthen the resources available to children, making marriage a luxury many couples cannot afford.

Remaking the Relationship between State and Family: From "Little Commonwealths" to "Separate Spheres"

While traditionalists like to present the marital family as timeless and enduring,[33] the change from an agricultural economy to an industrial one destabilized family arrangements. New family understandings ultimately took hold for the majority of the population only with the creation of a more robust state that took on the provisions of economic security as a critical public function. This earlier creation of a more interventionist state was a century in the making, and the source of considerable ideological division then and now. It nonetheless models the multifaceted aspects of state promotion of family regularity discussed above.

The United States began as an agricultural country with a limited state. This is turn made the family more independent of the state *and* more critical to the state's success in addressing the needs of its citizens. In the colonial era and the era immediately following independence, the state depended on the family as a basic unit of commercial *and* social reproduction, with readiness for marriage tied to male landownership. Farm households both produced products for sale and grew enough food and raised sufficient animals to feed their own residents. Farmwives made their own clothes; farm parents trained their children in the agricultural methods and crafts necessary to sustain an agricultural economy. The families of this era were described as "little commonwealths."[34] They were hierarchically organized, self-sufficient, interdependent households, with the husband's role as head of household tied to his property ownership, and all members contributing to its economic viability.[35]

The manufacturing era, which began in the Northeast before the Civil War, gradually altered these relationships and contributed to changes in the role and size of the state over the course of the next century. With industrialization, commercial production moved out of family households and into factories and offices. Wage labor replaced property ownership as the primary source of income for urban families, and urban households bought food and factory-produced clothes. Formal education became more important in the preparation of children for adult roles. Yet, the wage labor on which urban households depended could, in the early days of industrialization, be variable and insecure. Injuries, layoffs, and recessions threatened family well-being. And urban living conditions, especially in densely populated areas, could be unsanitary, unsafe, and demoralizing. In his report on the African American family, Assistant Secretary of Labor Daniel Patrick Moynihan observed that country life and city life "are profoundly different. . . . It was this abrupt transition [from rural to urban life] that produced the wild Irish slums of the 19th Century Northeast. Drunkenness, crime, corruption, discrimination, family disorganization, juvenile delinquency were the routine of that era."[36] As a result, the initial implementation of the new family system increased ethnic and regional inequality. The native-born white Protestants in the Northeast were the first to embrace the system, preparing their sons for leadership roles in the new economy while they more strictly policed their daughters' sexuality, encouraging their greater investment in a smaller number of elite children.[37] In the meantime, the newly created working classes dealt with the insecurity of wage labor by sending their children to work in the factories at young ages. For them, the benefits of the new family system were beyond reach. And the South opposed state investment in education before the Civil War and continued to fight child labor laws, unionization, and racial equality thereafter.

Over time, however, the state promoted and extended the benefits of the new system. The Married Women's Property Acts gave wives the ability to enter into contracts and retain ownership of their own property within marriage. The state also co-managed one of the family's primary functions: the preparation of children for adult roles. Over the course of the nineteenth century, the expanding farm communities of the American Midwest embraced the greater emphasis on formal education and women's enhanced moral status that came with it. Free public secondary education, which initially took hold in the nineteenth century, contributed to the expansion of the new system, with mandatory school attendance laws and the prohibition of child labor following in the twentieth century.

Because the families of the industrial era could no longer insulate their members from the ups and downs of a market economy, political support grew for the protection of workers and families. During the first half of the twentieth century, state regulation gradually addressed the regularity of wage labor, eventually strengthening unions, creating a broader-based social safety net, and regulating pay and working conditions. Unions helped create a political coalition that supported the creation of a male "family wage," and protectionist legislation kept women out of the better-paid parts of the workforce, further helping to boost male wages and reinforcing gendered notions of marriage.[38] Beginning in the Progressive Era, and expanding during the New Deal and the Great Society, the state also became more willing to provide for the elderly and aid children whose parents struggled to care for them, ultimately enacting "mothers' pensions," old-age provisions, and survivor and disability benefits.[39] Starting in the Progressive Era, as well, "child savers" and urban reformers sought to extend the benefits of education and maternal investment in children to the immigrants flooding American cities. And the expansion of the state that came with the New Deal and postwar reforms further reduced regional and class-based inequalities in education and income.

These developments fundamentally remade the relationship between state and family. The state no longer depended on family households for commercial production, but it continued to rely on the family to prepare children for citizenship, though in ways that differed by class, race, and region.[40] Parental investment in children became more critical in an era that placed greater emphasis on formal education—initially for the upper-middle-class professionals, scientists, and managers of the industrial era, but eventually for a large portion of the American workforce—and on inculcation of the right mores in a society that provided less direct supervision than the small towns of colonial America. The state supplemented the family role with free primary and secondary education, and relied on parents to insure school readiness and compliance with compulsory school attendance laws.

The state continued to oversee marriage, promoting it as necessary to family stability and administering it in accordance with patriarchal norms that tied family well-being to a male wage earner's income. Yet, within this new system, marriage became less unitary and more dissoluble, with the gradual liberalization of divorce terms giving spouses greater ability to leave intolerable unions or to remarry if one of the spouses deserted the other. The state no longer depended on the household as a unit that integrated commercial and domestic production, but rather on marriage as a way to coordinate husbands' and wives' distinctively gendered contributions to raising children.

By the fifties, the combination of marriage based on a stable male family wage and high rates of maternal investment in children had become a shared national ideal, an ideal that had become accessible to the working classes because of the creation of the state-sponsored institutions that supported it. By the end of the fifties, however, African American families, who had never fully shared in the benefits of the new family model, began to suffer from the increased instability that would later become a hallmark of the postindustrial era, and by the seventies, a new economy began to take hold in the country as a whole.

Remaking the Relationship between State and Family: From the Industrial to the Information Age

Today, we are in the midst of an equally momentous transformation in the relationship between state and family. Large, permanent institutions, whether public or private, dominated the industrial era. They are being replaced by more flexible networks. In the home, the industrial age enshrined the company "man" and his stay-at-home wife in fixed and gendered roles they assumed as part of the transition to adulthood. Today, in contrast, successful adults need to be nimbler, switching jobs, cities, and sometimes careers in search of better opportunities. Couples trade off work, domestic chores, and child-rearing duties to meet the changing needs of their employers, partners, and children. Those with the flexibility to adapt and those who succeed in forging enduring relationships that help them manage the transitions and the trade-offs in the new system will receive handsome payoffs. Those requirements also place the benefits of stable family life beyond the reach of a good part of the population. The state response to date has been continued valorization of the importance of marriage in securing family stability. That celebration of marriage without consideration of the alternatives contributes to growing inequality in American society.

This transformation in the relationship between family and state involves two overlapping shifts. The first is the dismantling of rigidly gendered family roles. This shift began with middle-class and elite women's increased participation in the paid labor market. By the sixties, economic growth had also fueled demand for the labor women had traditionally performed. As married women flooded into the labor market, they further spurred demand to hire other women (and labor-saving home products) to perform what has historically been seen as non-market labor.[41] Antidiscrimination laws increased women's access to higher education (Title IX) and better-paying jobs (Title VII, the Equal Pay Act), with women's increasing education fueling their move into the professional and managerial ranks in the eighties. By then, Supreme Court decisions had also guaranteed, as a matter of constitutional right, women's access to contraception and abortion, allowing women greater control of childbearing. Women today are more likely than men to graduate from college, and they constitute almost half of the labor force.[42] Their greater income and economic independence, in turn, accords women greater practical ability to raise children on their own.

The second shift is the change in the nature of employment. The state responded to the challenges posed by globalization and technological change by embracing a neoliberal ideological framework that accords greater deference to private decision-makers and withdraws the state from the active protection of worker interests through measures such as unionization, enforcement of workers' rights, and robust regulation of wages and hours that characterized the manufacturing era at its height. The result undermines support for worker-friendly policies. As a result, the state no longer promotes creation of either secure employment or "family wages" for anyone.[43] Job tenure has fallen across the economy.[44] Roughly a third of workers no longer hold full-time, permanent positions, and that figure is expected to rise as high as 50 percent in the next few years.[45] Work has become far more precarious, with the greatest impact on blue-collar men, who have seen their income and employment stability decline.[46]

The combination of these two shifts challenges the traditional marital family of male breadwinners and female homemakers. In its place, state-sanctioned marriage has become a legal relationship premised on formal equality that requires flexibility, maturity, and trust to endure.[47] Family law legislation and judicial decisions treat spouses as equals, holding that both spouses merit an equal share of the family's financial assets and that children's interests lie with continuing contact with both parents following a breakup. Those who succeed in finding a suitable spouse and manage to balance two jobs and family responsibilities still gain a measure of economic security through marriage. Two incomes offer more of a cushion than one for weathering economic difficulties, marshaling the economic resources to return to school or otherwise retool, and trading off family responsibilities that might exhaust a single parent. And the state continues to grant married couples various perquisites, such as family and medical leave privileges, Social Security benefits for surviving spouses and children, and more than a thousand other benefits. Well-educated couples are the primary beneficiaries of the new system. They invest considerably more material and emotional resources in their children than their parents did—and dramatically more than average families can hope to do. The class-based differences in children's lives have increased substantially.

This has occurred, at least in part, because the increasing complexity of family responsibilities compounded the challenges of managing such relationships. Changes in divorce laws made it even easier to end marriages, and two-thirds of divorces are initiated by women.[48] For the well-educated, the response has been a steady increase in the age of marriage. Elite couples continue to hold the line on improvident births that would derail education or careers and tend to form families only when they have achieved a measure of maturity and financial stability. When they do marry, they overwhelmingly marry each other. For the rest of the population, however, the average age of first birth has remained the same, with unintended pregnancies exceeding 50 percent of the total.[49] In the meantime, relationships outside the top third of earners have become more fragile. Indeed, while Tamara Metz notes in Chapter 2 of this volume that marriage serves to privatize dependence, even as the institution has been extended to same-sex couples, it is unable to perform that role for an increasingly large segment of the population, for whom economic insecurity is a constant theme.

The reasons the family has changed have nonetheless been a matter of dispute. Traditionalists point to cultural factors, including societal acceptance of non-marital sexuality and greater emphasis on personal fulfillment rather than duty or commitment. Modernists are more likely to tie shifts in family form to the changing economy and to bristle at any suggestion that women should be required to obey their husbands or to avoid sexual activity until marriage. Yet, there is little doubt that the combination of a changing economy and shifting gender roles plays a significant part in explaining family transformation. Family scholars agree that at least five factors contribute.

The first is the decline in stable male employment. Studies overwhelmingly report that women do not want to remain married to a man without a steady job.[50] Observers disagree on whether the jobs simply aren't there or men are unwilling to take and keep the low-wage positions that employers sometimes have trouble filling.[51]

The second is that uncertainty and variability may matter as much,

if not more, than low wages. Good measures of instability in employment are hard to come by, but smaller-scale studies report that income
variations, even from factors such as loss of overtime pay, destabilize
relationships and that uncertainty about the future makes couples more
reluctant to commit.[52]

The third is that breakups rarely come from low income alone. Instead, greater inequality, employment uncertainty, and perceived loss
of status also tend to correspond with increases in violence, substance
abuse, infidelity, and relationship tensions.[53] Ethnographic studies indicate that in poor communities, domestic violence is a factor in over half
of breakups, and sexual infidelity is a factor in another 40 percent.[54]

The fourth is that the lack of shared expectations about gender roles
exacerbate the first three issues. Women often respond to layoffs or cut-
backs in their hours by spending more time on the home and children.
Men may respond, particularly in the immediate period after a layoff,
by helping out less at home. If the women feel pressure to work longer
hours without increased assistance from their partners, relationship tensions increase.[55]

The fifth involves the role of mass incarceration policies in reducing
the available men in low-income and minority communities. Indeed, the
women in communities with higher incarceration rates tend to invest
more in their own education and employment than women elsewhere,
increasing their independence and often their reluctance to commit to
uncertain or poor-quality relationships.[56]

These findings suggest that the cultural and economic explanations
for family change are deeply interrelated. To the extent that economic
factors alter family practices, they do so because they modify behavior in
ways that contribute to changing cultural assumptions.[57] They also suggest that the existing state approach to promoting family stability cannot
work. Couples continue to see conventional markers of economic stability such as secure employment as the indicia of readiness for marriage,
yet the economy no longer makes such jobs available to a large portion
of the population. Parents continue to want autonomy in overseeing
their children's upbringing, yet the dominant middle-class model that
insists on recognition of two equal parents often undermines rather
than secures parental autonomy in the face of unstable relationships.
State promotion of greater income security or greater assistance with
early childhood might help, but deep political divisions obstruct the
most promising proposals.

As a result of these changes, the growing gulf in experiences between families has emerged as a marker of growing societal inequality, a sign of the growing gulf in status and experiences between families typical of their respective classes. Women who have graduated from college were once less likely to marry than high school graduates; today, they are the women most likely to marry.[58] And while better-educated women may have led the change in family roles in the seventies, with greater economic security seen as a factor in increasing divorce rates,[59] today the opposite is true. The only group in American society to see their marriage rates increase over the past forty years has been women in the top 10 percent of the income scale.[60] In the poorest communities, marriage has effectively disappeared. Divorce rates, which stabilized for college graduates, have continued to rise for the rest of the population, and a majority of the births to those without college degrees take place outside marriage.[61] Moreover, while more than half of the births to unmarried women occur in the context of cohabiting unions,[62] both marriage and cohabitation in working-class communities have become less stable. Racial differences have also remained large, with African Americans less likely to marry than whites at every educational level. State policies enshrined in family law reflect the norms of middle-class marriages; they rarely acknowledge the different understandings of working-class families, increasing the incentives for working-class couples to stay out of marriage and out of court.[63]

As a consequence of these developments, the class divide in children's experiences has sharpened dramatically. Yet, the ability to thrive in a networked economy and to navigate the shoals of relationships that require flexibility and trust depends on greater investment in children. The result challenges the sufficiency of existing institutional responses, raising the question of whether the state will ultimately need to create not only new responses, but new institutions as it did in dealing with the industrial era's challenges to family stability.

Values Polarization and Partisan Conflict

Broad agreement exists that the growing class divide in family form and well-being threatens societal well-being. Broad agreement also exists that parental investment is critical to the capacity of the next generation. The issue of what to do about it nonetheless divides American society on the question of how the state role in the economy and the state role in the family interact. The answers depend on two competing perspectives.

The first, which we have referred to as red traditionalism, combines neoliberal economic policies with state promotion of traditional values and private responsibility. (By neoliberal, we adopt Joan Tronto's characterization of it as "the economic system in which government expenditures are limited, the market is viewed as the preferred method for allocating all social resources . . . and social programs are limited to being a 'safety net.'"[64]) In this view, the state allows market forces to determine which firms prosper and which disappear, even if that means greater employment instability. Stable families can weather this greater commercial insecurity. These families need to instill norms of hard work and responsibility; privatize dependence by assuming responsibility for the young, the old, and the sick; channel reproduction exclusively into two-parent unions; and undertake child-rearing as a sacred obligation. Marriage is central to these arrangements, and to make marriage work requires that the state reinforce the authority of marriage as a societal command that encourages men to marry as the price of access to sexual relationships, women to invest in men's productivity and well-being, and parents to accept responsibility for their children. The most critical state role in this endeavor is promotion of the right moral values in the public square, emphasizing marriage as a time-honored moral command indispensable to private responsibility and individual well-being.

The alternative view, which we have termed blue modernism, rests on a fundamentally different view of the interrelationship of the state, the family, and the economy. In accordance with this view, the principal obligation of the state is to insure the equal citizenship and capacity for individual flourishing of all societal members. The modernist state should remain neutral toward different possible conceptions of the "good"; tolerance is a critical state obligation.[65] Instead, the state should remain open to varying outcomes as the values of the state change in accordance with the deliberations that emerge from democratic processes. For citizens to be able to make meaningful choices in such a democracy, however, the state must commit to what Linda McClain terms "fostering capacity" or "personal self-government."[66] McClain argues that it would violate principles of equal citizenship for the state to continue to privatize dependency through women's subordination within marriage or to disadvantage children because of the circumstances of the families in which they were born.[67] The state accordingly has an obligation, consistent with its commitment to tolerance, equality, and democracy, to insure the individual self-development of all of its citizens, with care work as a social as well as a personal and familial obligation.

These two systems fundamentally talk past each other about the relationship between the state and the family. This values divide, however, does not just entrench differing views about the family. It also makes intrinsically divisive cultural issues, like abortion, markers of political identity, and links political coalitions to psychological dispositions, such as preferences for hierarchy, authority, and in-group membership, rather than to policy preferences.[68] These more tribal identities, which also correspond to deep-seated values preferences, divert attention from the broad social and economic forces producing family change and frustrate the creation of a political coalition that favors a far-reaching state response. At its core, the historical state strategy for family well-being has been to reinforce the identity between family formation and the resources necessary for child-rearing, primarily by defining and policing entry into and exit from marriage. Where marriage does not or cannot secure the resources necessary for child-rearing, it ceases to be universal. In this context, neoliberal traditionalists tend to insist that the response should be state policies that double down on moral exhortation and personal responsibilities, while modernists are more inclined to support state policies that enhance families' individual choices.

Missing in this conflict, however, is a more considered response to the unfolding change in the nature of employment. The initial part of this change, as we indicated above, involved the combination of women's increased workforce participation and the decimation of the male family wage, upending the industrial age's marriage bargain. The next development has been the "casualization" of labor, as an increasing part of the workforce has access only to temporary or part-time jobs. The step about to unfold may well be dramatically greater automation of routine tasks, increasing unemployment on a global basis. The question for the family is what the state responses to these developments will be.

The initial stages of the change have given rise to a new marriage model that replaces a gendered assignment of family rights and obligations with a more egalitarian one. McClain's argument for greater state investment in all children to encourage a more capable, informed, and flexible citizenry is also a proposal to increase family stability: more capable children are also likely to be more capable partners, better equipped to establish stable families. This analysis, however, fails if those more capable children find that meaningful and secure employment is unlikely to be there for them. The impoverishment or the marginalization of large portions of the population will undermine the stability of the family, whether the state attempts to promote marriage or whether it accepts and supports alternative family forms.

The missing piece, therefore, in the discussion of the relationship between state and family is the recreation of the state to meet the information age's needs for stability and security. At this point, we do not know from where the resources of the future necessary to support family life will come, but without a more robust state effort to order the terms of the new age, the result is likely to be even greater family instability and inequality in the future. Just as industrialization and urbanization increased inequality and undermined family stability, so too has the information age destabilized the family forms of the industrial age. And just as the industrial age required the reinvention of the state to address these circumstances, so too will the information age require the reinvention of the state to insure individual—and family—stability. This reinvention, like the ones before it, will involve the following three elements.

First, how will the state develop policies on family formation and the state resources available to support children? With the transition to the industrial age, those resources shifted from landownership to male wage labor. Currently, many and perhaps soon the majority of American families will lack secure sources of sustenance. It is possible, however, to imagine a future with greater distribution of capital ownership (i.e., more widespread ownership of stocks and bonds tied to economic performance),[69] a universal jobs guarantee that offers every citizen a job paying the minimum wage and accommodating health care needs,[70] or some form of minimum income,[71] or more modest state interventions that promote private sector employment and tighten labor markets.[72] The terms on which such benefits are available will be important in determining the form of future families, and whether family form will simply continue to vary with personal choices or converge on new, widely accepted forms. They require in turn the redesign of the state to deliver such benefits, and the construction of a political coalition to support that redesign. If that does not happen, it is also possible to imagine a future in which existing trends continue, and family form will still reflect entrenched class differences. Such families, however, will not really be "families of choice," and they will reflect state-created, rather than personal, moral decay.

Second, how will the state's allocation of responsibility between public and private sources define the terms of family autonomy? The question of parental autonomy will depend both on cultural agreement on child-rearing authority and on the sources of self-sufficiency that make autonomy possible. Perhaps most critical in this respect is reproductive autonomy for everyone. Families that choose the timing of reproduction enjoy greater stability in adult relationships and provide better for their children. In addition, increased public support for children, in the form of early childhood care, universal preschool education (which is as great an imperative today as free secondary education in the nineteenth century), family-friendly workplaces, and universal health care, would make it easier to respect all parents' autonomy in the decisions they make for their children. State systematization of reproductive autonomy, which is a product of access to contraception and the norms that encourage its use, together with state support for care work, will be critical to reinforcing parental authority and children's well-being.

Third, how will the state promote the circumstances that make family well-being possible? The critical economic transformation in today's economy has been the shift from large public and private institutions that offered lifelong employment to more flexible and rapidly changing networks. The largest employers in 1960 were mostly the same as those in 1910. Many of today's large companies did not exist fifty years ago. While such companies may still dominate the economic landscape, they routinely sell off entire divisions, mechanize plants, and create high-paying jobs in specialties that did not exist a few years before. Fifty percent of computer science majors will leave the field within a decade of graduation, in part because their skills will be outmoded. Will the state assist individuals in acquiring the capacities to respond more quickly and nimbly to changing economic circumstances? This will require not only greater investment in children and more public support for education and training, but greater efforts to balance commercial and domestic needs. Because of state deference to powerful private actors, neoliberal policies have stood in the way of the creation of the more family-friendly workplaces the vast majority of the public wants.

Conclusion

The state has historically sought to encourage family stability and economic security by linking family formation to the husband's ability to secure the resources necessary for family support. By the mid-twentieth century, the state's goal in promoting family stability involved policies fostering steady employment, a family wage for men, and a gendered assignment of family roles. Today, in contrast, there is no institutionalized political support either for a direct state role to ensure the family's economic stability or for a state-imposed definition of family formation that ties legal regulation to acquisition of the prerequisites for economic security. Indeed, even on such basic issues as the importance of marriage or contraceptive access, there is no systematic effort to ensure that the entire population has realistic access, with the result that elite families not only have ready access to reliable contraception, but use it in accordance with strong norms against unintended pregnancies, while the rest of the population has neither secure access nor broadly shared norms about the importance of contraceptive use or the importance of avoiding early pregnancy in encouraging stronger families. Similarly, the amount of money spent on marriage promotion reflects diverging views on the privatization of care and men's breadwinning roles, with some traditionalists seeing conventional gender roles as essential to marital vitality, while others view the lack of commitment to egalitarian values as a primary obstacle to stable family life.[73] As a result, not only is there is no agreement on overall direction, there is no consistent construction of the state institutional capacity to influence family practices.

To reforge the links between state and family requires assembling a political coalition to redefine the substantive source of family economic security. The state relationship to the family has always rested on assumptions about the links between the economy and the family, and as the economy has changed, so too has the nature of state intervention in the family. The state successfully addressed the industrial age's destabilization of the family only with the creation of the administrative state of the New Deal and its promotion of the private measures, such as unions and employer-provided benefits, that contributed to family stability. The state, whether a libertarian or a socialist one, will be able to effectively address the family needs of the information age only when it reinvents itself to be able to promote individual and family resilience in a networked age. Partisan conflicts not only prevent agreement on new family values strategies but also distract attention from the need to redesign the state so that tomorrow's families can thrive. Transformation and a degree of convergence are possible as the irrevocability and destructiveness of economic change become more apparent. After all, both Donald Trump and Nancy Pelosi agree that creating more "good jobs" ought to be a critical measure of political success.

Notes

Our thanks to Maryam Gueye for research assistance.

1. Julie Novkov and Carol Nackenoff, Introduction to this volume (p. 4); Carol Nackenoff and Julie Novkov, *Statebuilding from the Margins: Between Reconstruction and the New Deal* (Philadelphia: University of Pennsylvania Press, 2014).

2. For a complete explanation of these terms, see Naomi Cahn and June Carbone, *Red Families v. Blue Families: Legal Polarization and the Creation of Culture* (New York: Oxford University Press, 2010).

3. Priscilla Yamin, *American Marriage: A Political Institution* (Philadelphia: University of Pennsylvania Press, 2012); and Martha Fineman, *The Neutered Mother, the Sexual Family, and other Twentieth Century Tragedies* (New York: Routledge, 1995).

4. Cahn and Carbone, *Red Families v. Blue Families.*

5. Carol Nackenoff, "Groundhog Day Again? Is the 'Liberal Tradition' a Useful Construct for Studying Law, Courts, and American Political Development?" *The Good Society* 16, no. 1 (2007): 43.

6. Linda C. McClain, "The Family, the State, and American Political Development as a Big Tent: Asking Basic Questions about Basic Institutions," *Polity* 48, no. 2 (April 2016): 228.

7. Karen Orren and Stephen Skowronek, *The Search for American Political Development* (New York: Cambridge University Press, 2004), 123.

8. Carl E. Schneider, "The Channelling Function in Family Law," *Hofstra Law Review* 20, no. 3 (1992): 495.

9. Ann Laquer Estin, "Family Law Federalism: Divorce and the Constitution," *William & Mary Bill of Rights Journal* 16, no. 2 (2007): 409.

10. Anne C. Dailey, "Federalism and Families," *University of Pennsylvania Law Review* 143, no. 6 (1995): 1790.

11. Jill Elaine Hasday, "Federalism and the Family Reconstructed," *University of California Law Review* 45 (1998): 1299.

12. Nackenoff, "Groundhog Day"; *Obergefell v. Hodges*, 576 U.S. __ , 135 S. Ct. 2584 (June 26, 2015).

13. Susan Moller Okin, *Justice, Gender, and the Family* (New York: Basic Books, 1989); see also Carole Pateman, *The Sexual Contract* (Stanford, CA: Stanford University Press, 1988).

14. Joan C. Tronto, *Caring Democracy: Markets, Equality, and Justice* (New York: New York University Press, 2013), xi; Tronto, "Responsibility for the Well-Being of Families," Foreword to this volume.

15. Novkov and Nackenoff, Introduction to this volume, p. 1.

16. Maxine Eichner, *The Supportive State: Families, Government, and America's Political Ideals* (New York: Oxford University Press, 2010).

17. Patricia Strach, *All in the Family: The Private Roots of American Public Policy* (Stanford, CA: Stanford University Press, 2007), 18.

18. Michael R. Haines, "Long-Term Marriage Patterns in the United States from Colonial Times to the Present," *The History of the Family* 1, no. 1 (January 2012): 15–17.

19. Martha Fineman, "What Place for Family Privacy?" *George Washington Law Review* 67, no. 5 (1999): 1207–1224.

20. Naomi R. Cahn, "Family Law, Federalism, and the Federal Courts," *Iowa Law Review* 79, no. 3 (1994): 1094–1095.

21. June Carbone, *From Partners to Parents: The Second Revolution in Family Law* (New York: Columbia University Press, 2000).

22. June Carbone and Naomi Cahn, "The Triple System of Family Law," *Michigan State Law Review* 2013 (2013): 1185.

23. June Carbone and Naomi Cahn, "Nonmarriage," *Maryland Law Review* 76 (2016): 55.

24. Clare Huntington, "Postmarital Family Law: A Legal Structure for Nonmarital Families," *Stanford Law Review* 67, no. 1 (January 2015): 167.

25. Indeed, Martha Fineman advocates protection of the nurturing role associated with motherhood, whether performed by men or women. Fineman, *The Neutered Mother.*

26. Cahn and Carbone, *Red Families v. Blue Families.*

27. Schneider, "The Channelling Function in Family Law."

28. June Carbone, "Out of the Channel and into the Swamp: How Family Law Fails in a New Era of Class Division," *Hofstra Law Review* 39 (2011): 859.

29. Yamin, *American Marriage,* 19.

30. *Obergefell v. Hodges,* 576 U.S. ___ (2015).

31. Charles Murray, *Coming Apart: The State of White America* (New York: Crown Forum, 2012).

32. Eileen McDonagh, "The Family-State Nexus in American Political Development: Explaining Women's Political Citizenship," *Polity* 48, no. 2 (2016): 203.

33. *Obergefell,* at 2613 (Roberts, C. J.), citing James Q. Wilson, *The Marriage Problem: How Our Culture Has Weakened Families* (New York: Harper Collins, 2002).

34. John Demos, *A Little Commonwealth: Family Life in Plymouth Colony* (New York: Oxford University Press, 1970), quoted in Michael Grossberg, *Governing the Hearth: Law and the Family in Nineteenth-Century America* (Chapel Hill: University of North Carolina Press, 1985), 4–5.

35. Anne C. Dailey, "Constitutional Privacy and the Just Family," *Tulane Law*

Review 67 (1993): 964–965. This "little commonwealth" of family life was public not only in the economic sense, but as the phrase implies, in the full political sense as well.

36. *The Negro Family: The Case for National Action (The Moynihan Report)*, US Department of Labor, Office of Policy Planning and Research, March 1965, http://www.blackpast.org/primary/moynihan-report-1965.

37. Mary Ryan, *Cradle of the Middle Class: The Family in Oneida County, New York, 1790–1865* (Cambridge: Cambridge University Press, 1981).

38. Marion Crain, "Between Feminism and Unionism: Working-Class Women, Sex Equality, and Labor Speech," *Georgetown Law Journal* 82 (1994): 1903.

39. Theda Skocpol, *Protecting Soldiers and Mothers: The Political Origins of Social Policy in the United States* (Cambridge, MA: Harvard University Press, 1992); Janet Zollinger Giele, "Social Policy and the Family," *Annual Review of Sociology* 5 (August 1979): 275–302.

40. For freed slaves, marriage became both a necessary part of preparation for citizenship and a potential source of oppression. Yamin, *American Marriage*; Katherine Franke, *Wedlocked: The Perils of Marriage Equality* (New York: New York University Press, 2015); Julie Novkov, *Racial Union: Law, Intimacy, and the White State in Alabama, 1865–1954* (Ann Arbor: University of Michigan Press, 2008).

41. Carbone, *From Partners to Parents,* 48.

42. Mark DeWolf, US Department of Labor Blog, March 1, 2017, https://blog.dol.gov/2017/03/01/12-stats-about-working-women.

43. Barbara Ehrenreich, *Nickel and Dimed: On (Not) Getting By in America* (New York: Holt Paperbacks, 2001).

44. "Employee Tenure Summary," Economic News Release, US Department of Labor, Bureau of Labor Statistics, September 20, 2018, https://www.bls.gov/news.release/tenure.nr0.htm.

45. Martin Konrad, "Freelancers Make Up 34 Percent of the U.S. Workforce: Here's How to Find, Hire, and Manage Them," *Entrepreneur* magazine, May 24, 2016, https://www.entrepreneur.com/article/275362.

46. June Carbone and Naomi Cahn, *Marriage Markets: How Inequality Is Remaking the American Family* (New York: Oxford University Press, 2014).

47. Carbone and Cahn, "Nonmarriage."

48. Margaret F. Brinig and Douglas W. Allen, "These Boots Are Made for Walking: Why Most Divorce Filers Are Women," *American Law and Economics Review* 2, no. 1 (January 2000): 128 (stating that two-thirds of those filing for divorce are women and custody laws affect willingness to file).

49. Kay Hymowitz et al., "Knot Yet: The Benefits and Costs of Delayed Marriage in America," National Marriage Project, http://nationalmarriageproject.org/wp-content/uploads/2013/03/KnotYet-FinalForWeb.pdf.

50. Alexandra Killewald, "Money, Work, and Marital Stability: Assessing Change in the Gendered Determinants of Divorce," *American Sociological Review* 81, no. 4 (2016): 696; Carbone and Cahn, *Marriage Markets*, 98.

51. Charles Murray, *Coming Apart: The State of White America* (New York: Crown Forum, 2012).

52. Carbone and Cahn, *Marriage Markets*, 77, 100–101.

53. Richard Wilkinson and Kate Pickett, *The Spirit Level: Why Greater Inequality Makes Societies Stronger* (New York: Bloomsbury Press, 2009).

54. Kathryn Edin and Maria Kefalas, *Promises I Can Keep: Why Poor Women Put Motherhood Before Marriage* (Los Angeles: University of California Press, 2005), 81.

55. Paul Amato et al., *Alone Together: How Marriage in America Is Changing* (Cambridge, MA: Harvard University Press, 2007), 123–124.

56. Stéphane Mechoulan, "The External Effects of Black Male Incarceration on Black Females," *Journal of Labor Economics* 29, no. 1 (January 2011): 1–35.

57. Carbone and Cahn, *Marriage Markets*.

58. Lindsey Cook, "For Richer, Not Poorer: Marriage and the Growing Class Divide," *US News*, October 26, 2015.

59. Mary Ann Glendon, *The Transformation of Family Law: State, Law, and Family in the United States and Western Europe* (Chicago, IL: University of Chicago Press, 1989).

60. Shawn Fremstad and Melissa Boteach, "Valuing All Our Families," Center for American Progress, January 12, 2015, p. 33 of the downloadable report, https://www.americanprogress.org/issues/poverty/reports/2015/01/12/104149/valuing-all-our-families/.

61. Ben Casselman, "Marriage Isn't Dead—Yet," *FiveThirtyEight*, September 29, 2014, http://fivethirtyeight.com/features/marriage-isnt-dead-yet/, accessed January 5, 2016.

62. Though less so for black women. Key facts about births to unmarried women can be found at "Births to Unmarried Women," Child Trends, http://www.childtrends.org/indicators/births-to-unmarried-women/.

63. Carbone and Cahn, "Nonmarriage."

64. Joan Tronto, *Caring Democracy*, 37.

65. Edward L. Rubin, *Soul, Self, and Society: The New Morality and the Modern State* (New York: Oxford University Press, 2015).

66. McClain, "The Family, the State, and American Political Development as a Big Tent," 4.

67. McClain, 5.

68. Cahn and Carbone, *Red Families v. Blue Families*.

69. Robert Ashford, "Economics, Democracy, and the Distribution of Capital Ownership," *Forum for Socio-Economics* 40 (2011): 361.

70. L. Randall Wray et. al., *Public Service Employment: A Path to Full Employ-*

ment, Levy Economic Institute of Bard College, report, April 2018, http://www
.levyinstitute.org/pubs/rpr_4_18.pdf.

71. Benjamin Sadlek, "United States: The American Enterprise Institute Releases a Proposal for a Universal Basic Income," Basic Income Earth Network
(BIEN), July 16, 2017, https://basicincome.org/news/2017/07/united-states
-american-enterprise-institute-releases-proposal-universal-basic-income/.

72. Edmund S. Phelps, *Rewarding Work: How to Restore Participation and Self-
Support to Free Enterprise* (Cambridge, MA: Harvard University Press, 1997).

73. Compare W. Bradford Wilcox and Steven L. Nock, "What's Love Got to
Do with It? Equality, Equity, Commitment, and Women's Marital Quality," *Social
Forces* 84, no. 3 (2006): 1321–1345, with Naomi Cahn et al., *Unequal Family
Lives: Causes and Consequences in Europe and the Americas* (New York: Cambridge
University Press, 2018).

2 | *Obergefell,* Marriage, and the Neoliberal Politics of Care

Tamara Metz

Introduction: Underbelly of a Victory

On June 6, 2015, the Supreme Court's decision in *Obergefell v. Hodges* made same-sex marriage legal throughout the United States. While the decision was widely—and rightly—celebrated as a victory for justice and civil rights, the case and its vision of marriage emerge as accomplices to a politics that undermines the social and material conditions upon which common life depends.

Obergefell turns on an account of marriage that has come to dominate US public imagination and policy since the 1970s. At its core, this account sentimentalizes individuals and their families and places all responsibility on them for caring for each other, which serves the neoliberal order by simultaneously securing and obscuring the radical privatization and deeply flawed distribution of the costs and benefits of care. Celebrated in terms that do not quite cohere—individual rights, private choice, and freedom; *and* a pre-political institution with sacred duties and significance; *and* evidence of limited government; *and* a key site of the state as an ethical authority—this vision of marriage is one of many contradictions that fuels the operations of the neoliberal political project. For all else that it is, *Obergefell* offers a perfect summary of the role, ideological and material, that the institution of marriage has come to play in the consolidation of our neoliberal social formation.

Scholars have long argued that in the *liberal* tradition marriage functioned to secure the essential labor of care even as it hid the costs and gendered inequalities associated with the provision of this labor under a veil of sentiment, consent, and companionate, if separate, equality.[1] Early defenders of liberalism relied heavily on this vision of marriage to make their political case; it would remain central to the tradition well into the twentieth century.[2] In many ways, the idealized white, middle-class, marital family of the United States in the 1950s is the exemplar of the liberal vision: ostensibly founded in consent but dominated by sentiment, a separate but equal companionship that forms the haven in a heartless world essential to the social, cultural, and political reproduction of citizens.

To many in the United States, the challenges to marriage in the 1960s thus seemed to portend the end of a long-standing phenomenon: marriage's utility as servant to liberal capitalism.[3] Divorce was on the rise, feminists and counter-culturalists vociferously criticized the institution, and policy shifts like no-fault divorce shook the foundational place of marriage in American imagination and practice. In retrospect, the downfall of marriage alongside the emergence of neoliberal cultural logic should not have been at all surprising.

And yet, by the early 1980s the pendulum had swung in the opposite direction. In public rhetoric and policy, if not exactly practice, marriage was back in favor.

This reversal occurred just as the political, economic, and cultural shifts of neoliberalism took hold in the United States.[4] Neoliberal politics operates on the fuel of a grand ruse: that a world populated by self-investing individuals whose fortunes are determined by choice, not structures of class, race, gender, or national history, is possible and desirable. Personal responsibility and entrepreneurial spirit are the cardinal virtues.[5] Competition and contract are the dominant modes of interaction. Over the last half century, this logic has been matched by tectonic shifts in policy and economies.

In short, one might think that the public reputation of marriage would have suffered in a world dominated by market logic and entrepreneurial individualism. In fact, as this chapter shows, the opposite has occurred. It turns out that marriage, in a version both familiar and novel, crystalized in *Obergefell*, has been essential to the consolidation of the neoliberal social formation. From the perspective of how marriage functions in the neoliberal political project, the landmark decision is notable less for its radical break from the heteropatriarchal history of the institution, and more, as I shall argue, for its continuation of the celebration of a deeply incoherent but clearly popular account of marriage and its relationship to the state. The result is that *Obergefell*, like all of its neoliberal compatriots, uses the language of individual freedom and personal responsibility to secure and then obscure the real costs and benefits of care in our world, as well as the inequalities that structure their distribution.

Neoliberal marriage is a vigorously inclusive choice that no responsible person would refuse. Extended first to "interracial" (with the US Supreme Court decision *Loving v. Virginia* in 1967) and then to same-sex couples, marriage is cast at once as an individual freedom—"a fundamental right"—and, at the same time, as an institution that forms the cornerstone of society. And while *Obergefell* appears to dethrone compulsory heterosexuality, it rests heavily on a vision of care that has always depended on and, it turns out, continues to depend on gender, race, class, and legal status. Now more than ever, private families are affirmed as responsible for securing great swaths of essential and costly social reproductive labor. Whether marital families are providing care firsthand or, as is increasingly the case, secondhand by paying people lower down on the socioeconomic scale, the vision of marriage that animates *Obergefell* affirms responsibility for the production and well-being of consumer-citizens as a wholly private matter, shunting the real costs and benefits of this work from public attention and off the public ledger. Put another way: ideologically, marriage has helped justify and obscure the consequences of the death of embedded liberalism and the welfare state of the postwar period.

The Neoliberal Politics of Care

Scholars point to the 1970s as the moment when the growing force of neoliberal policy, economic, and cultural trends dislodged "embedded liberalism" in the United States.[6] The shifts included the expansion of "free market" mechanisms into new arenas; the deregulation of industry, capital flow, and finance; and an emphasis on market health as the key indicator of social and political health. As the market was valorized, government support for social welfare was villainized. Postwar public policy that helped spread the gains of a robust economy across the population contracted. Corporations and the wealthy saw their taxes fall steadily. Workfare replaced welfare. Public goods, from education to prisons, parks, and the postal service, were increasingly privatized and/or outsourced.[7] Provision of last-ditch "safety nets" was deemed the only appropriate function of government.[8] This "great risk shift" moved responsibility for life's universal and inevitable moments of vulnerability from the commons to private shoulders.[9] Broadly, the neoliberal economy witnessed an upward redistribution of resources from the poor, working, and middle classes to an international capitalist class, and a marked increase in income and wealth inequality between the ultra-rich and the rest.[10]

The material impact of these changes on care has been profound. For the purposes of this chapter, by "care" I refer to labor associated with meeting the basic material, social, and psychological needs that extend from the fact of human vulnerability, which in the United States is historically associated with the private sphere, women, low social status, and, when paid, low pay.[11] In the United States, "right-to-work" policies weakened labor unions and the living wages and ample benefits they had secured. Economic necessity and new gender norms shepherded into the paid labor force an increasing number of American women who had previously provided significant proportions of unpaid domestic labor. Public policy failed to respond to the resulting decrease in available caregivers. Indeed, just the opposite occurred. The reimagining of good governance as market growth and fiscal discipline led to deep cuts in social insurance programs and shifted more of the onus for meeting the basic risks of life onto increasingly atomized individuals and families.[12] These trends produced what scholars have called a "care crisis." Individuals and their caregiving networks now bear an increased responsibility for the costs of care with fewer resources.[13] Women who entered the paid labor force, in effect, joined the ranks of their less-advantaged peers of earlier generations, now working two shifts, one at home and one outside it.[14] And the pressure on private intimate caregiving units in the global north—paradigmatically, "the family"—fuels an increase in paid intimate care and a burgeoning of a global care chain wracked with inequalities.[15]

As always, the material shifts are matched by ideological shifts, or as Wendy Brown puts it, shifts in the dominant political rationality. The neoliberal political rationality not only reorients and reshapes the state, but also "govern[s] subjects themselves and every institution on the landscape.... Not itself an instrument of governing, [this political rationality is] the condition of possibility and legitimacy of its instruments."[16] This is a worldview in which politics serves the market, and economic health, rather than political health, is the guiding value. Market values reach beyond the world of the economy and now extend into *all* spheres of life, becoming embodied in self-regulating, self-investing, responsible subjects.[17] The neoliberal subject is entrepreneurial to the core: driven by the imperative to self-invest, the neoliberal subject has little interest in the public good.[18] Each is a singular entrepreneur responsible for improving her own human capital (measured in market, not religious, political, social, or poetic terms). The state's task is to secure "free" markets, to produce economic growth, and, at most, to secure the conditions that allow responsibilized citizens to increase their value.

This thinking is the foundation of Margaret Thatcher's famous claim, "There is no such thing as society. There are individual men and women . . . and their families."[19] But, as Brown and others have noted, Thatcher's ellipsis points to the embarrassing impossibility of the neoliberal imaginary, this world of unencumbered, deal-making individuals. The neoliberal vision of human life is at odds with reality; no human being survives, much less thrives, on her own. We enter, leave, and often spend extended unpredictable stretches in between, utterly vulnerable. And the care we receive generates, in our caregivers, "derivative vulnerability."[20] In the normal course of life, "individuals" cannot do without "families" (or some source of care for which they cannot bargain, whom they cannot be guaranteed to pay back).

Like its liberal democratic forebear but with a vengeance, neoliberal politics are parasitic on institutions, norms, and practices they deny. The new politics witness both an intensification and a shift in the content of this relationship.[21] The neoliberal politics of care continues to treat the family as a black box that produces citizens—now conceived of as individual market actors—magically, and free of charge. The inherently nested nature of care—caring for the utterly vulnerable creates derivative needs for care that, in turn, create their own needs for care—is occluded.[22] Thus, when responsible, self-maximizing individuals are not produced, a moralizing rhetoric of dysfunction places blame on private families.

But where embedded liberalism admitted, if tacitly, vulnerability and necessary interdependence and provided structures of support for meeting the needs individual humans cannot meet on their own— albeit, unequal in many ways—neoliberalism exalts only "personal responsibility" multiplied, however incoherently, by "care for one's own." Slipped in under cover of the rhetoric of individualism and an ellipsis, the realities of human vulnerability and the resulting, unavoidable interdependence are denied and hidden from public view. "Familialism," the cult of the private family, Brown rightly argues, "is an essential requirement, rather than an incidental feature of the neoliberal privatization of public goods and services."[23] Neoliberal logic cannot acknowledge or explain the essential costly labor of care and the institutions that supply it. But because it depends on that labor, it must secure those goods and commitment to their provision off the books in the private sphere.

This is where marriage comes in.

Because families are tasked with the increasingly impossible task of providing care to their members in a neoliberal political economy, and because every individual is an entrepreneur responsible for themselves, "the family" needs to sound like a good deal. Marriage is the key means by which state and society market this bill of goods. This is a familiar strategy. Decades ago, Susan Moller Okin argued that marriage served *liberal* politics as an ideological cover and mechanism for reinforcing patriarchal relations upon which they depended but could not justify. Alongside the story of a union of equals in "companionate" marriage, the sentimental veil of marriage proffered an account of gender and separate spheres that cast a deeply unequal relationship as natural. In *Justice, Gender, and the Family*, Okin showed how the interplay of ideas and practices entrenched and normalized a gendered division of labor across the purported public-private divide in liberal theory and practice. Marriage simultaneously secured and obscured the costs and benefits of essential kinds of care by casting a sentimental veil over a thoroughly gendered institution.[24]

The marital family of *neoliberalism* plays a similar role, but one molded to the particular needs of the new social formation. Marriage—now of any color, now gay or straight—wraps a sentimental shroud tailored to the new political rationality around the era's impossible economic and social structures. On stark display in *Obergefell*, marriage under neoliberalism is characterized by three functions.

First, it combines an aggressively individualist logic with the tradition of marriage as a comprehensive social institution, the authority of which exceeds the political. Thus, civil rights advocates describe the "freedom to marry" and argue that "marriage is a fundamental right," while marriage remains a "cornerstone of society."

Second, neoliberal marriage revivifies the sentimental veil that marriage has long placed over the private family as the privileged site of responsibility for care. Thus, it takes the assumption of that responsibility of bearing the risks and costs of care outside the market logic that dominates but cannot account for those costs.

Finally, neoliberal marriage is blind to difference, yet intimately tied to intensified inequalities based on race, class, national status, and gender.

For all that *Obergefell* did to advance civil rights, the vision of marriage (and its function in the polity) expressed in the decision hits all of these notes. In that sense, as we shall see, the cunning of history has this landmark decision turn on a vision of marriage that is part and parcel of a broader politics that threatens the values it purports to uphold. Equality realized by marriage reworked to embrace gays and lesbians simultaneously serves to bolster a neoliberal social formation that undermines broad material equality across divides of sex/gender, race, class, and legal status.

Marriage as Handmaiden to the Neoliberal Politics of Care

The shadow side of the political victory in *Obergefell* is evident in light of the history of marriage in the service of the neoliberal politics of care. Whether we look to early responses to the skyrocketing rates of divorce in the 1970s and 1980s, efforts to use marriage as poverty prevention, the same-sex marriage battles, the cries of a marriage crisis among African Americans, or the work-life balance discourse, we see the same story: marriage is hailed at once as a fundamental individual political right *and* a timeless, pre-political institution; a source of supreme existential meaning and romantic connection *and* the privileged, primary site of essential care; a personal choice that no responsible person would fail to make. Woven through this story are strands of race, class, and sex/gender that both construct and obscure the operations of these categories in the neoliberal politics of care. What is perhaps most striking about this phenomenon is the range of political constituencies that have bought into a neoliberal view of marriage. Even groups that have, for good reason, been suspicious of the state's investment in pro-marriage policies have adopted the framework of marriage as a personal right and civil responsibility.

To appreciate just how marriage morphed to fit the emerging politics, it is necessary to consider what it looked like in the practices, policy, and rhetoric of the 1960s and early 1970s, in the period before the consolidation of neoliberal politics in the United States. Evidence of the demise of marriage was everywhere. Changing economic realities were disturbing the traditional gendered model of marriage: women were moving into the paid labor force in record numbers, and male wages—and with them, the prevalence of the so-called family wage—were declining.[25] The necessity of marriage, especially for women who were no longer so dependent on men for financial means, seemed less obvious. Feminist criticisms of the institution found eager audiences not only among women and counter-culturalists broadly, but also capitalists happy to have another argument that seemed to support the growing reserve of workers (male and female) and the resulting depressed wages.[26] Reverberations of free love also shook the hold marriage had on the American imagination: pop culture was happy to escape the confines of the institution. Legal changes such as the Supreme Court's 1965 *Griswold v. Connecticut* decision legalizing the use of contraception by married couples, the 1972 *Eisenstadt v. Baird* decision establishing the same right for unmarried people, and the 1973 *Roe v. Wade* decision legalizing abortion, as well as medical advances such as the birth control pill, helped decouple sex from procreation and weaken the taboo against premarital sex.[27] Even religious institutions were relaxing their hold on marriage—for example, the Catholic Church allowed easier access to annulments.[28]

No change better captures the spirit of the era than no-fault divorce. By the late 1960s, the discrepancy between the law, which required couples to establish fault, adultery, or cruelty, and social reality, wherein more people wanted to leave marriage and were willing to perjure themselves to do so, was clear enough to legal professionals that they initiated efforts to reform the law.[29] Following the model of the insurance world, proponents of no-fault divorce argued that marriage should not be treated as a morally exceptional contract. The state needed only to ensure that people and property were safe and fairly treated. In the air of the late 1960s, these arguments by a relatively small band of lawyers were convincing. In 1969, Ronald Reagan, then governor of California, signed the first no-fault divorce bill into law, and by 1985, no-fault divorce was secured in all but a few states. For the first time in US history, one party could unilaterally end a marriage for "irreconcilable differences."[30] As a legal matter, breaking up had never been easier to do.

In the United States in the 1970s, marriage appeared to be losing its pull. And, in many ways, this fit comfortably with the neoliberal political rationality that was coming to dominate US public life. Born in the mountains of Switzerland, nurtured by scholars at the University of Chicago, and experimented with in Chile after Augusto Pinochet took power in a coup, this vision of politics and society was drawn into public discourse and policy in the United States first by conservative politicians reacting to the economic crisis of the 1970s. Candidate and then President Ronald Reagan (1981–1989) was an early and vociferous adopter, touting the benefits of free markets, small government, and personal responsibility as he cut taxes on corporations and the wealthy, reduced public spending on social welfare programs, deregulated industry, and waged war against trade unions. By the 1980s, the neoliberal world view was ascendant. In this context, one might expect that the social institution of marriage, with its affective ties and unlimited obligations, might lose its attraction.

Obituaries for marriage, however, were premature. In fact, with alacrity, actors on both the right and left of the political spectrum turned to marriage as a key component of shifting public policy. Social conservatives initiated the return. Activists such as Phyllis Schlafly and Anita Bryant focused on marriage as they campaigned against threats to the traditional sex and gender norms of the heteropatriarchal family.[31] Drawing energy and focus from these efforts, in the 1980s President Reagan made marital family values a central plank of his politics. In the 1990s, efforts to defend marriage coalesced in the proliferation of "conservative institutes, think tanks, and programs focused on marriage . . . [such as] the National Marriage Project, Focus on the Family, Smart Marriages, Marriage Savers, the Center for Marriage and Family at the Institute for American Values, and the Institute for Marriage and Public Policy," and the neoconservative marriage movement was born.[32] An outpouring of popular, quasi-scholarly work, such as James Q. Wilson's *The Marriage Problem* and Linda Waite and Maggie Gallagher's *The Case for Marriage,* identifying marriage as both cause of and solution to social ills, followed in the early 2000s.[33] The vision of marriage that emerged was both a familiar conservative one and also new, marked with distinctly neoliberal inflections. Marriage is a pre-political institution *and* fundamentally a civil institution, a cornerstone of society *and* an individual choice, a source of timeless traditions of sex, gender, and sexuality *and* entirely compatible with the new norms of gender equality, at once a source of supreme existential meaning *and* the primary source of basic social welfare provision.

One persistent question about the rise and consolidation of neoliberal politics in the last half century in the United States is how it is related to the rise of neoconservative forces.[34] The story of marriage suggests that these developments are symbiotic. Even as the neoconservative celebration of marriage sounded many traditional notes, it also struck novel ones. The new defense of marriage emphasized rights and choice and, even among social conservatives, often endorsed a kind of gender equality. Reagan, in his 1986 radio address on family values, captures the sentiment: "They understood that all those aspects of civilized life that we most deeply cherish—freedom, the rule of law, economic prosperity and opportunity—that all these depend upon the strength and integrity of the family. . . . All of our lives, it's the love of our families that sustains us when times are hard. And it is perhaps above all to provide for our children that we work and save."[35] Freedom, rule of law, and economic prosperity could have been taken straight out of those books of the neoliberal bible, Friedrich Hayek's *The Road to Serfdom* and Milton Friedman's *Capitalism and Freedom.*[36]

Eight years later, George H. W. Bush's vice president Dan Quayle struck a related note when he chided Murphy Brown—the fictional forty-something divorced news anchor played by Candice Bergen—for her decision to have a child outside marriage: "Bearing babies irresponsibly is simply wrong. . . . Failing to support children one has fathered is wrong. We must be unequivocal about this. It doesn't help matters when prime-time TV has Murphy Brown, a character who supposedly epitomizes today's intelligent, highly paid professional woman, mocking the importance of fathers by bearing a child alone and calling it just another lifestyle choice."[37] Quayle does not criticize Brown for her success in the world of paid labor—on the contrary, he seems to approve—but for her failure to make the responsible choice to have a child in marriage.

Understanding marriage as a uniquely significant social institution—the site and source of personal fulfillment and responsibility—is, perhaps ironically, intimately linked to the politics of poverty prevention and social welfare programs of the Great Society era. A foundational document in this shift was Assistant Secretary of Labor Daniel Patrick Moynihan's 1965 report, *The Negro Family: A Case for National Action.* What came to be known as the Moynihan Report traces the roots of problems facing black communities to family structure. Moynihan wrote, "At the heart of the deterioration of the fabric of Negro society is the deterioration of the Negro family"; "at the center of the tangle of pathology is the weakness of the family structure."[38] Relatively low marriage rates and high divorce rates, and the fact that black women are more likely than white women to have children out of wedlock, Moynihan argued, explains why black children receive public assistance.[39] He urged the government to intervene, and to help "strengthen the Negro family so as to enable it to raise and support its members as do other families."[40]

His story is clear: There were problems peculiar to "Negro society," not society as a whole or poor communities generally. Lack of marriage, more than histories and structures of racialized inequalities or lack of public support for social reproductive labor, was the acute source of the problem and thus the proper location of state intervention.

This trope would recur and evolve, generating bipartisan consensus, over the next five decades. Ronald Reagan sewed up his unsuccessful 1976 run for the Republican nomination for president with a speech that would introduce the figure of "the welfare queen"—the black, unwed, single mother living carefree off the taxpayers' largesse—into popular imagination. The next administration continued the tradition. Quayle's 1992 speech is best remembered for the Murphy Brown bit, but it was delivered in response to the violence that erupted after the white Los Angeles police officers whose beating of Rodney King was captured on videotape were acquitted. In the speech, titled "On Family Values," Quayle noted that while on a trip to Japan, he "was asked many times . . . about the recent events in Los Angeles." Those with whom he met abroad asked why the riots happened. "In a nutshell," Quayle said, "I believe the lawless social anarchy which we saw is directly related to the breakdown of family structure, personal responsibility, and social order in too many areas of our society. For the poor the situation is compounded by a welfare ethos that impedes individual efforts to move ahead in society."[41] There was a problem in the black society, and lack of marriage was its cause.

In their push for "welfare reform," neoliberal Democrats took up this racialized trope with unrelenting vigor. Despite the fact that more white Americans relied on public assistance than black Americans, Democrats sold their reform by replaying the images of the welfare queen from two decades earlier.[42] Welfare was again cast as a black problem caused by lack of marriage that could be solved by marriage promotion.[43] In 1996, President Bill Clinton made good on his promise to "end welfare as we know it," signing into law the Personal Responsibility and Work Opportunity Reconciliation Act (PRWORA). The opening line in the act reminds us that "marriage is the foundation of a successful society." The key aims of the act, the document continues, are "promoting job preparation, work, and marriage." Mirroring not only the rhetoric but also the policy goals of the neoconservative marriage movement, the act gave block grants to states to support marriage promotion and abstinence-only sex education that "teaches that a mutually faithful monogamous relationship in context of marriage is the expected standard of human sexual activity." The act promotes a specific vision—two-parent, sexually contained, amatonormative,[44] and, at the time, heterosexual, family, and asserts that "personal responsibility" is a public value realized through participation in marriage and the paid labor force. To enforce the second part of that equation, the act strictly limited the amount of time families can receive aid to sixty months and makes that aid contingent upon recipients participating in "job preparation, work, and support services [that would] enable them to leave the program and become self-sufficient."[45] Wedding high romance with responsibility and sentiment with economic prudence (and very low cost to government), PRWORA is a perfect snapshot of how marriage served the neoliberal political goal of shrinking support for social reproductive labor.

Since the late 1990s, new iterations of the message have made their way into public discourse. The neoconservative marriage movement of the late 1990s and early 2000s spurred a cottage industry of social scientific research on the links between marriage and socioeconomic stability. Commentators were confident in their findings that marriage "produces goods for the partners, for their children, and for the rest of society."[46] The research gave the imprimatur of science to the social theories they espoused and helped justify the political conclusions the movement defended. As Bradford Wilcox of the conservative Heritage Foundation put it: "marriage is really the original Department of Health and Human Services. When marriage disappears, the state has to step in as . . . a provider to broken families."[47] As a presidential primary candidate, Barack Obama gave a Father's Day speech focused on the crisis of "missing" black fathers that closely echoed Reagan: "Of all the rocks upon which we build our lives, we are reminded today that family is the most important."[48] As president, he expanded this message into a wider policy initiative called Responsible Fatherhood that focused largely on promoting employment, financial responsibility, and marriage.[49] Though Democrats endorsed limited expansions of benefits to low-income parents and children, the resounding message from the White House was that absent fathers, and by implication, non-marital families, "[leave] a hole in a child's heart that a government can't fill."[50]

By identifying African Americans as the cause of and solution to "their own" social, economic, and political woes, these racial and moral politics of marriage align seamlessly with the sex-, gender-, race-, and class-blind institution represented in *Obergefell*.[51] The classic story of marriage as timeless and pre-political, constructing a private, heteropatriarchal family responsible for its own, was augmented by commitments to freedom, rights, and even a certain kind of gender equality, overlaid with the promise of economic flourishing. The latter set of commitments came straight from the neoliberal quiver. On the other side of the political spectrum, already more comfortable with the rhetoric of rights, freedom, and equality, the center-left embraced this distinctly neoliberal vision of marriage as the privileged site and source of responsibility for care. Marriage for both conservatives and centrist-progressives became a personal choice that no responsible citizen could fail to make—the sign of respectability; an essential ingredient to financial and physical health, wealth, and happiness; the key to securing privacy and protection from intrusion by others.

If the embrace of this vision by some in the African American community seems somewhat disconcerting, its embrace by many feminists is outright surprising. Feminists are better known for criticizing the conjugal institution than commending it. In recent decades, however, some of the most prominent self-proclaimed feminists have taken to extolling the virtues of marriage. Staking ground in the "work-life balance" discussion, major figures have singled out marriage as key to women's success in the world of paid work. By the early 2000s, hand-wringing about how women might manage "work" and "life" had become something of a national pastime. Widely portrayed as evidence of feminism's arrival into mainstream consciousness, the topic filled the pages and screens of the nation's news and social media.

More than one commentator has noted the decidedly tame tenor of so-called feminist contributions to this wider discussion.[52] For our purposes, what stands out is the place and particular vision of marriage in these contributions. As we have seen before, marriage is cast as a romantic choice that no prudent person would fail to make.

In her 2011 Barnard College commencement address, Facebook executive Sheryl Sandberg told graduates, "The most important career decision you're going to make is whether or not you have a life partner and who that partner is."[53] As she would make clear in her best-selling *Lean In*, and in the press following the sudden death of her husband, marriage to the right person was essential to her success. The impossible demands of neoliberal capitalism are cast as a personal, logistical, and psychological challenge, not a structural political problem. That challenge is to find "balance" between competing demands of "work" and "life." And the most important part of the solution is simple: marry the right person.

Even as she worked up a disagreement with Sandberg, Ann Marie Slaughter concurred on this point: "I could never have had the career I have had without my husband."[54] Economist Sylvia Ann Hewlett, chief executive officer at the Center for Talent Innovation and mother of four, also pointed to marriage as the essential ingredient in "having it all": "It's terribly important to have the wherewithal to have a loving, supportive spouse. And while it does take a lot of imagination, emotional intelligence is our strong point, take the time to find your mate."[55]

The message is clear: the impossible demands of neoliberal capitalism on traditional sites and sources of care—women and the private family—is, first, a women's problem; second, a personal, not a structural problem; and third, a problem that individual action can solve. No revolution or even deep critique of neoliberal political capitalism is required. Rather, the ideal woman has it all, and she secures "it all" by learning to lean in, to embrace "flexible" work arrangements, to rely on minor policy tweaks like mandating family or paid maternity leave, and most importantly, marrying (the right person).

For women ensconced in the upper echelons of social, political, and economic life, the emphasis on marriage is notable. Indeed, it is an essential element of a feminism that makes peace with the impossible demands of neoliberal capitalism. The work-life balance problem is solved not by ensuring that everyone has more time and resources for "life," but rather by marriage. Marriage is a veil behind which the costs of care are paid for and distributed out of view of the markets and the governments that support them.

Same-Sex Marriage and the New Politics of Care

The ideology of sentimentalized marriage in service of the neoliberal politics of personal responsibility and radically privatized care is perhaps nowhere more obvious than in the same-sex marriage debates. These battles brought the celebration of neoliberal marriage—with its profound tensions—to a fevered pitch that reached a crescendo in the landmark Supreme Court decision *Obergefell v. Hodges.*[56] And so, the cunning of history: this very real advance for civil liberties is part and parcel of a politics that threatens the very ground upon which the exercise of these liberties depend.

Gay Marriage Movement Finds Its Neoliberal Footing

When same-sex marriage first appeared as a potential political aim in the gay community, queer and especially queer feminist critics warned that marriage came at a serious cost to real equality and freedom, both as it is tied to care and to normative forms of intimacy and family.[57]

But the mainstream LGBTQ community was unmoved. Marriage became *the* focus of gay politics in the United States in the second half of the twentieth century. Commentators have argued that the key to the stunningly rapid turn in public opinion was the "rebranding" effected by defenders of same-sex marriage, a point complicated by Ellen Andersen in Chapter 3 of this volume.[58] After a number of false starts, proponents settled on the rhetoric of individual freedom and familial responsibility and by the dawn of the twenty-first century had convinced a majority of Americans. The shift from equality to freedom worked, I propose, precisely because it tapped into broader neoliberal politics of care in which marriage is cast at once as a free and private choice, and as *the* site of responsible intimate care, hence a choice no conscientious citizen would refuse. This is precisely the version of marriage that has been deployed by a politics that "responsibilize[s] freedom—where you are free *to take care of yourself*[59] or, crucially, as Joan C. Tronto puts it, "care for one's own."[60] Gay or straight, the ideal neo-sentimental family is wrapped in the marital shroud.

In the early years, starting with the 1971 Minnesota case *Baker v. Nelson*, defenders of same-sex marriage spoke in the idiom of equality.[61] To be sure, those such as Tom Stoddard used language echoing the conservative marriage movement, calling marriage "the centerpiece of our entire social structure," something that "inspires sentiments suggesting that it is something almost suprahuman."[62] Likewise, Andrew Sullivan, whose "Case for Gay Marriage" would become the standard-bearer of the conservative argument for same-sex marriage, emphasized responsibility and care: "Like straight marriage, [gay marriage] would foster social cohesion, emotional security, and economic prudence."[63] But the dominant strategy of the early same-sex marriage movement turned on claims of equality.

This strategy bore disappointing results. In 1971 and then again in 1993, arguments in the courts that same-sex marriage was not prohibited by state law and that equal protection and due process demanded its recognition failed. In 1996, President Bill Clinton signed the Defense of Marriage Act expressly prohibiting same-sex marriage at the federal level, further evidence that the language of equality was persuading neither the American public nor national institutional actors. Even the victory in Vermont in 2000, when the legislature voted into law the nation's first civil unions regime, fell well short of proponents' ultimate goal. And despite a decisive 2004 win in Massachusetts, which became the first state in the nation to legalize same-sex marriage, efforts to secure the right nationally stalled, even backslid, in the immediate aftermath. As Molly Ball wrote in *The Atlantic*, "After 2004, when voters in eleven states approved constitutional amendments, top Democrats blamed gay marriage for John Kerry's loss in the presidential election, and some gay-rights leaders publicly wondered if the push for marriage should be shelved."[64] Then in 2008, the movement lost big again: Proposition 8, the California referendum to ban gay marriage, won a surprising victory.[65]

The loss pushed activists to rethink their strategy. Coordinated research bore a clear and surprising finding: the language of equality was not working. "The message gay-marriage campaigners had been using—an appeal to reason that enumerated the benefits of marriage that were being denied to gay people—wasn't persuasive at all."[66] What Americans needed was to be convinced that gays and lesbians did not want to change marriage but wanted to join it—as responsible citizens.

Proponents changed their message. Harkening back to the early conservative defenses of same-sex marriage by Stoddard, Sullivan, Jonathan Rauch and the like, the new message emphasized freedom *and* responsibility.[67] Evan Wolfson's aptly named Freedom to Marry spearheaded the campaign to convince straight voters that gays and lesbians were not sex-crazed radicals but responsible "family-folk" who just wanted to join the ranks of the responsible in society. "'It was old-lady lesbians who we found were the best messengers,' Erickson Hatalsky said. 'Nobody thought about sex when they saw them.'"[68] The shift bore results. By 2012 the tide had turned, and by 2015 the case was won.

Obergefell's Lineage

Obergefell v. Hodges, the 2015 Supreme Court decision, was groundbreaking in many ways. Most obviously, of course, it legalized same-sex marriage nationwide. The victory for civil liberty was unequivocal. From the perspective of how marriage functions in the neoliberal political project, however, the decision is notable less for its radical break from the heteropatriarchal history of the institution and more, as I shall argue, for its continuation, and indeed revivification of a deeply incoherent but clearly compelling vision of marriage and its relationship to the state. In this, *Obergefell* draws on and alters existing resources to secure and then obscure the real costs and benefits of care and in our world, and the race-, gender-, and class-based inequalities that structure their distribution.

My claim here is twofold. First, *Obergefell* is characterized by deep, and, for anyone who is paying attention, familiar tensions. These tensions—between principles of limited, secular government and the actual, existing establishment of marriage—have characterized the Supreme Court's (and lower courts') decisions from the earliest days. They are evident in the rise, fall, and uneasy coexistence of two incompatible accounts of marriage and the state that animate that history. They are also (merely) reflections of age-old tensions in the liberal tradition's treatment of the relationship between marriage and the state. Supreme Court Justice Anthony Kennedy replicates and exacerbates the incoherence that has always plagued the Court's effort to defend an arrangement, namely the establishment of marriage, that the liberal logic of the Constitution cannot sustain.

My second claim is that *Obergefell* does something new with these tensions. The decision trades in the same incoherent logic but shifts the emphasis in just the way neoliberalism needs in order to expand and obscure the intensified privatization of the costs of care upon which all of society depends.

Kennedy's decision in *Obergefell* concludes that the state must make marital status available to all of its citizens, including same-sex couples, by way of what I call both the liberal and institutionalist accounts of marriage.[69] While relying on these two incompatible accounts simultaneously is not a new strategy, the particular way in which Kennedy does so is. First, with all but one of his peers (ever the contrarian, Clarence Thomas), Kennedy affirms that marriage is a fundamental right: "the

court has long held the right to marry is protected by the Constitution";
"the Court has reiterated that the right to marry is fundamental . . .
marriage is fundamental under the Constitution."[70] As I explain elsewhere, this familiar strategy—the liberal account of marriage—dominates much of twentieth-century jurisprudence.[71] It is easy to see why.
In construing marriage as a right that warrants the most stringent protection, the justification for state concern with the institution is clear
and simple: liberal political theory and US constitutional jurisprudence
hardly assign a more basic task to the state than securing rights. But the
strategy does not quite do all of the work that the conclusion needs.
After all, what is this a right *to*? The same-sex marriage debates made
clear and courts recognized, it is a right *to* something. *But to what?* What
is the content and significance of the status? The liberal account does
not have the resources to answer these questions.

In his second step, Kennedy answers that question by offering what I
call an institutionalist account of the status and the state's role therein.
The Court first proffered this account in the 1888 case *Maynard v. Hill*,
on which Justice Kennedy and his peers draw extensively.[72] Marriage, Justice Stephen Field wrote, "is an institution, in the maintenance of which
in its purity the public is deeply interested, for it is the foundation of the
family and of society, without which there would be neither civilization
nor progress." That is, marriage is the foundation of social order. Its
reach is expansive, from money, to morals, and character. It creates webs
of rights, duties, and obligations, "relations" like "fatherhood and son-
ship," but not agreements framed within a contractual setting. Marriage
creates families and embeds them in society; as such, it is a creation of
and "for the benefit of the community." Its terms, though consented to
by the parties, are neither determined nor alterable by them. Marriage
is thus distinguished from a "mere contract" by the source of constraints
on individual choice "higher than any contract" that are imposed by
the legislature and emanate from "public authority," whether the state
or "a higher source." Though marriage "does not require any religious
ceremony for its solemnization," it does require "certain acts" beyond
consent.[73] For these reasons, marriage is an institution in which government has a fundamental interest and in which it plays a defining role.

The institutionalist account has the virtue of capturing key features
of the understanding of marriage that dominates the American tradition. It invokes public meaning, morality, character, and belief. We
might say it does good by marriage. But it also assumes (and avoids) too

much. Until recently, under pressure from the political and logical demands exposed in the same-sex marriage debates, jurists who presented institutionalist accounts did little more than gesture at the substance of the institution they celebrated. Further, they never offered full-fledged explanations of why and how involvement by the limited state embodied in the US constitutional tradition is essential, or why the state must, in practical or principled terms, be so involved in reproducing goods such as morality and character. The shortcomings of this line of reasoning explain, I have argued, its almost complete disappearance from the courts' reasoning during most of the twentieth century.

Nonetheless, Kennedy unflinchingly deploys the institutionalist account. Indeed, not since *Maynard* has the institutionalist vision of marriage found such forceful defense in a Supreme Court decision. Kennedy's marriage is sacred to those who live by their religions and offers unique fulfillment to those who find meaning in the secular realm. Its dynamic allows two people to find a life that could not be found alone, for a marriage becomes greater than just the two persons: "The centrality of marriage to the human condition makes it unsurprising that the institution has existed for millennia and across civilizations . . . marriage has transformed strangers into relatives, binding families and societies together."[74] Marriage, here, is much more than a simple legal status that supplies a traditional fundamental right—such as the freedom of speech—that guarantees freedom from interference, or even one that supplies concrete, clearly defined civic benefits—one that might be easily replaced with a registered domestic partnership. Kennedy paints a picture of an institution that far exceeds the staid confines of the limited government embodied in the US Constitution. The union, as he casts it, meets the existential cries of the human heart: "Marriage responds to the universal fear that a lonely person might call out only to find no one there. It offers the hope of companionship and understanding and assurance that while both still live there will be someone to care for the other."[75]

Given the shortcomings of the liberal story, primarily that it is unable to supply an account of what marriage *is*, Kennedy's revival of the institutionalist tradition is not entirely surprising. It had become unavoidably clear as same-sex marriage cases rolled through the US court system that the basic questions the courts had to answer were, "What *is* marriage? And why must the state serve in the pivotal role of defining and controlling the content of this fundamental right?" These questions became especially pressing in light of the proliferation of alternative statuses, such as registered domestic partnership, that provided every benefit of marriage except the name.

And yet, even as he brashly resuscitates the institutionalist argument, Kennedy leans heavily on and even expands the liberal account in his answer to how this fundamental right, which has always been conceived of in opposite-sex terms, should apply equally to same-sex couples. He acknowledges the opposite-sex history of the right defined by the Court and the importance of history to the case. The problem, he argues, is that the dissenters focus on the wrong features of the wider tradition. He finds four principles that are more essential, "more instructive," to the history of the right and its fundamental nature than the sex of the parties to marriage. Kennedy lays out what he takes to be the core— that is, secular liberal, not heterosexist—reasons government has, and should, create and control marital status: individual autonomy, the fundamental right to intimate association and privacy therein, safeguarding children and families, and marriage as the cornerstone of social order.[76]

The first three principles are drawn from the liberal playbook in the Court's treatment of marriage. And this is precisely the tradition Kennedy intends to engage. He explicitly distinguishes these types of reasons from those such as religion and mere tradition that we now, he says, understand as unjust, such as not accepting gays and lesbians as equal. The first three reasons for state control of marriage pass the test of the liberal constitution. The fourth principle, however, reiterates the institutionalist account Kennedy sketches early in the *Obergefell* decision. Citing Alexis de Tocqueville and *Maynard v. Hill,* Kennedy writes:

> Marriage remains a building block of our national community. For that reason, just as a couple vows to support each other, so does society pledge to support the couple, offering symbolic recognition and material benefits to protect and nourish the union. Indeed, while the States are in general free to vary the benefits they confer on all married couples, they have throughout our history made marriage the basis for an expanding list of governmental rights, benefits, and responsibilities.[77]

This vision, as we've seen, conflicts with the liberal account. Still he hangs on to both, whereas earlier courts emphasized one over the other and, in the twentieth century, always privileged the liberal.

Arguably, the "four principles," including Kennedy's account of marriage as a comprehensive social institution, constitute the best or, at

least, the most direct attempt at a full-throated justification for the establishment of marriage. And while the argument is rife with philosophical
inconsistencies, it clearly succeeds on a political level. Marriage today
is more firmly established—defined, controlled, and doled out by the
state—than ever before in history.

That few commentators question the decision's untenable assumption that the establishment of marriage is justified or notice related
tensions speaks in part to what an old, well-connected tradition it is.
That Kennedy can deploy the institutionalist argument as an effective
defense of the establishment of marriage, gay or straight, solidifies—in
combination with the liberal story of marriage as a right—the concept
of marriage in the neoliberal context.

Conclusion

Kennedy's confused defense of same-sex marriage fits the mood of our
moment and mirrors the vision of the institution that has gained prominence in the last fifty years. Contemporary romanticizations of marriage
cannot be reduced to a conservative defense of traditional institutions
and virtue, though they certainly complement neoconservative politics.
Obergefell offers a distinctly neoliberal picture of marriage, marriage as,
at once, a fundamental right *and* a hyper-sentimentalized (or -sacral-
ized) relationship: at once merely a private option *and the* site of responsible intimate care. So Kennedy's account squares with the vision
of marriage that has served a perfect helpmeet to a politics that says that
you are free to care for your own precisely at the moment that public
support for unavoidable, inevitable dependency is being dismantled by
the logic and policies of neoliberalism.

Obergefell, of course, casts marriage's net of legitimation and imposed responsibility wider. The decision welcomes a new group—gays
and lesbians—into the fold, ostensibly decoupling the distribution of
social reproductive labor from its previous heteropatriarchal norms and
forms. In fact, though, the decision alters the fundamental function
and form of marriage very little. It ties responsibility for the provision
of now more costly and risky care to a hyper-sentimentalized (amorous
and quasi-religious) and socially conservative (amatonormative, sexually, economically, and socially contained) unit of "one's own," even as
the demands of neoliberal political economy mean that the provision of

care is intimately linked to inequalities based on race, class, national status, and gender. In this way, *Obergefell* reflects and extends a time-tested strategy of liberal capitalism to simultaneously secure and obscure the real costs and unequal benefits and burdens of care—those labors and goods upon which common life depends but which neither capitalism nor liberal democratic politics incorporates fully and equally—by sentimentalizing the private family and making it responsible for those costs. Neoliberal marriage aligns citizens' expectations with the state's disinvestment from social welfare by encouraging people to embrace responsibility for themselves and their increasingly isolated families. The cunning of this history is that this battle in the larger struggle for gay and lesbian civil rights advances a rationality that conflicts in significant ways with our commitments to real freedom and equality for all.

Notes

The author wishes to thank Amanda Ufheil-Somers, Ophelia Vedder, the editors of this volume, and the Stillman Drake and Ducey Funds of Reed College for their contributions to the completion of this chapter.

1. Susan Moller Okin, *Justice, Gender, and the Family* (New York: Basic Books, 1989).

2. Mary Lyndon Shanley, *Feminism, Marriage, and the Law in Victorian England, 1850–1895* (Princeton, NJ: Princeton University Press, 1989).

3. Steven L. Nock, "Marriage as a Public Issue," *Future of Children* 15, no. 2 (Autumn 2005): 13–32; Andrew J. Cherlin, "The Deinstitutionalization of American Marriage," *Journal of Marriage and Family*, 66, no. 4 (November 2004): 848–861; Frank F. Furstenberg, "Will Marriage Disappear?" *Proceedings of the American Philosophical Society* 159, no. 3 (September 2015): 241–246.

4. There is much to the worry that "neoliberal" functions more as a term of disparagement than analysis, but the concept can be useful in identifying underlying, unifying features of political, economic, and social changes since the 1970s. Theorists of neoliberalism upon whom I draw in this chapter include David Harvey, *A Brief History of Neoliberalism* (New York: New York University Press, 2005); Wendy Brown, *Undoing the Demos: Neoliberalism's Stealth Revolution* (New York: Zone Books, 2015); Jamie Peck, *Constructions of Neoliberal Reason* (Oxford: Oxford University Press, 2010); Joan C. Tronto, *Caring Democracy: Markets, Equality and Justice* (New York: New York University Press, 2013); and Loïc Wacquant, "Crafting the Neoliberal State: Workfare, Prisonfare and Social Insecurity," *Sociological Forum* 24, no. 2 (2010): 197–220.

5. See, for example, Harvey in *A Brief History of Neoliberalism*, 65: "while per-

sonal and individual freedom in the marketplace is guaranteed, each individual is held responsible and accountable for his or her own actions and well-being."

6. Karl Polanyi, *The Great Transformation* (Boston, MA: Beacon Press, 1957). Polanyi's canonical analysis of embedded liberalism has inspired much recent work on the subject. See, for example, Nancy Fraser, *The Fortunes of Feminism: From State-Managed Capitalism to Neoliberal Crisis* (New York: Verso, 2013).

7. Wacquant, "Crafting the Neoliberal State." For a more detailed story, see Joe Soss, Richard C. Fording, and Sanford Schram, *Disciplining the Poor: Neoliberal Paternalism and the Persistent Power of Race* (Chicago, IL: University of Chicago Press, 2011).

8. Maxine Eichner, "Market-Cautious Feminism," *Studies in Law, Politics, and Society* 69 (2016): 141–187.

9. Jacob Hacker, *The Great Risk Shift: The Assault on American Jobs, Families, Health Care, and Retirement and How You Can Fight Back* (New York: Oxford University Press, 2006); Eichner, "Market-Cautious Feminism."

10. Harvey, *A Brief History of Neoliberalism*; Thomas Piketty, *Capital in the Twenty-First Century*, trans. Arthur Goldhammer (Cambridge, MA: Belknap Press, 2014).

11. See Joan C. Tronto, *Moral Boundaries: A Political Argument for an Ethic of Care* (New York: Routledge, 1993); Virginia Held, *The Ethics of Care: Personal, Political, Global* (Oxford: Oxford University Press, 2006), Daniel Engster, *The Heart of Justice* (Oxford: Oxford University Press, 2007).

12. Eichner, "Market-Cautious Feminism"; Tronto, *Caring Democracy*; Alissa Quart, *Squeezed: Why Our Families Can't Afford America* (New York: HarperCollins, 2018).

13. Tronto, *Caring Democracy*; Eichner, "Market-Cautious Feminism."

14. Arlie Russell Hochschild, *The Second Shift: Working Parents and the Revolution* (New York: Avon Books, 1990).

15. Arlie Russell Hochschild, "Global Care Chains and Emotional Surplus Value," *On the Edge: Globalization and the New Millennium* (London: Sage Publishers, 2000): 130–146; Gillian Hewitson, "The Commodified Womb and Neoliberal Families," *Review of Radical Political Economics* 46, no. 4 (2014): 489–495.

16. Brown, *Undoing the Demos*, 121.

17. Tronto, *Caring Democracy*, 38.

18. Tronto, 38.

19. Brown, *Undoing the Demos*, 100.

20. Martha Fineman, *The Neutered Mother, the Sexual Family, and Other Twentieth Century Tragedies* (New York: Routledge, 1995).

21. Brown, *Undoing the Demos*. Brown uses this language to describe what happens to gender under neoliberalism.

22. Brown, *Undoing the Demos*; Tronto, *Caring Democracy*; Engster, *The Heart of Justice*.

23. Brown, *Undoing the Demos*, 105–106. See also Elizabeth Bernstein, "Carceral Politics as Gender Justice? The 'Traffic in Women' and Neoliberal Circuits of Crime, Sex, and Rights," *Theory and Society* 41, no. 3 (2012): 233–259.

24. Okin, *Justice, Gender, and the Family*.

25. David Autor, David Dorn, and Gordon Hanson, "When Work Disappears: Manufacturing Decline and the Falling Marriage Market Value of Young Men," National Bureau of Economic Research Working Paper Series (Cambridge, MA: NBER, 2017); W. Bradford Wilcox and Wendy Wang, "The Marriage Divide: How and Why Working-Class Families Are More Fragile Today," *Opportunity America–AEI–Brookings Working Class Group*, September 2017; Sharon Sassler and Amanda Jayne Miller, *Cohabitation Nation: Gender, Class, and the Remaking of Relationships* (Oakland: University of California Press, 2017).

26. Nancy Fraser, "Feminism, Capitalism, and the Cunning of History," *New Left Review* 56 (March–April 2009): 97–116.

27. *Griswold v. Connecticut*, 381 U.S. 479 (1965); *Eisenstadt v. Baird*, 405 U.S. 438 (1972); *Roe v. Wade*, 410 U.S. 113 (1973).

28. Herbert Jacob, *Silent Revolution: The Transformation of Divorce Law in the United States* (Chicago, IL: Chicago University Press, 1988), 27.

29. Naomi R. Cahn, "The Moral Complexities of Family Law," *Stanford Law Review* 50, no. 1 (1997): 225–271; Andrew J. Cherlin, *Labor's Love Lost: The Rise and Fall of the Working-Class Family in America* (New York: Russell Sage Foundation, 2014); Andrew J. Cherlin, *The Marriage Go-Round: The State of Marriage and the Family in America Today* (New York: Alfred A. Knopf, 2009); Dan Hurley, "Divorce Rate: It's Not as High as You Think," *New York Times*, April 19, 2005; Claire Cain Miller, "The Divorce Surge Is Over, but the Myth Lives On," *New York Times*, December 2, 2014.

30. Nancy Cott, *Public Vows: A History of Marriage and the Nation* (Cambridge, MA: Harvard University Press, 2000); Lenore J. Weitzman, *The Divorce Revolution: The Unexpected Social and Economic Consequences for Women and Children in America* (New York: Free Press, 1985); Stephen D. Sugarman and Herma Hill Kay, *Divorce Reform at the Crossroads* (New Haven, CT: Yale University Press, 1990); Nancy D. Polikoff, *Beyond (Straight and Gay) Marriage* (Boston, MA: Beacon Press 2008); Priscilla Yamin, *American Marriage: A Political Institution* (Philadelphia: University of Pennsylvania Press, 2012); Jacob, *Silent Revolution*.

31. Polikoff, *Beyond (Straight and Gay) Marriage*, 40.

32. Yamin, *American Marriage*, 103–104.

33. James Q. Wilson, *The Marriage Problem* (New York: HarperCollins, 2002); Linda J. Waite and Maggie Gallagher, *The Case for Marriage: Why Married People are Happier, Healthier, and Better Off Financially* (New York: Doubleday, 2000).

34. Wendy Brown, "American Nightmare: Neoliberalism, Neoconservatism, and De-Democratization," *Political Theory* 34, no. 6 (2006): 690–714; Melinda

Cooper, *Family Values: Between Neoliberalism and Neoconservatism* (New York: Zone Books, 2017).

35. Ronald Reagan, "Radio Address to the Nation on Family Values," December 20, 1986, The American Presidency Project, University of California at Santa Barbara, http://www.presidency.ucsb.edu/ws/index.php?pid=36826.

36. Hayek, *The Road to Serfdom* (Chicago, IL: University of Chicago Press, 1976); Friedman, *Capitalism and Freedom* (Chicago, IL: University of Chicago Press, 1962).

37. Dan Quayle, "On Family Values," presented at the Commonwealth Club of California, May 19, 1992.

38. Daniel P. Moynihan, *The Negro Family: The Case for National Action* (Moynihan Report), US Department of Labor, Office of Policy Planning and Research, March 1965, pp. 5, 30.

39. Moynihan, *The Negro Family*, 5–12.

40. Moynihan, 47.

41. Quayle, "On Family Values."

42. Soss, Fording, and Schram, *Disciplining the Poor.*

43. On marriage and the racialization of welfare, see Angela Onwuachi-Willig, "The Return of the Ring: Welfare Reform's Marriage Cure as the Revival of Post-bellum Control," *California Law Review* 93, no. 6 (December 2005): 1647–1696.

44. Elizabeth Brake, *Minimizing Marriage* (Oxford: Oxford University Press, 2012).

45. The Personal Responsibility and Work Opportunity Reconciliation Act of 1996, https://aspe.hhs.gov/report/personal-responsibility-and-work-opportunity-reconciliation-act-1996. See also Nancy Cott, *Public Vows: A History of Marriage and the Nation* (Cambridge, MA: Harvard University Press, 2000), 221; and Rebecca M. Blank, "Trends in the Welfare System," *Welfare, the Family, and Reproductive Behavior: Research Perspectives* (Washington, DC: National Academy Press, 1998), 44.

46. Waite and Gallagher, *The Case for Marriage*, 17.

47. Bradford W. Wilcox, Paul Taylor, and Chuck Donovan, "When Marriage Disappears: The Retreat from Marriage in Middle America," *Heritage Lectures*, no. 1179 (2001): 9.

48. "Obama's Father's Day Remarks," *New York Times*, June 15, 2008, https://www.nytimes.com/2008/06/15/us/politics/15text-obama.html.

49. The White House, "Promoting Responsible Fatherhood," June 2012, https://obamawhitehouse.archives.gov/sites/default/files/docs/fatherhood_report_6.13.12_final.pdf.

50. Barack Obama, address to a Young Men's Barbeque, June 20, 2009, https://obamawhitehouse.archives.gov/blog/2009/06/19/a-town-hall-fatherhood.

51. The sleight of hand here, of course, is particularly misleading. It not only obscures the original sin of the republic and the contemporary inequalities it continues to produce, but also the ways in which those inequalities are essential to feeding a key supply line of the underpaid providers of care for the rest of America.

52. Catherine Rottenberg, *The Rise of Neoliberalism Feminism* (Oxford: Oxford University Press, 2018); Rottenberg, "Happiness and the Liberal Imagination: How Superwoman Became Balanced," *Feminist Studies* 40, no. 1 (2014): 144–168; Karen Vintges, *A New Dawn for the Second Sex: Women's Freedom Practices in World Perspective* (Amsterdam: Amsterdam University Press, 2017), 129–164.

53. Sheryl Sandberg, "Barnard College Commencement," New York, May 17, 2011.

54. Anne-Marie Slaughter, "Why Women Still Can't Have It All," *Atlantic*, July–August 2012.

55. Hewlett, quoted in Kerima Greene, "Work-Life Balance: Can Women Have It All?" CNBC, July 7, 2014.

56. An increasing number of scholars have made arguments in this spirit. See Lisa Duggan, *The Twilight of Equality? Neoliberalism, Cultural Politics, and the Attack on Democracy* (Boston, MA: Beacon Press, 2003); Priya Kandaswamy, "State Austerity and the Racial Politics of Same-Sex Marriage in the US," *Sexualities* 11, no. 6 (2008): 706–725; Jaye Cee Whitehead, "Risk, Marriage, and Neoliberal Governance: Learning from the Unwillingly Excluded," *Sociological Quarterly* 52, no. 2 (2011): 293–314; Cooper, *Family Values*.

57. Claudia Card, "Against Marriage and Motherhood," *Hypatia* 11, no. 3 (1996): 1–23; Lisa Duggan, "Beyond Same-Sex Marriage," *Studies in Gender and Sexuality* 9, no. 2 (2008): 155–157; Judith Stacey, *Brave New Families: Stories of Domestic Upheaval in Late-Twentieth-Century America* (Berkeley: University of California Press, 1990); Paula Ettelbrick, "Since When Is Marriage a Path to Liberation?" *Out/Look: National Lesbian & Gay Quarterly* 6 (1989): 14–16.

58. Katherine Franke, *Wedlocked: The Perils of Marriage Equality* (New York: New York University Press, 2015).

59. David Scott, *Refashioning Futures: Criticism after Postcoloniality* (Princeton, NJ: Princeton University Press, 1999).

60. Tronto, *Caring Democracy*.

61. It would also be correct to say that they spoke in the language of civil rights. But for the purposes of the present argument, this language confuses the matter because "civil rights" refers to a fundamental freedom from unequal treatment, whereas "civil liberties" refers to specific rights enshrined in law. It is the latter toward which proponents of same-sex marriage eventually turned, thus emphasizing individuals' rights and choice versus the equality of the earlier "civil rights" approach. For the sake of clarity, I thus leave out reference to civil rights. See *Baker v. Nelson*, 291 Minn. 310, 191 N.W.2d 185.

62. Jane S. Schacter, "The Other Same-Sex Marriage Debate," *Chicago-Kent Law Review* 85, no. 2 (April 2009): 388.

63. Andrew Sullivan, "Here Comes the Groom: A (Conservative) Case for Gay Marriage," *New Republic*, August 27, 1989.

64. Molly Ball, "How Gay Marriage Became a Constitutional Right," *Atlantic*, July 1, 2015.

65. Jesse McKinley and Laurie Goodstein, "Bans in 3 States on Gay Marriage," *New York Times*, November 5, 2008; Jessica Garrison, Cara Mia DiMassa, and Richard C. Paddock, "Voters Approve Proposition 8 Banning Same-Sex Marriages," *New York Times*, November 5, 2008.

66. Ball, "How Gay Marriage Became a Constitutional Right."

67. Ellen Andersen's contribution to this volume confirms and expands this reading of the politics of same-sex marriage. See Chapter 3, "Constituting Families: Marriage Equality Activism and the Role of the State."

68. Ball, "How Gay Marriage Became a Constitutional Right."

69. For discussion of this history in Supreme Court jurisprudence on marriage, see Tamara Metz, *Untying the Knot: Marriage, the State and the Case for Their Divorce* (Princeton, NJ: Princeton University Press, 2010), chap. 2.

70. *Obergefell v. Hodges*, 576 U.S. _____ 135 S. Ct. 2584 (June 26, 2015), 11–12.

71. Metz, *Untying the Knot*, chap. 2.

72. The Court addressed the question of whether it was within the purview of state legislatures to grant divorce. The nature of marriage and the government's role therein were at the heart of the case, forcing the justices to say something about both. In his majority opinion, Justice Field gave the early defining statement of the view that marriage is a foundational institution.

73. *Maynard v. Hill*, 125 U.S. 190 (1888), 212–213.

74. *Obergefell*, 3.

75. *Obergefell*, 14.

76. *Obergefell*, 12–16.

77. *Obergefell*, 15–16.

3 | Constituting Families

Marriage Equality Activism and the Role of the State

Ellen Ann Andersen

Something huge happened for marriage equality activists in 2012; they began winning at the ballot box. Voters in Maine, Maryland, and Washington approved measures opening marriage to same-sex couples, while voters in Minnesota rejected an effort to amend their state's constitution to bar same-sex couples from marrying. Prior to this string of victories, marriage equality activists had lost thirty-two of thirty-three ballot measures seeking to restrict the relationship rights of same-sex couples.[1] All the measures prohibited states from authorizing or recognizing same-sex marriages; a significant subset also barred states from authorizing or recognizing relationships, such as civil unions, that approximated marriage.

The 2012 victories were widely credited to a tactical choice made by marriage equality activists.[2] Rather than discussing marriage in the language of equality and rights as they had done in most earlier ballot campaigns, activists framed their discussion of marriage in the language of love and commitment. In other words, marriage equality advocates emphasized marriage's *private* dimensions rather than its *public* ones.[3]

The primary justification for this new emphasis came from polling and focus group data. These data showed both that voters described marriage primarily in terms of love and commitment and that many voters thought same-sex couples wanted to marry for different reasons than did heterosexual ones.[4] For example, a 2009 survey of voters commissioned by Basic Rights Oregon asked respondents why "couples like you" married, giving them only two options: "to publicly acknowledge their love and commitment to each other" or "for rights, and benefits, like tax advantages, hospital visitation, or sharing a spouse's pension."[5] When forced to choose one option, 72 percent of the respondents said couples like them married for love and commitment, while 18 percent said they married for rights and benefits. In sharp contrast, only 36 percent of the respondents said that same-sex couples wanted to marry in order to publicly acknowledge their love and commitment. The plurality—42 percent—thought same-sex couples wanted marriage for its rights and benefits.[6]

Importantly, voters who thought same-sex couples wanted to marry for love and commitment were inclined to support marriage equality, while voters who thought gay and lesbian couples wanted marriage for its associated rights and benefits were inclined to oppose it. Data from a 2011 Third Way survey are illustrative: 60 percent of voters who thought gay and lesbian couples wanted to marry for love and commitment favored marriage equality, while 60 percent of voters who thought same-sex couples wanted marriage for its rights and benefits opposed it.[7]

In a similar vein, voters who thought same-sex couples were trying to *join* the institution of marriage were far more comfortable with the concept of same-sex couples marrying than were voters who thought lesbians and gay men were trying to *change* the institution of marriage. The 2011 Third Way survey asked voters how comfortable they were with the idea of marriage for same-sex couples on a scale of zero to ten, with higher scores indicating increasing comfort. Nearly two-thirds of those who thought same-sex couples were trying to change marriage indicated they were highly uncomfortable with the concept of same-sex couples marrying, rating themselves a zero or one on the scale. Less than a tenth of voters who thought same-sex couples were trying to join marriage did the same.[8]

The primary message Freedom to Marry, the Movement Advancement Project, and a host of other marriage equality organizations drew from these sorts of survey results was that talking about marriage using the language of rights and equality was, at best, ineffective and, at worst, counterproductive. The task of activists, then, was to persuade voters that same-sex couples who wanted to marry were no different than their heterosexual counterparts—that they wanted to marry in order to "take on the commitment and responsibility that marriage brings" rather than "get married for rights."[9] In this way, they were seeking to join marriage rather than to change it.

A 2012 set of talking points developed by the Movement Advancement Project, a Colorado think tank founded in 2006 to assist equality advocates by conducting rigorous research, laid out this strategy. When talking about marriage, the guide recommended, activists should emphasize "marriage values" and use sentences such as "Marriage is about loving, committed couples who want to make a lifelong promise to take care of and be responsible for each other, in good times and bad."[10] Under a heading titled "Things to Avoid," the guide warned: "DON'T talk about marriage as a 'right' or as a package of 'benefits.'" The guide also cautioned activists to "be careful when using the term 'marriage equality,'" because the phrase might "create confusion and barriers to understanding" for voters not already strongly supportive of the concept.

Survey and focus group data collected after the 2012 elections added additional support to the argument that activists should emphasize love and commitment and avoid rights-based discussions when discussing marriage equality. A Third Way/Grove Insight poll conducted shortly after Washington State voters opted to open marriage to same-sex couples asked voters why they thought gay and lesbian couples wanted to get married. As before, two options were offered: "to officially acknowledge their love and commitment to each other" or "for rights, and benefits, like tax advantages, hospital visitation, or sharing a spouse's pension." Of the 43 percent of respondents saying that same-sex couples wanted to marry for love and commitment, a whopping 85 percent indicated that they had voted in favor of marriage equality. Of the 35 percent of respondents believing that lesbian and gay couples wanted marriage in order to access rights and benefits, only 26 percent voted for marriage equality.[11]

It is the belief by voters that "love and commitment" is a better, more acceptable reason to marry than "rights and benefits" that I wish to address in this chapter. This belief is predicated on the premise that marriage is, at its core, a private institution; that the legal consequences of marrying are peripheral. From this perspective, those who seek to marry for rights and benefits are marrying for base motives. At best they are ignorant or incapable of understanding the transcendent private purpose of marriage. At worst they are greedy people focused on financial perks rather than interpersonal responsibility and commitment.

I make three major claims. First, I argue that the premise that marriage is primarily a private institution is, stated baldly, *ignorant*. I draw on the literature examining the role of marriage in American political development to show that marriage and the state are deeply intertwined.

On the micro-level, marriage is a key mechanism for the distribution of a host of public and private benefits.[12] More broadly, laws regulating who may marry have been used throughout American history to encourage certain kinds of family formations and discourage others.[13]

Second, I argue that voters' disparagement of the desire to marry as a mechanism for obtaining legal rights is *ironic*. Here I draw on survey data of same-sex couples who married in four different states (California, Massachusetts, Oregon, and Utah) over the decades-long struggle for marriage equality in the United States. I show that couples who said they married to gain legal rights and benefits were disproportionately likely to live in states with more hostile legal regimes and also disproportionately likely to have experienced legal harms because of their lack of legal ties to one another. These couples married to protect their relationships from the harms caused by their prior inability to marry. In other words, they married for the very reason voters found laudable: to "take on the commitment and responsibility that marriage brings."[14]

My final claim is that voters' conceptions of acceptable and unacceptable motivations to marry are *illuminating*. That some citizens can ignore or minimize the ways in which the laws governing marriage shape the very capacity of citizens to form and maintain intimate relationships highlights the existence of what Suzanne Mettler calls "the submerged state" and Jacob Hacker calls the "subterranean" one.[15] Both terms refer to the mechanisms by which public policies in the United States are often enacted, mechanisms that tend to obscure the role of the state itself as an actor. As Mettler explains, "Our government is integrally intertwined with everyday life from healthcare to housing, but in forms that often elude our vision: governance appears 'stateless' because it operates indirectly, through subsidizing private actors."[16] Marriage, I argue, is a prime example of the submerged state in action: an institution permeated by the government that nonetheless appears to exist beyond its reach.

Juxtaposing voters' conceptions of *acceptable* reasons to marry with same-sex couples' *actual* reasons for marrying also reveals that the power of the state is far more visible to marginalized groups than to mainstream ones. Many of the same-sex couples surveyed were keenly aware of the public functions of marriage, in no small part because they had grappled with the legal consequences of being unable to marry. Those (presumptively heterosexual) voters who devalued the public functions of marriage, in contrast, lived in a world where access to marriage—and its legal benefits—was already assured. At the risk of causing metaphor fatigue, I argue that the marital state is only submerged when viewed from above; its role is very evident to those watching from below.

Marriage as a Public Institution

That voters deciding whether to open marriage to same-sex couples placed primacy on the private dimensions of marriage is understandable. Marriage in the United States is often construed as an intensely private event, an agreement by two people in love to merge their lives together, ideally forever. Ann Swidler calls this understanding the "mythic culture of love" in which weddings are the centerpiece, the moment when "true love" is affirmed by the joining together of two individuals who will, in the most perfect form of the myth, live happily ever after.[17]

But although marriage is often spoken of in the language of love and commitment, privacy and intimacy, it is undeniably a public institution as well. Marriage "is constituted by the state; its form and requirements are created by public authority and it operates as systematic public sanction, bringing rights and privileges along with duties."[18] I consider two of marriage's key public functions here: first, as a legal contract creating a dense web of rights and obligations and, second, as a mechanism used by the state to sanction—in both the positive and negative senses of the word—intimate private relationships.[19]

Marriage as a Legal Contract

At the most concrete level, marriage is a legal contract creating a dense web of legal rights and obligations at both the state and federal levels. A Government Accounting Office (GAO) report issued in 2004 itemized 1,142 separate federal benefits, rights, or privileges dependent on marital status.[20] Hundreds of additional rights and responsibilities fall under the auspices of state law. George Chauncey has aptly described marriage as "the nexus for the allocation of a host of public and private benefits."[21]

Some of the legal consequences of marrying are relatively trivial. Under Vermont law, for example, the spouses of deceased veterans may continue to mark their cars with a special license plate indicating military service.[22] But many are much more serious. Among the more important financial consequences are the following: Married couples usually inherit from each other automatically in the absence of a will. They can transfer property between each other tax-free while living and upon death. They receive Social Security, Medicare, survivorship, and disability benefits for their spouses. Their tax status changes. (For couples with unequal incomes, marrying usually reduces the taxes they owe. Couples with roughly equivalent incomes are often subject to the so-called marriage penalty.) Married couples can partake in employer-provided benefits such as access to health insurance, life insurance, and pension protections.

The legal consequences of marrying in the context of familial rights are also significant. Foreign spouses of American citizens receive special consideration when applying for citizenship. Married couples are generally treated as each other's next of kin for purposes of medical decision-making, hospital visitation, and burial arrangements. They are automatically considered the parents of children born into their relationship, are permitted to adopt children jointly, and are given joint rights and responsibilities in parenting. They can take bereavement or sick leave to care for each other.

However, because marriage is a creature of both federal and state law, the legal consequences of marriage can and do vary significantly from state to state. A 2004 report on Washington State's legal code uncovered 423 separate provisions detailing the legal consequences of marriage, while a 2002 report on Connecticut's legal code detailed 588 statutes turning on marital status.[23] This difference suggests that marital status may affect a wider array of rights and responsibilities in Connecticut than in Washington.

But even when state laws address the same aspect of marriage, different states may develop different policies. To the extent there is common awareness of interstate variation in the legal consequences of marriage, it tends to be centered around divorce law. Some states are "community property" states, treating all assets accumulated by the couple during the course of the marriage as jointly owned and thus subject to division during divorce, while other states are "separate property" states. In these latter states, assets titled in one person's name are generally considered to be individual assets, even if they were acquired during the marriage.[24]

But interstate differences in the legal consequences of marriage go far beyond the rules for dividing property in divorce. In some states, for example, spouses can be cut out of wills, while in other states they cannot.[25] In some states, the existence of a valid marriage at the time of childbirth makes a man the irrebuttable legal father of the child, even if he is not the biological father of that child, while in other states marriage does not operate in this fashion.[26]

In short, the legal consequences of marriage in the United States are enormous. Marriage binds legal strangers together into a unit and gives the members of that unit a powerful set of tools for protecting one other, helping them navigate childbirth, child-rearing, illness, death, and dying, and enabling them to accrue and transfer wealth. Importantly, couples can obtain relatively few of these economic and familial benefits for each other outside the ambit of the state. The private ordering of relationships through contractual agreements can offer proxies for only a small handful of marriage's legal consequences.[27] At the same time, to the extent marriage is governed by state law, the legal consequences of marriage are variable.

Marriage as Public Sanction

In November 1999, the Vermont Supreme Court ruled that same-sex couples could not constitutionally be excluded from the benefits and protections state laws provided to different-sex married couples. However, the majority ruling in *Baker v. State of Vermont* distinguished between the rights, benefits, and obligations provided by marriage and the right to obtain a marriage license, deferring the latter question to another day.[28] In its instructions to the state legislature, the Court noted that creating "an alternative legal status to marriage for same-sex couples" would be a permissible solution to the issues at stake in *Baker*.[29]

The *Baker* Court's distinction between the rights *of* marriage and the right *to* marry helps illuminate the complicated terrain upon which marriage is located. In addition to creating a web of legal rights and obligations, marriage operates as a status that confers cultural worth to those deemed eligible. This cultural worth is evident in all sorts of ways. For example, marriage is seen as a key rite of passage.[30] It is a marker of prestige and personal achievement.[31] Weddings, in particular, have become status symbols.[32] This is especially true for women, who have been socialized to place primacy on their weddings in ways that men have not.[33] Yet married men are often viewed as more mature than their single counterparts, in part because marriage is seen as the "paradigm of enduring commitment."[34]

Importantly, and as the *Baker* decision shows, the state itself is centrally implicated in using marriage as a mechanism for conferring and reinforcing cultural worth. By separating the rights *of* marriage from the right *to* marry, the *Baker* court bifurcated marriage-as-contract from marriage-as-status and gave the Vermont legislature the option of reserving the status of marriage to different-sex couples. And, indeed, that is precisely what the legislature did. Four months after the *Baker* ruling, the legislature created civil unions, which gave same-sex couples all the state-level rights and benefits of marriage under a different name.

Vermont's approach to bifurcating the rights of marriage from the right to marry was not particularly unusual. Between 1999, when *Baker* was decided, and 2015, when *Obergefell v. Hodges* instituted marriage equality across the nation, roughly a dozen states followed Vermont's lead by creating mechanisms through which same-sex couples could receive most or all of the state-level rights and responsibilities of marriage under another name. In one instance (Oregon), the legislature created a new legal status for same-sex couples (domestic partnerships) as a way to get around a constitutional provision explicitly limiting marriage to heterosexual couples. But as a general rule, states turned to mechanisms such as civil unions and domestic partnerships specifically to accord same-sex couples the rights of marriage without the status of being married.[35]

The Massachusetts Supreme Judicial Court, in contrast, specifically considered and rejected the bifurcation approach. In *Goodridge v. Department of Public Health*, its 2003 decision establishing the right of same-sex couples to marry, the majority wrote, "The Massachusetts Constitution affirms the dignity and equality of all individuals. It forbids the creation of second-class citizens."[36] When the state legislature asked the court to clarify whether creating an alternative legal status for same-sex couples would be acceptable, the court responded, "The dissimilitude between the terms 'civil marriage' and 'civil union' is not innocuous . . . It is a considered choice of language that reflects a demonstrable assignment of same-sex, largely homosexual, couples to second-class status."[37]

Allocation and demarcation of status are, in fact, among the core state interests in marriage. Marriage laws have long been used in the United States to define what Priscilla Yamin calls "the boundaries of civic membership."[38] The dramatic shift in marriage laws during the Progressive Era illuminates this boundary-demarcating function. Between 1880 and 1920, twenty states and territories expanded prohibitions on interracial marriage, most commonly by expanding the number of people categorically prohibited from marrying white people. The great majority of states enacted laws proscribing "feeble-minded" people from marrying. Some states likewise prohibited, "drunkards," "habitual criminals," and/or poor people from marrying.[39] The federal government likewise used marriage to demarcate the boundaries of civic membership. For example, marrying an American male citizen automatically conferred citizenship on the spouse in the years between 1855 and 1922. In contrast, the 1907 Expatriation Act divested citizenship from American women who married non-citizens.[40] These sorts of laws in essence divided citizens into three classes: responsible citizens, free to marry; irresponsible citizens, allowed to marry each other but not to pollute responsible citizens; and dangerous citizens, unworthy of marriage at all.[41]

In short, marriage is more than a legal contract, as important as that is. It is also a marker of responsible citizenship as well as a status reserved to responsible citizens. Moreover, significant evidence suggests that both state actors and private citizens care more about protecting the status function of marriage than its contractual function. Several states were willing to grant the rights and responsibilities of marriage to same-sex couples years before moving to make marriage itself available to same-sex couples.[42] Pew Research Center surveys of public opinion revealed that support for civil unions remained roughly fifteen percentage points higher than support for same-sex marriage between 2003 (the first year a civil unions question was asked) and 2013 (the last year a civil unions question was asked).[43] The same surveys found that support for civil unions exceeded the 50 percent threshold in 2005, while support for same-sex marriage did not exceed the 50 percent threshold until 2013.[44] From this perspective, the debate over whether same-sex couples should be permitted to marry was less about whether same-sex couples deserved the rights that accompany marriage and more about whether lesbians and gay men were worthy beneficiaries of the status of marriage.

Ignorance Revisited

Recall that the survey and focus group data collected by marriage equality activists revealed that voters articulated the meaning of marriage primarily in terms of its private dimensions. Marriage, they believed, was primarily—and appropriately—about love and commitment. Voters who believed that same-sex couples shared their vision of marriage were more likely to support marriage equality than voters who believed that same-sex couples were seeking marriage in order to access its legal rights and benefits.

I claimed then and reiterate now that this belief system reveals a profound ignorance of the public functions of marriage. As I described generally above—and will show specifically below—the laws surrounding marriage are designed to make it easier for socially desirable family units to thrive while making it more difficult for socially undesirable family units to do so. In all fairness, the voters' sense that the contractual aspects of marriage reside outside the essential core of marriage appears to be widely shared. Yet voters also seem either unaware of or unwilling to recognize marriage's undeniable role in conferring and reinforcing cultural worth. In contrast, same-sex couples who desire to marry are keenly aware of these functions. I turn to that now.

Same-Sex Couples and the Public Functions of Marriage

Surveys of same-sex couples who married in four different states during the struggle for marriage equality in the United States offer a unique opportunity to juxtapose voters' conceptions of acceptable reasons to marry with same-sex couples' actual reasons for marrying. This juxtaposition reveals several things. First, same-sex couples surveyed valued the private dimensions of marriage, just as voters did. Second, they were also keenly aware of the public functions of marriage. And third, those couples who said they married to gain legal rights and benefits were disproportionately likely to live in states with more hostile legal regimes. They commonly articulated their desire for legal rights and benefits as a way to protect their families. In other words, they recognized that their very capacity to maintain their integrity as a family unit was dependent on the scaffolding provided by the law.

The Data

The data I employ here come from four different mail surveys. Three surveys targeted participants in wedding waves, an iconic feature of the marriage equality movement. Wedding waves occur when same-sex couples amass to take advantage of brief windows of opportunity to obtain marriage licenses. The two largest wedding waves occurred in 2004, when local officials in San Francisco, California, and Multnomah County (Portland), Oregon, began issuing marriage licenses to same-sex couples, notwithstanding state laws limiting marriage to different-sex couples. By the time courts in each state forced local officials to cease issuing licenses, over four thousand couples in San Francisco and three thousand couples in Portland had seized the chance to marry. All the marriage licenses were subsequently invalidated by the courts. A smaller wave occurred in Utah during the sixteen days between December 20, 2013 (when a federal district court struck down Utah's ban on same-sex marriage), and January 6, 2014 (when the Supreme Court stayed the lower court's decision). During that time 1,362 same-sex couples grabbed the chance to marry; the validity of these licenses was subsequently upheld.[45]

The fourth survey targeted the more than 5,700 same-sex couples who married in Massachusetts from 2004 through 2006, a period of time in which Massachusetts was the only state in the nation formally embracing marriage equality. Unlike the wedding wave participants, there was little need for couples in Massachusetts to rush to the altar. These weddings occurred under the auspices of the Massachusetts Supreme Judicial Court ruling in *Goodridge*, and there was no immediate danger that the state would suddenly cease issuing licenses or that those licenses would be invalidated, although there was concern that the state might enact a constitutional amendment foreclosing future same-sex marriages.

One thousand couples were randomly selected from each of the 2004 wedding waves, as were 2,000 couples from Massachusetts and 587 couples from Utah. The San Francisco and Portland couples were surveyed in the fall of 2006, the Massachusetts couples in the fall of 2007, and the Utah couples in the spring of 2015. Couples in the first three surveys were mailed questionnaires, while the Utah couples were mailed letters containing login information for a web survey. All respondents were urged to participate in the survey even if their spouse chose not to do so; the samples were drawn at the couple level, but the unit of analysis was the individual.[46]

In addition to a series of questions about demographic attributes, political attitudes, and political activities, the surveys asked respondents about various aspects of their spousal relationships, including how long they had been together prior to getting married, whether they had children, and whether they had ever experienced problems as a result of their lack of legal ties to one another. The surveys also asked respondents to describe their motivations to marry.[47]

Responses to the San Francisco and Portland surveys were analyzed using thematic analysis. In thematic analysis, the respondents' own words are used to develop coding categories (themes).[48] Themes and sub-themes were identified by two coders working independently until saturation was reached and no new themes emerged. This coding schema was subsequently applied to the Massachusetts and Utah surveys. As with the initial surveys, two coders worked independently. They were instructed to look for motivations that fell outside the initial coding schema, but no new themes emerged.

Motivations to Marry

No matter where they married, the respondents' motivations for marrying fell into four broad categories: to express their love and commitment, to gain rights and benefits, to achieve recognition and validation for their relationships, and to make a political statement.[49]

Roughly 40 percent of the respondents said that they married for reasons that clearly fall within the "love and commitment" framework so prized by the voters. These respondents said they married to express their love for their spouse and/or to deepen or reaffirm their commitment to each other. Phrases like "We've always wanted to marry" and "We've always felt married" were common. Two things about these responses are particularly worth noting. First, among the 60 percent of the respondents who did not describe their motives explicitly in terms of love and commitment, many responses presupposed its existence. For instance, one Oregonian married "because our love and relationship deserve the same value and respect and benefits as heteros get. We need the law on our side for medical decisions etc." Second, only about 10 percent of the respondents limited their responses to the "love and commitment" framework. Instead, the vast majority of the respondents articulated reasons to marry that invoked marriage's public dimensions in addition to or instead of marriage's private dimension.

About 40 percent of respondents indicated they married for instrumental purposes: they wanted access to the legal rights and protections that accompany marriage. Some respondents spoke in general terms, but others were more specific. In the context of familial rights, respondents spoke of their desire to protect the integrity of their spousal relationship against external interference, especially in three milieus: hospital visitation, medical decision-making, and end-of-life events. One Utah woman encapsulated the concerns expressed by many respondents:

> In 1996 Maggie my wife was involved in an ATV crash and was flown to the hospital. When I got [to the hospital] they would not tell me anything, and [would] not let me see her until her mom got there. Thank God her mother has always been wonderful to me and she and I went back to see her. [Maggie] was in the hospital for a week and if her family had said no I could not see her, then [the hospital] would have not let me in. Maggie and I have talked about what we would like to happen if one of us should pass away and until we were able to get married I would not have a say about it, only her mother or family would, even though I know her wishes and have been there now for 19 years. Now I have the say.[50]

In the context of marriage's financial implications, access to health insurance was a predominant theme. "We intended to get married to support same sex marriage but did it as quickly as we did because Rebecca needed health insurance," one Massachusetts woman explained. The desire to protect spouses and families from financial hardship was also a prevalent theme. An Oregonian wrote that she married primarily because she "wanted to protect my kids' security and my spouse's security should something happen to me, the primary breadwinner of our family." End-of-life concerns abounded. "[We] wanted to ensure that what we built together would (without question) belong to the other in the event of a tragedy," one person wrote.

These sorts of instrumental motivations to marry speak directly to the contractual functions of marriage. But respondents were also keenly aware of the ways that legal marriage confers status. Thirty percent of the respondents said that they married at least in part to gain legitimation and validation for their relationships. One Utahan explained her motivations this way: "There is a way in which society legitimizes the relationship when you are married. Despite the fact that my partner and I had been together for many years, and people knew, they behaved differently when they found out we were getting married. Suddenly the relationship felt more real to other people." Another woman who married in San Francisco stated her reasoning more succinctly: "Marriage is society's stamp of approval."

Finally, nearly 50 percent of the respondents said they married as an act of political contestation. These respondents spoke of "taking a stand," "being counted," "making a statement," and fighting for equal rights. Like those who sought validation and legitimation through marrying, respondents using the language of political contestation and equality recognized the ways that legal marriage confers status.

In sum, the respondents in all four surveys articulated motivations to marry that invoked both the private and the public functions of marriage. The percentages discussed above do not sum to 100 percent because respondents commonly gave multiple reasons for marrying. For example, one Portland man said he married when he did "Because we love each other. Because we would want to be on the same health insurance. Because it is an important sociopolitical movement." Motivations to marry are distinguishable in theory but deeply intertwined in practice. Notably, only 10 percent of the respondents stayed entirely within the love and commitment framework when describing their reasons for marrying. The great majority were drawn to marriage at least in part because of its public functions.

Marrying for "Rights and Benefits": How Law Matters

While the respondents' motivations for marrying fell into four broad categories no matter where they married, separating out the responses by wedding location shows that the percentage of respondents articulating particular rationales for marrying shifted dramatically across locale, most strikingly so with respect to marrying for legal protections (see Figure 3.1 below). Roughly three-quarters of the respondents who married in Utah said they did so at least partly because of marriage's legal consequences. Only half the respondents who married in Massachusetts said the same. Fewer than a third of those who married in Portland articulated rights and benefits as a motivating force to marry, while only about a sixth of those who married in San Francisco did so.

When other factors—such as respondents' age, gender, and parenthood status—are accounted for, the effect of wedding location on motivations to marry looms even larger. Participants in the Utah wedding wave were more than three times as likely as those who married in Mas-

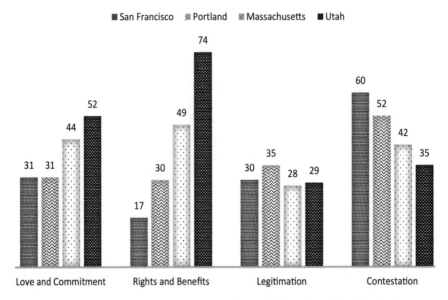

Figure 3.1. Percentage of Respondents Articulating Specific Motivation to Marry.

sachusetts to say they married to secure legal rights and benefits. They were over seven times as likely as the Portland respondents to say so. And they were more than *fourteen times* as likely as the San Francisco respondents to say so.[51]

Of course, other factors affected the likelihood of marrying to secure legal rights and benefits as well. Respondents who had experienced legal problems as a result of their lack of legal ties to their partner were about 50 percent more likely than individuals who had not experienced such legal problems to say they married to secure legal rights and benefits. Parents were about 30 percent more likely than non-parents to say they were motivated by legal rights and benefits. Individuals who had been coupled with their partner for fewer than five years were about 50 percent less likely to cite legal consequences as a motive for marrying. These are not small effects. But they are dwarfed in magnitude by the effects of wedding location.

Part of the explanation for the outsized role wedding location plays in shaping motivations to marry may come from the varying legal certainty of the weddings. Many of the people who decided to marry in San Francisco and Portland knew that the validity of the marriage licenses would be subject to debate. And, indeed, all the licenses were subsequently invalidated. The Massachusetts and Utah weddings took place on firmer legal ground, occurring as they did under the auspices of judicial rulings. Yet the legal certainty, or lack thereof, of the weddings is at best a partial explanation. The weddings in both San Francisco and Portland both occurred amid great legal uncertainty, yet the Portland respondents were far more likely than the former to invoke the legal benefits of marriage as a reason to wed. The Massachusetts and Utah weddings were both on reasonably firm legal ground, but Utahans were far more likely than Bay Staters to be motivated by marriage's legal consequences.

I argue here that the stark differences revealed in Figure 3.1 reflect systematic variations in the legal consequences of marrying. Couples who married in San Francisco in 2004 had the least to gain in the way of new legal protections. Over three-quarters of the respondents who married in San Francisco were already registered as domestic partners, a status that offered same-sex couples many of the state-level rights and protections of marriage. Moreover, the state had already amended its domestic partnership law to expand protections further. The revised law, which was set to go into effect in 2005, made domestic partnerships nearly equivalent to marriage insofar as state law was concerned. At the time of the San Francisco wedding wave, California was second only to Vermont in the rights afforded to same-sex couples.

Couples who married in Oregon and Massachusetts in 2004 had greater need for the contractual protections offered by marriage. At that time, neither state provided a mechanism for same-sex couples to legally link their lives together in the absence of marriage, although several localities in Massachusetts—including Boston—did have domestic partnership registries. These registries offered a small handful of the legal protections of marriage, most commonly hospital and jail visitation. Some Bay State employers also offered health care benefits to registered domestic partners, although some of those employers signaled their intent to discontinue providing health care benefits to registered domestic partners once legal marriage was an option.

Couples who married during the 2013–2014 Utah wedding wave had the most to gain in the way of new legal rights and protections. Utahans were similar to their Portland and Massachusetts counterparts in that the state offered no mechanism for same-sex couples to legally link their lives together in the absence of marriage. But they differed from everyone else in two key legal respects. First, the Utah weddings took place after the Supreme Court's 2013 decision in *United States v. Windsor*, which struck down Section 3 of the Defense of Marriage Act defining marriage as the union of one man and one woman for all purposes of federal law.[52] The legal consequences of marrying were thus much broader for the Utahans than for the other three survey populations, because marriage brought with it hundreds of federal benefits, including the ability to file federal taxes jointly and to access a spouse's Social Security and Medicare benefits.

The Utah couples also differed from the other three survey populations in that they faced a uniquely hostile legal regime. In 2008, the Utah legislature amended the state's adoption provisions to explicitly forbid unmarried, cohabiting couples from adopting children.[53] This provision of the Utah Adoption Act was enacted specifically to fence out same-sex couples from adopting children, even in circumstances where one member of the couple was the biological parent of the child.[54] While single LGBT people remained eligible to adopt, the only way for both partners in a same-sex couple to obtain parenting rights to their children in the absence of legal marriage was to temporarily relocate to another state and complete the adoption process before returning to Utah.

Many respondents indicated that they were marrying either because they were planning to have children or because they were seeking to protect the children they already had. For example, one woman wrote that she married in large part because "we have a son who Jan was allowed to adopt but I was not allowed to adopt due to the laws in Utah. It was important to him and to me to have me legally adopt him and confirm to him that he was my son legally, financially and emotionally." Another woman reported that she had given birth two days before the weddings began in Utah. Her partner, she said, "spent the night out in the snow to make sure she was at the beginning of the line at the [Salt Lake City] Clerk's Office" because getting married would allow both women to be listed on the child's birth certificate.

In short, marrying had significantly greater legal consequences for some of the survey respondents than for others. Marriage offered relatively little in the way of additional legal rights and protections for couples who wed during the San Francisco wedding wave. For couples in Utah, however, the legal consequences of marrying were enormous. Among the four populations studied, they had the least ability to protect their families from external forces in the absence of marriage. And because the Utah weddings were the only ones to occur after the *Windsor* decision, they were the only ones to include access to the plethora of federal rights, benefits, and protections.

Irony Revisited

The survey data collected by marriage equality activists showed that voters who thought same-sex couples wanted to marry "for rights, and benefits, like tax advantages, hospital visitation, or sharing a spouse's pension" were much less likely to favor marriage equality than voters who thought same-sex couples wanted to marry "to publicly acknowledge their commitment to each other." Contrasting voters' perceptions of why same-sex couples want to marry with the actual reasons why same-sex couples in four different locations got married reveals those voters' profound misunderstanding of the relationship between the legal consequences of marriage on the one hand, and the private domain of "love and commitment" on the other. Same-sex couples who married to access the rights and protections of marriage did not do so in lieu of marrying as a declaration of love and commitment. In fact—and here is the first irony—the Utah respondents, who were the most likely to indicate they married for "rights and benefits," were also the most likely to say that they married for "love and commitment."

Instead—and here is the second irony—respondents motivated by the legal consequences of marriage often saw marriage as helping them to fulfill their romantic and parental commitments. Respondents married because "I was diagnosed with cancer [the year before]. I want to do all I can to ensure my husband Anthony will be protected by the rights accorded to married couples." They married so that they could share health and retirement benefits. They married "so our adopted children would have some security and so that we would have peace of mind in case of disaster." Unsurprisingly, those respondents who lived in states with more hostile legal regimes were the most likely to recognize that the laws governing marriage shaped their very capacity to form and maintain their intimate relationships, because they were the most keenly aware of the real and potential harms caused by their prior inability to marry.

Marriage and the Submerged State

Polling and focus group data collected from 2009 to 2012 consistently showed that voters arrayed motivations to marry along a hierarchy. Voters who believed same-sex couples wanted to marry to express their love and commitment to each other were inclined to support marriage equality, while voters who believed that same-sex couples wanted to marry to access legal rights and benefits were inclined to oppose it. That is, voters generally found "love and commitment" a more virtuous reason to marry than "rights and benefits." Yet, as I have demonstrated, the laws governing marriage in the United States shape the very capacity of citizens to form and maintain intimate relationships. In other words, the rights and benefits of marriage play a critical role in enabling couples to actually care for each other.

So how is it that the surveyed voters could be so unaware of the ways that marriage and the state are deeply intertwined? How can an institution so permeated by government be seen as essentially private? Suzanne Mettler's concept of the "submerged state" is useful here. Mettler uses the term to describe the accumulation of government policies that operate to shroud the role of the state itself as an actor, most commonly by "incentivizing and subsidizing activities engaged in by private actors and individuals."[55] These policies, she argues, have made the functioning of the state invisible to most citizens, even those who directly benefit from particular policies.

Marriage, I argue, is an example of the submerged state in action.[56] An institution that is enveloped in a thicket of law, marriage is nonetheless situated as fundamentally private and pre-political. That the voters surveyed by marriage equality activists conceptualized marriage in this fashion is clear. Importantly, though, this understanding of marriage is also advanced by state actors. Consider Justice William O. Douglas's opinion in *Griswold v. Connecticut* (1965), describing marriage as "a coming together for better or for worse, hopefully enduring, and intimate to the degree of being sacred. It is an association that promotes a way of life, not causes; a harmony in living, not political faiths; a bilateral loyalty, not commercial or social projects. Yet it is an association for as noble a purpose as any involved in our prior decisions."[57]

Justice Anthony Kennedy's opinion in *Obergefell v. Hodges* (2015)—the case that instituted marriage equality nationwide—described marriage in similar tones: "The nature of marriage is that, through its enduring bond, two persons together can find other freedoms, such as expression, intimacy, and spirituality." Later in the decision, Kennedy opined, "No union is more profound than marriage, for it embodies the highest ideals of love, fidelity, devotion, sacrifice, and family. In forming a marital union, two people become something greater than once they were."[58]

Elected officials have likewise framed marriage as private and prepolitical in nature. In 2004, for example, then president George W. Bush used his weekly radio address to call for a constitutional amendment to limit marriage to one man and one woman. In it he described marriage as the most "enduring" and "fundamental" institution of civilization. "Ages of experience," he said, "have taught us that the commitment of a husband and a wife to love and to serve one another promotes the welfare of children and the stability of society." By "recognizing and protecting marriage"—presumably from incursion by same-sex couples—government "serves the interest of all."[59]

Note both the minimization of government's role in regulating marriage and the implied causality in President Bush's words. The love and commitment of two private actors promotes not only the welfare of children, but also the very stability of society. Private commitments, in other words, produce public goods, seemingly with no assistance from the state other than some nebulous form of "protection" and "recognition."

Marriage's framing by government actors as essentially private exemplifies the submerged state in action. Even as state actors literally employ the power of the state to shape and constrain marriage, they position marriage as existing beyond the power of the state. No wonder the voters surveyed by marriage equality activists ignored or minimized the importance of rights and benefits. State actors actively work to obscure the public functions of marriage.

My study has shown, however, that marriage is only "submerged" from the perspective of those citizens who comfortably fall within the institution's existing parameters. Same-sex couples were keenly aware of marriage's public functions, in no small part because they grappled with the legal consequences of being unable to marry. The ability to see marriage as a private institution, then, constitutes a form of privilege.

Conclusion

Marriage, situated as private, is neither perceived by many citizens nor by state actors as thoroughly connected to the state. This allows some citizens to fundamentally misconstrue the relationship of citizens to the state, blinding them to the ways in which marriage is a central aspect of governance. And while this shapes their understanding of what marriage is and who should be permitted to marry, it does more than that.

The rights and benefits of marriage conferred by the state are not only about legal recognition of affective ties and about wealth transfers; they are vital to the provision of care for couples and their biological or adoptive children. In Chapter 2 of this volume, Tamara Metz argues that a core political function of marriage today is to privatize the risks, responsibilities, and costs of caring for youth, the elderly, and other vulnerable citizens. My research adds to hers by showing that the state's reliance on familial relations to perform care work heightens the stakes for marriage. Many of the same-sex couples I surveyed sought to marry because of the difficulty in providing care work in the absence of marriage. By establishing privatized care work as a relational expectation and then making it difficult, if not impossible, for couples in committed relationships to care for each other outside marriage, the state is not isolating family in the private realm. It is actively intervening to structure and privilege some families over others, thereby "freeing" the family as an institution to heighten inequality.

Notes

1. Their one earlier victory—the failure of Arizona's Proposition 107 in 2006—was short-lived; two years later voters approved Proposition 102, thereby amending the state's constitution to restrict marriage to one man and one woman.

2. Molly Ball, "How Gay Marriage Became a Constitutional Right," *Atlantic*, July 1, 2015, http://www.theatlantic.com/politics/archive/2015/07/gay-marriage-supreme-court-politics-activism/397052/; Frank Bruni, "Examining the Support for Same-Sex Marriage," *Frank Bruni's Blog, New York Times*, December 12, 2012, https://bruni.blogs.nytimes.com/2012/12/12/examining-the-support-for-same-sex-marriage/; David Dodge, "Why Marriage Won: Right-Wing Messaging and the 2012 Elections," Political Research Associates, December 13, 2012, https://www.politicalresearch.org/2012/12/13/why-marriage-won-right-wing-messaging-and-2012-elections; Lanae Erickson Hatalsky and Sarah Trumble, "How Marriage Won in Washington State," Third Way, December 2, 2012, https://www.thirdway.org/report/how-marriage-won-in-washington-state; Carrie Wofford, "Why Equality Is Winning," *US News & World*

Report, March 26, 2014, https://www.usnews.com/opinion/blogs/carrie-wof ford/2014/03/26/how-did-public-opinion-on-gay-marriage-shift-so-quickly. All URLs in this chapter were working as of September 28, 2019.

3. Tamara Metz discusses this tactical shift in Chapter 2 of this volume. She argues that it was successful because it tapped into the prevailing neoliberal politics of care, a politics that positions marriage as the primary site of essential caretaking.

4. Lanae Erickson, "Why Marriage Matters: The Research Behind the Message," Third Way, March 16, 2011, http://content.thirdway.org/publications /377/Third_Way_Fact_Sheet_-_Why_Marriage_Matters.pdf; Marc Solomon, *Winning Marriage: The Inside Story of How Same-Sex Couples Took on the Politicians and Pundits and Won* (Lebanon, NH: ForeEdge, 2014), 230; "Winning at the Ballot," Freedom to Marry, http://www.freedomtomarry.org/pages/Winning -at-the-Ballot.

5. Solomon, *Winning Marriage,* 230.

6. It is worth noting that 22 percent of the respondents were unable or unwilling to pick either of the two options in the context of same-sex couples, while 10 percent were unable or unwilling to do in the context of "couples like you." Some or all of these respondents may have rejected the either/or framing of the question. In other words, some respondents may have thought that couples—whether same-sex or different-sex—married for both reasons and were unwilling or unable to prioritize one over the other.

7. Erickson, "Why Marriage Matters."

8. Lanae Erickson Hatalsky, "Commitment: The Answer to the Middle's Questions on Marriage for Gay Couples," Third Way, November 7, 2011, https://www.thirdway.org/report/commitment-the-answer-to-the-middles -questions-on-marriage-for-gay-couples-1.

9. Erickson, "Why Marriage Matters."

10. "An Ally's Guide to Talking about Marriage for Same-Sex Couples," Movement Advancement Project, 2012, http://www.lgbtmap.org/file/allys -guide-talking-about-marriage.pdf.

11. Voters were similarly split when they were asked whether they thought "gay and lesbian couples who want to get married were trying to join the institution of marriage or change the institution of marriage." Half of the respondents believed same-sex couples wanted to join marriage. Of these respondents, 92 percent said they had voted to open marriage to same-sex couples. In sharp contrast, 93 percent of the respondents who thought same-sex couples were seeking to change marriage voted to bar them from marrying.

12. George Chauncey, *Why Marriage? The History Shaping Today's Debate over Gay Equality* (New York: Basic Books, 2005), 71.

13. Priscilla Yamin, *American Marriage: A Political Institution* (Philadelphia: University of Pennsylvania Press, 2012), 9.

14. Erickson, "Why Marriage Matters."

15. Suzanne Mettler, *The Submerged State: How Invisible Government Policies Undermine American Democracy* (Chicago, IL: University of Chicago Press, 2011); and Jacob S. Hacker, *The Divided Welfare State: The Battle over Public and Private Social Benefits in the United States* (New York: Cambridge University Press, 2002).

16. Mettler, *The Submerged State*, 6.

17. Ann Swidler, "Culture in Action: Symbols and Strategies," *American Sociological Review* 51, no. 2 (1986): 273–286.

18. Nancy F. Cott, "Marriage and Women's Citizenship in the United States, 1830–1934," *American Historical Review* 103, no. 5 (1998): 1441.

19. Tamara Metz persuasively argues in Chapter 2 of this volume that marriage serves another major public function: to privatize the responsibilities and costs of caring for youth, the elderly, and other vulnerable citizens.

20. General Accounting Office, "Defense of Marriage Act: Update to Prior Report" (Washington, DC: GAO, 2004).

21. Chauncey, *Why Marriage?*, 71.

22. 23 V.S.A. (Vermont Statutes Annotated) Chapter 7 § 304 (j).

23. Jamie D. Pederson, "The RCW Project: An Analysis of the Benefits and Burdens of Marriage Contained in the Revised Code of Washington," for the Legal Marriage Alliance of Washington, 2004, PDF in author's possession; Susan Price-Livingston, "Connecticut Laws Involving Marital Status," Office for Legislative Research, 2002, https://www.cga.ct.gov/2001/rpt/2001-R-0606.htm.

24. Ellen Ann Andersen, "The Gay Divorcee: The Case of the Missing Argument," in *Queer Mobilizations: LGBT Activists Confront the Law* (New York: New York University Press, 2009), 281–319.

25. Angela M. Vallario, "The Elective Share Has No Friends: Creditors Trump Spouse in the Battle over the Revocable Trust," *Capital University Law Review* 45 (2017): 333.

26. June Carbone and Naomi Cahn, "Marriage, Parentage, and Child Support," *Family Law Quarterly* 45, no. 2 (2011): 219–240.

27. Andersen, "The Gay Divorcee"; Jennifer Wriggins, "Marriage Law and Family Law: Autonomy, Interdependence, and Couples of the Same Gender," *Boston College Law Review* 41 (1999): 265.

28. "While some future case may attempt to establish that—notwithstanding equal benefits and protections under Vermont law—the denial of a marriage license operates per se to deny constitutionally-protected rights, that is not the claim we address today." *Baker v. State of Vermont*, 170 Vt. 194 (1999).

29. *Baker v. State*, 170 Vt., 225.

30. Joseph R. Gusfield and Jerzy Michalowicz, "Secular Symbolism: Studies of Ritual, Ceremony, and the Symbolic Order in Modern Life," *Annual Review of Sociology* (1984): 417–435.

31. Andrew J. Cherlin, "The Deinstitutionalization of American Marriage,"

Journal of Marriage and Family 66, no. 4 (2004): 855, https://doi.org/10.1111
/j.0022-2445.2004.00058.x.

32. Cherlin, "The Deinstitutionalization of American Marriage," 855; Chrys
Ingraham, *White Weddings: Romancing Heterosexuality in Popular Culture* (New
York: Routledge, 2014).

33. Ingraham, *White Weddings*.

34. Milton C. Regan, Jr., *Alone Together: Law and the Meanings of Marriage:
Law and the Meanings of Marriage* (New York: Oxford University Press, 1999), 7.

35. For example, Connecticut instituted civil unions in 2005 via legislation that
simultaneously limited marriage to different-sex couples (Conn. Stat. § 46b-38rr).

36. *Goodridge v. Department of Public Health*, 440 Mass. 309 (2003).

37. *Opinions of the Justices to the Senate*, 440 Mass. 1201 (2004).

38. Priscilla Yamin, "The Search for Marital Order: Civic Membership and
the Politics of Marriage in the Progressive Era," *Polity* 41, no. 1 (2009): 88.

39. The restrictions were expressly eugenic in intent, an effort to prevent
the so-called feeble-minded from creating additional unfit citizens, who would
become burdens on the state. See Matthew J. Lindsay, "Reproducing a Fit Citizenry: Dependency, Eugenics, and the Law of Marriage in the United States,
1860–1920," *Law & Social Inquiry* 23, no. 3 (1998): 541–585.

40. Leti Volpp, "Divesting Citizenship: On Asian American History and the
Loss of Citizenship through Marriage," *UCLA Law Review* 53 (2005): 405; Cott,
"Marriage and Women's Citizenship in the United States, 1830–1934."

41. Nor are these sorts of regulations entirely a product of the distant past.
In 1987, the Supreme Court overturned a Missouri correctional policy prohibiting inmates from marrying without the express permission of the prison
superintendent, an approval that was conditioned on the existence of some sort
of "compelling" reason, most commonly pregnancy or childbirth. See *Turner v.
Safley*, 482 U.S. 78 (1987).

42. Six states took this path: Connecticut, Delaware, Illinois, New Hamp-
shire, Rhode Island, and Vermont.

43. "In Gay Marriage Debate, Both Supporters and Opponents See Legal
Recognition as 'Inevitable,'" Pew Research Center, June 6, 2013, 4, http://
www.people-press.org/2013/06/06/in-gay-marriage-debate-both-supporters-
and-opponents-see-legal-recognition-as-inevitable/.

44. "In Gay Marriage Debate," Pew Research Center.

45. For more on wedding waves in these three locations, see Ellen Ann
Andersen, "The State of Marriage? How Sociolegal Context Affects Why Same-
Sex Couples Marry," in *LGBTQ Politics: A Critical Reader* (New York: New York
University Press, 2017), 374–393.

46. For detailed information on the sampling process and response rate, see
Andersen, "The State of Marriage?"

47. The wording differed slightly among the surveys. The San Francisco

and Portland questionnaires asked respondents why they and their spouses "decide[d] to apply for a [marriage] license." The Massachusetts and Utah questionnaires asked why respondents and their spouses "decided to marry." The wording difference may have colored the nature of responses.

48. Richard E. Boyatzis, *Transforming Qualitative Information: Thematic Analysis and Code Development* (Thousand Oaks, CA: Sage Publications, 1998).

49. These findings are consistent with other studies. See, for example, Kimberly D. Richman, *License to Wed: What Legal Marriage Means to Same-Sex Couples* (New York: New York University Press, 2013); Verta Taylor et al., "Culture and Mobilization: Tactical Repertoires, Same-Sex Weddings, and the Impact on Gay Activism," *American Sociological Review* 74, no. 6 (December 1, 2009): 865–890, https://doi.org/10.1177/000312240907400602; M. V. Badgett, "Social Inclusion and the Value of Marriage Equality in Massachusetts and the Netherlands," *Journal of Social Issues* 67, no. 2 (2011): 316–334; Ellen Schecter et al., "Shall We Marry? Legal Marriage as a Commitment Event in Same-Sex Relationships," *Journal of Homosexuality* 54, no. 4 (2008): 400–422.

50. The names of respondents and their spouses have been changed to preserve their privacy.

51. These numbers come from binomial logistic regression analysis, where a variable capturing whether or not respondents said they married to obtain legal protections was regressed against the location of the weddings as well as the following control variables: respondent age, gender, parenthood status, religiosity, level of political activism, self-identification as liberal or highly liberal, and whether respondents had experienced legal problems as a result of their lack of legal ties to their partner. For a fuller explanation of the model, see Andersen, "The State of Marriage?"

52. *United States v. Windsor*, 570 U.S. 12 (2013); and *Defense of Marriage Act (DOMA)*, Pub. L. No. 104–199, § 7, 1 United States Code (n.d.).

53. Utah Code Ann. § 78B-6-117 (2008).

54. See Shane A. Marx, "A Best-Interest Inquiry: The Missing Ingredient in Utah Family Law for Children of Alternative Families—Jones v. Barlow," *Journal of Law & Family Studies* 11 (2008): 157.

55. Suzanne Mettler, "Reconstituting the Submerged State: The Challenges of Social Policy Reform in the Obama Era," *Perspectives on Politics* 8, no. 3 (2010): 804.

56. I am taking some liberties with Mettler's concept here. Her submerged state is in large part the product of deliberate political decisions to obscure the state's involvement. I am less certain that political actors have *intentionally* sought to shroud the state in the context of marriage.

57. *Griswold v. Connecticut*, 381 U.S. 479 (1965).

58. *Obergefell v. Hodges*, 576 U.S. ___, 135 S. Ct. 2584 (June 26, 2015).

59. George W. Bush, "The President's Radio Address," georgewbush-whitehouse.archives.gov, June 3, 2006.

4 | The Legal Construction of Motherhood and Paternity

Interracial Unions and the Color Line in Antebellum Louisiana

Gwendoline Alphonso and Richard Bensel

Like every other state in the antebellum South, Louisiana was committed to slavery as an economic system. Because the cotton and sugar that slaves produced underpinned the entire economy of Louisiana, slavery created interests in its own maintenance among many people who did not own a slave. The state of Louisiana's commitment to slavery thus extended beyond its enforcement of property rights in black labor to include an ongoing obligation to reproduce all social relations. As the edifice upon which the slave economy depended, these social relations pivoted on the creation and maintenance of a color line demarcating a boundary between the black and white races. The resultant legal and social stakes attending racial identity were very high.[1] As slave property increased in value during the decades before the Civil War, the precise and predictable ascertainment of racial identities became ever more important.

Despite the increasingly high material stakes involved in policing the color line, it was difficult to maintain in practice and depended in large part on the ongoing regeneration of beliefs in white superiority and in the moral legitimacy of black slavery among slaveholders and non-slaveholders. For one thing, slaves could and did run away from their masters. Given that the state of Louisiana maintained only a minuscule police force, the recovery of runaway slaves largely depended on the voluntary action of citizens who, for that reason, had to be both oriented toward the policing of the racial boundary (e.g., any black person could be presumed to be a slave) and willing to enforce the social relations that monitored that boundary (including the apprehension of runaway slaves). These were not demands that could be imposed on reluctant citizens; they had to have internalized them in the form of more or less spontaneously self-reproducing beliefs and ethical principles.

These self-reproducing beliefs undergirding white supremacy and black subordination were one of the most characteristic aspects of ante-bellum Louisiana (and southern) culture and constituted a distinctive "social practice" of slavery, collectively reproducing slavery as a social and economic system.[2] The legal construction of a color line distinguished blacks from whites and enabled the state to uphold the social practice of slavery by making racial identity one of the central organizing principles of social relations and belief systems.[3]

However, these commitments to a color line and the social practice of slavery came up against the state's commitment to another pivotal social institution: the white family. As growing scholarship on the family in American political development as well as the chapters in this volume amply show, the state has an abiding, and historically contingent, interest in recognizing, constructing, and accommodating family relations to uphold its economic and political imperatives.[4] In the context of a slave-based political economy, the southern white family was of paramount interest to the state to the extent that it was the primary unit responsible for physical reproduction of "white" identities as well as essential to the social reproduction of racially delineated social and economic values from generation to generation.

Yet the very nature of the family belied its easy appropriation by the state. Families are both legal constructions and bundles of emotional ties. As legal constructions, they orient mothers, fathers, and their children toward each other as groups of people with shared and interdependent interests. The law, on the one hand, enshrines and protects these interests and, on the other, creates them.[5] Among other things, much of the law's focus on the family concerns the assignment of responsibility to provide for, nurture, and socialize the young.

However, the formal assignment of responsibility does not ensure that parents will, in fact, properly provide and care for their children. As with policing the color line in everyday life, parents must desire these things in their own right and share a belief that they must provide for their children in these ways. That motivation arises when a family also becomes a bundle of emotional ties and shared beliefs in which the interests of family members take on real meaning and importance for other members of the family.

In a world ideally suited for the reproduction of slavery as a system, the legal construction of the family and the affective ties between separate white and black units of mothers, fathers, and their children would have exactly coincided. If this had been the case in the antebellum South, racial identity as a legal status would have rested on a much more secure and durable foundation. However, in addition to their sexual exploitation of slaves, white men sometimes became intimately involved with black women, free and enslaved, and in some of those cases assumed the affectionate and material guardianship of their resultant children.[6] The courts were reluctant to deny the existence of these emotional ties, particularly those of white men of wealth, as these were viewed as the natural and rightful parental feelings of a patriarch, an important component in the legal construction of the white family.[7] Moreover, politically and ideologically, white patriarchal affection was also very closely aligned with beliefs in white superiority. The assumption that the white patriarch, either as father or master, was paternalistic, chivalrous, honorable, and affectionate provided much of the ideological rationale for slavery as a socioeconomic system.[8] However, the courts could not clothe white paternal affective ties across the color line with the sanctity of law without undermining the racial distinctions and ideology that underlay slavery.

Three interrelated elements came to a head through the antebellum state's dual commitments to family and slavery: (1) the ideological construction of physical racial difference as indelible evidence of white superiority; (2) the reliance on emotional attachments between white fathers, mothers, and children as the mainspring for the reproduction of moral and ethical values in the society; and (3) the practical impossibility of containing white patriarchs' sexual relations and affective attachments within the white family.

As this chapter will show, antebellum courts played a central role in reconciling such tensions in the state's commitment to slavery and the white family by developing specific family-based frames (biological maternity and public paternity) for the assignment of racial identity and for adjudicating the claims of white fathers regarding their mixed-race children. In so doing the courts linked racial status to the legal construction of the family in ways that upheld, but also revealed the tension between, both commitments. In this chapter we thus suggest how the state of Louisiana legally constructed race to reconcile and adjust the tensions between slavery and the family, shaping both slavery and the legal construction of the family in the process. Much like Carol Nackenoff and Julie Novkov's discussion in Chapter 7 in this volume of how the messiness of family life as a social experience complicated the state agenda (to restrict Chinese immigration) and invited "modest independent governing authority" on the part of the courts vis-à-vis administrative agencies, the following narrative will highlight how family relations complicated, and in some cases contravened, the state's commitment to racially determined slavery, in turn making way for the courts to play an active role in the race-based and gendered production of family in the antebellum era.

Summary of Argument

We assemble and analyze two frames in the legal construction of race through which, we argue, the courts attempted to align Louisiana's commitments to slavery and to family: the biological certainty of maternity linked to black mothers (biological maternity) and public acknowledgment of paternity by white fathers (public paternity). In trials involving juridical policing of the color line, biological motherhood played a primary role. For example, in cases in which the racial identity of an individual was physically indeterminate, maternal descent was often offered as the decisive criterion. The mother's physical characteristics (e.g., the width of her nose and the straightness of her hair), along with how her neighbors regarded her, would be entered into evidence and that evidence would "tell the tale" with respect to her children. In these cases the courts were not interested in evidence that might have established white paternity. For one thing, maternity was usually much more easily established as a biological fact than paternity. But even more importantly, the courts were very reluctant to acknowledge the existence of interracial sexual relationships or to recognize the legal consequences that might attach to such unions between white men and black women (especially enslaved but also free).

The tables were turned in cases in which a white father wished to acknowledge paternity over mixed-race children. In such trials, the issue was not the determination of racial identity but the property or inheritance rights of the children for whom the public assertion of paternity by the white father was a central consideration. In some instances, such as wills or notarized acknowledgments, paternity was formally acknowledged. But paternity was also informally demonstrated through public displays of fatherly affection and responsibility in which, for instance, the father would openly regard the children as his own before friends, neighbors, and relatives. These informal demonstrations of paternal affection assumed legal significance in the determination of material questions, such as disputes over inheritance and property between the mixed-race children and other white heirs. Through the frame of public paternal acknowledgment, the otherwise condemned sexual conduct of the white patriarch was reconciled with legal fealty to the individual prerogatives of a father and his lawful emotional ties toward his child that underpinned the legal integrity of the white family. As a result, his children were often granted some of the privileges ordinarily limited to white children even though they themselves were legally black.

Taken alone, these two frames, biological maternity and public paternity, were superficially consistent. Where the father was not brought into evidence, the race of the mother was decisive. Where the father publically acknowledged paternity, the race of the mother was largely irrelevant (but not entirely so because, in practice, the burden of proof was higher if the mother was black). Both frames thus depended on and shaped a commonly shared construction of the color line.[9]

The rest of this chapter proceeds as follows: after a discussion of our anticipated contribution to the literature, the following section discusses antebellum Louisiana as a site for investigating the complex legal relationship among family, race, and slavery. The next two sections assemble the frames of biological maternity and public paternity as invoked by courtroom attorneys, judges, and witnesses in cases involving the color line. The conclusion summarizes the implications of our analysis.

Contribution to the Literature

Although slavery and gender initially spawned mostly separate literatures, much of recent scholarship on the antebellum South has blended the two themes, largely through the heuristic of family.[10] In that connection, the historical and legal literature has repeatedly documented the unique characteristics of the southern antebellum (white) family and its pivotal relation to the construction of the social and economic organization of slavery.[11] Much of this work presents the patriarchal white family and slavery as organically interdependent in that the southern state simultaneously reproduced both slavery and family by constructing and maintaining a racial and gendered hierarchy of legal statuses within family and in society at large.[12] In this literature the slippage between family and slavery in southern antebellum law, a slippage that required active judicial management, pivoted on the tension between the individual rights of the (white) patriarch on one hand, and the communal demands of slavery, as a predictable, legally coherent system on the other.

We suggest, however, that the southern state's dual commitments to family and slavery contained another source of tension that the existing literature glosses over, one that involves racial determination and the policing of the color line. This is seen in judicial cases when (1) an individual's racial identity was physically ambiguous and called into question his family and/or slave status and (2) a white patriarch formed familial relations with a black woman that resulted in mixed-race progeny whom he wished to legally benefit and support. These cases challenged some of the foundational ideological assumptions underpinning both slavery and the patriarchal family, and the courts consequently extended and created legal principles and interpretations *of race* to police the "borderlands" of Louisiana society, a terrain in which complex racial realities and social relations defied the formal constructions assumed in statutes and court decisions.

Although existing scholarship has highlighted the close relationship of family to slavery, other work examining the practices and logics involved in the determination of racial identity has largely focused on individuals, paying scant attention to how conceptions of family shaped legal construction of the color line.[13] As we will suggest, family provided the primary social context through which racial identities were assigned to individuals as they engaged in social and economic relations with one another. These social practices created shared expectations and recognition of bloodlines that charted a family's racial identity over time, and judicial construction and regulation of the color line often drew upon these practices. In this way we hope to highlight the missing "family" piece in the literature on racial determination while simultaneously illuminating the overlooked role of "racial determination" in scholarship on the legal construction of family and slavery in the antebellum South.

With respect to a larger perspective on American political development, we build on Julie Novkov's *Racial Union* on the regulation of interracial marriage in Alabama following the Civil War. Novkov argues that southern states sought to create new boundaries for racial categories in the wake of abolition and that their efforts almost immediately centered on the white family. The white family thus came to replace slavery as a key site for southern efforts to reconstruct white supremacy and racial hegemony.[14] Our chapter contributes to this narrative by demonstrating the role played by family before the Civil War in constructing and maintaining the color line, which is, in both her and our accounts, an essential element in a white supremacist regime. As Novkov posits, slavery was "a powerful proxy for black subordination and construction of black racial inferiority"; however, as we show, the empirical reality of everyday antebellum life revealed contradictions within slavery, many of them related to the complex character and "messiness" of emotional attachments created by long-term family-like unions. Maintaining slavery as a racial hegemonic system required an active, ongoing effort on the part of courts to produce racial categories that were both interpretable in actual social practice and compatible with the ideological presumptions of white supremacy.

In sum, this chapter contributes to at least three literatures: on the southern family and law, on race and racial determination in the South under slavery, and to the broader literature on American political development in which the legal constructions of race and family have helped shape contemporary society.

Louisiana as a Research Site: Methodology and Sources

Louisiana had been ruled by the Spanish and then by the French before the United States purchased the colony in 1803.[15] As the agricultural economy expanded and New Orleans became an increasingly important port, slavery became an ever-more-prominent element in Louisiana society as a social order and a labor system.[16] Responding to pressure from whites (Americans, French- and Spanish-speaking Creoles, and West Indians alike), Louisiana began to harden the legal construction of racial categories as it imposed increasingly harsh restrictions on people of color. In 1806, the new American territory adopted a Black Code that more strictly regulated racial categories than had been the case under Spanish law. This new three-tiered racial caste system distinguished between whites, *gens de couleur libre* (free people of color), and slaves.[17] Other laws prohibited slaves from purchasing their own freedom (a long-standing practice called "coartacion"), limited manumission by masters, and curtailed the emigration or settlement of "free negroes or malattos."[18] Both the hardening of racial categories and the increasing discrimination between whites and blacks meant that the courts were compelled to decide more and more cases in which the determination of race was a central issue.[19]

All of this took place after the acquisition by the United States had unsettled the traditions and practices of civil law in Louisiana. That civil law tradition had been an integral part of Louisiana's French and Spanish colonial history. After the United States acquired the territory, many Louisiana citizens feared that their new rulers would impose the American common law system, which was much more reliant on judge-made law than upon a formal code.[20] Among other differences, the American common law system protected individual rights through such mechanisms as trial by jury, the presumption of innocence, the writ of habeas corpus and stare decisis. These mechanisms were largely unknown in the civil law tradition.[21]

In 1812, in drawing up a constitution prefatory to statehood, Louisiana resisted the introduction of American common law by forbidding the legislature from imposing that system upon the state and by requiring the newly created Supreme Court to justify each and every decision by citing specific acts of the legislature or articles in the Civil Code.[22] However, most of the judiciary in the antebellum period, including justices appointed to the Louisiana State Supreme Court, immigrated to Louisiana from states in which the common law tradition prevailed. Trained in that tradition, they tended to graft common law principles onto their adopted state's civil law foundation.[23] Similarly, the state legislature increasingly incorporated American common law principles into statutes, interweaving judicial discretion and individual rights with the traditional civilian emphasis on formally codified law.[24]

In the cases we examine, Louisiana judges mostly followed the injunction to uphold the legislative will and dutifully cited statutory law as support for their decisions. However, they sometimes also followed common law practice and cited precedents while elaborately and creatively interpreting legislative intent or simply ignoring legislative dicta.[25] In many ways, then, the legislature and courts ensured that Louisiana law became Americanized following statehood as the white citizenry became increasingly integrated into national social, commercial, and political networks. Within a generation, Louisiana had emerged as one of the most "southern" of American states, with a very repressive slave regime that mimicked those of its neighbors. Moreover, through the 1840s and 1850s the status of free people of color in Louisiana, like that of those elsewhere in the South, was increasingly eroded.[26] These developments occurred despite the state's racial and ethnic diversity, the complexity of its social relations, and its distinctive legal history.[27]

Louisiana thus represents a particularly interesting site for an investigation of the legal construction of family and black subordination in the antebellum slave South. Although we must carefully qualify the conclusions that we draw from studying this case, the evidence from this racially and ethnically complex society amply illustrates the stress that social practice imposed on increasing legal enforcement of fundamental commitments to the patriarchal white family and to slavery.

We examine the trial manuscript records of the Supreme Court of Louisiana from 1803 to 1860, archived at the University of New Orleans. Although these records are now partially digitized, this was not the case at the time our research was conducted. We thus read each handwritten trial record in its entirety, including the arguments of attorneys, depositions, written interrogatories, bills of exceptions, the clerk's summary of the evidence, the original opinions, appeal briefs, and the judgments and opinions of the trial judges and Supreme Court justices (the latter were often edited with commentary in the margins and sections crossed out and then revised). This rich record details the complex social contexts in which people lived and in which the courts functioned as they attempted to reinterpret extremely messy social relations so that they conformed to coherent legal principles and logic.

We identified cases involving the color line by searching the indexes and texts in the following sources: Helen T. Catterall, *Judicial Cases Concerning American Slavery and the Negro*; the *Louisiana Digest: 1809 to Date*; Ariela J. Gross, "Litigating Whiteness: Trials of Racial Determination in the Nineteenth-Century South"; and Judith Schafer, *Slavery, the Civil Law, and the Supreme Court*.[28] In this survey, we first identified all cases associated with race and skin color by using keywords such as "color," "white," "black," and "mulatto." We selected only those in which a person's racial identity was a legal issue. Within this subset, we identified those involving persons of "mixed" color (referred to as mulattoes, griffes, or quadroons). We focused on these cases, along with those in which racial identity was ambiguous, because light-skinned people of color, both enslaved or free, could often cross the color line in Louisiana.[29] After thus winnowing down the archive, our sample was composed of twenty-one case transcript files, each ranging from fifty to four hundred pages of material. Through a process of close induction, discourse, and content analysis, we then identified the kinds of racial frames that the courts and participants in these cases constructed and, in particular, how those frames invoked families and parenthood.

Maternity and the Construction of Racial Identity

Throughout the nineteenth century, racial identity was assumed to be a "natural," self-evident fact that was visibly inscribed on a person's physiognomy. People recognized that skin color and other physical characteristics varied across a range from black to white and thus developed subcategories in which, for example, they would label individuals as quadroons (one-fourth black), octoroons (one-eighth black), and griffes (those with a black and a mulatto parent). In the racial understandings of the period, these subcategories were based on a very high, if not precise, correlation between an individual's lineage and their physical appearance.[30] However, the assignment of these subcategories to particular individuals was often uncertain in practice. For example, the physical appearance of individuals with lighter skins often had to be buttressed with a social reputation (e.g., how they had been regarded within their communities) before racial identity could be firmly assigned.[31]

With the exceptions of Virginia and Alabama, no southern states formally defined racial categories in their statutes.[32] Although American racial categories evolved over time, they consistently relied on biological descent to construct race in legal proceedings.[33] In the context of slavery maternal descent in particular, as opposed to descent from the father, played a central role in the construction of race. In Louisiana (as in the South generally), descent from a slave mother automatically conferred slave status on the child, and since only blacks could be legally enslaved, a mother's slave status also raised the presumption of blackness of the child.[34]

In 1820, the Louisiana Supreme Court confirmed that skin color was a crucial factor in deciding who could and who could not be enslaved.[35] Yet, the firm predication of slave status on maternal lineage meant that in most cases, regardless of skin color (i.e., how white a person might physically appear to be), the slave status of the mother would decisively determine the child's enslaved status. This reliance on maternal lineage also extended to free blacks, wherein the race of children was similarly determined by the racial status of their mother, even if she was free. As a result, cases involving racial identity often involved not merely a physiological interrogation of the physical features of the claimant but, almost invariably, an investigation of those features as exhibited by his or her mother and, in some cases, grandmother.

For example, when Alexina Morrison, a slave in Jefferson Parish in Louisiana, ran away from her master James White in 1857 and sued him for her freedom on the basis that "she was born free and of white parentage" and had been kidnapped into slavery in Arkansas, the social relations and implied slave status of her mother and siblings were used to contradict her claims. One witness stated that "the general reputation in this [Matagorda] county," Texas, was that Alexina "was a slave" and that this reputation was derived, in part, "from the fact that her mother was and is a slave." The witness went on to say that he could vouch for these facts because he himself had known the mother for "nearly twenty years." He had "bought said Alexina as a slave together with her mother and several other children" who were her "brothers and sisters." However, it was clear from his description of Alexina's physical appearance that maternal lineage, not conformance to a racial stereotype, was the decisive criterion for her enslavement. "Her age as near as I can judge is about fifteen years, her complexion was very fair for a mulatto. She had yellow flaxen hair and light blue eyes, would have passed for a white child anywhere if not known. I cannot say what her size is now, not having seen her since I carried her to Little Rock. She was then rather slender and delicate." The witness had taken Alexina to Little Rock, Arkansas, so that she could be lodged with his nephew's family "for the purpose of having her taught to sew and do house work." After that, he had lost track of her.[36]

Alexina Morrison's appearance would have had little or no bearing on the racial identities of the other members of her family, particularly her mother, who was a documented slave of the Morrison family in Arkansas and Texas. However, the skin tone and physical characteristics of an enslaved person often implicated the racial status of other members of the family in the maternal lineage in other instances. Such implications were an integral part of daily life in Louisiana. For example, 90 percent of the people sold in the New Orleans slave market were described in their Acts of Sale in terms of their imagined blood quantum (most commonly, negro, griffe, mulatto, or quadroon). Walter Johnson notes that "those words described pasts not visible in the slave pens by referring to parents and grandparents who had been left behind with old owners . . . buyers made the same move from visible to the biological . . . buyers were seeing color, but they were looking for lineage."[37] That lighter-skinned people were in the slave pen implied that their mother had been enslaved, while their skin color implied that they had a white male ancestor (or ancestors) somewhere in their lineage.

Other social and economic histories were implied by skin color as well. Black or dark skin tone implied descent from dark-skinned slave mothers who were frequently field hands and/or manual laborers, whereas light skin tones and other "white features" conjured up descent from mothers who had been house servants, seamstresses, or cooks, skills with a higher market value.[38] Lighter-skinned slaves, if they were young women, thus commanded a far higher price in the slave market than darker-skinned slaves. Touting their fair skins and describing their "slender" frames, "delicate" facial features, and sound teeth, slave merchants clearly justified the relatively high market value of a lighter-skinned female slave and her descendants.

The strong implications that maternal physical features had for a person's racial identity carried over into suits involving slander. In such cases, light-skinned men (all the cases involved only men as plaintiffs) sued those who had publicly declared them to be "colored." In the subsequent court proceedings, the physical characteristics of the plaintiff's mother were almost always interrogated. In *Boullemet v. Phillips* (1836), for example, Stephen Boullemet charged that Alexander Phillips had publically claimed that Boullemet's mother was a colored woman (i.e., with African lineage) with the clear and unavoidable implication that he, her son, was also colored.[39] In a remarkable confirmation that his own physical appearance was not at issue, Stephen Boullemet himself never testified. Instead, witnesses for both the plaintiff and the defendant focused on his social standing in the community (e.g., where he had gone to school, his membership in the militia, and other social relations). Since they were blood relations descended from the same mother, Boullemet's brothers' social standing and social relations (e.g., membership in volunteer fire companies) were similarly brought into evidence but, again, not their physical characteristics.[40]

While the context of their social relations was important (because it demonstrated how they had been received by the white community), the trial proceedings largely consisted of testimony regarding the physical features of Stephen Boullemet's mother and grandmother. Witnesses for both the plaintiff and the defendant agreed that they had darker complexions than those normally expected of a white person. The witnesses for the plaintiff attributed their skin color to descent from a Caribbean Indian tribe in order to claim that he was not "colored." Witnesses for the defendant, in contrast, claimed that the mother and grandmother were descended from blacks. For example, Mrs. Lavigne, who lived near the Boullemet family, gave the following description of Stephen Boullemet's grandmother and mother:

> The features of the old lady were rather those of an Indian than those of an African. She had coarse black hair, which came as low as her hips. They were very straight. She had the face of an Indian and also the colour. She had thin lips and her nose was very large but rather sharp. Her daughter, Mrs. Boullemet [Stephens' mother], here present [in the courtroom as Lavigne testified], favoring her very much although she looked more like an Indian than [her daughter] does.[41]

Despite the fact that Lavigne's testimony supported the plaintiff, Norbert Vandry backed the defense when he reported that "the grandmother's hair was black, long and a little curley [sic]," adding that she also had "a large mouth and thick lips . . . Her nose was neither flat nor sharp, by no means an Indian nose." He also claimed that Stephen Boullemet's mother "has black hair, black eyes, same nose as her mother, pretty near the same mouth also."[42]

Although Judge Charles Marrian of the New Orleans Parish Court upheld the jury's decision to award $4,000 (a remarkably large amount) to Stephen Boullemet, the judge also reported that he did not agree with the verdict.[43] When the case reached the Louisiana Supreme Court on appeal, Chief Justice Francois Xavier Martin both substantially reduced the jury's award and declared that the court shared the trial judge's "dissatisfaction with the finding of the jury . . . our view of the evidence, like his, totally differing from theirs."[44] Contrary to the jury, both the trial judge and the appellate judges appear to have found that Stephen Boullemet was in fact not white based on the testimony pertaining to the physical features of his mother and grandmother, as seen in the following handwritten notes that were crossed out in the original manuscript and thus did not form part of the recorded Supreme Court decision.

The testimony shews that the plaintiff's mother is not a white person absolutely; two of the plaintiff's witnesses deposing that her mother was of Indian
descent, to wit from the Carabee Indians. The witnesses on both sides declared that the plaintiff's mother is of a very dark complexion. Those of the
defendant attest that she is considered as a coloured woman [in her social
relations in the community], that she has a brother who was considered as a
coloured man and some of her children are thought so; that she lived with a
barber as his menagerie in the manner of which women of colour often do.[45]

Stephen Boullemet's father had passed away before the trial, but his
physical features were never at issue because all the witnesses conceded
that he was white in skin color and social reputation. In fact, they reported that he "was a very worthy, good man" who had run a boarding
house and billiard room patronized by white men and also owned a
plantation outside the city. There was some question of whether or not
the father and mother were married, but their marriage had been recorded by the Catholic Church and it was said that the Church never
knowingly solemnized a union between white and black persons. On the
one hand, the respect thus shown for Boullemet's father tended to favor
the mother's non-black status as well. On the other hand, the father and
mother did not always present themselves as husband and wife because
the mother seemed more than a little deferential to the father.[46] But the
larger point is this: in Louisiana, a father's racial identity was never interrogated because it was commonly assumed that a clearly white mother
would never have intimately associated with someone whose racial identity was suspect.[47] The mother's features and lineage were interrogated
in the Boullemet case precisely because the white father was not presumed to have restricted his sexual relationships to white women.[48]

In other slander cases, descriptions of the father's or grandfather's
skin color or physical appearance were not entered into evidence even
when the plaintiff's grandmother had been a "mulatress of light color"[49]
or that "they had seen and known [plaintiff's] grandmother" and "that
she was a real mulatto woman."[50] However, the courts usually discounted
these claims if there existed documentary evidence such as marriage
and birth certificates that "traced his [the plaintiff's] descent through
unmixed blood for upwards of a century."[51] But even when such evidence was introduced, the mother's and maternal grandmother's physical features were interrogated, not those of the father.

The physical features of a mother and daughter were similarly at issue in *Gottschalk v. DeLaRosa* (1834). Lino DeLaRosa had bought Polly and her child, Mary, at a slave auction but had subsequently refused to pay the $560 price to the plaintiff because, DeLaRosa claimed, both mother and child were white and had been only been represented as enslaved after they had been kidnapped in Alabama. Asserting that "Polly and her child are whiter than quateroons which circumstance alone raises the presumption of liberty in their favor," DeLaRosa declared that he would "produce said Polly and her child in open Court."[52]

In this instance, testimony regarding the physical features of the mother was presented as more important than those of the child because, if the mother, Polly, were found to be white, then her child, Mary, could not be held as a slave regardless of whether she was found to be white or black. So freedom for the both of them depended on Polly's racial identity. John H. Hand, a "practitioner of Medecine [*sic*]" from Mississippi, testified for the defendant and said that Polly had been imported into Louisiana under a certificate originally made out for another woman named Judy who was "about sixteen years old, very dark mulattoe, very dark hair and little curled. Front teeth large and very close." According to Dr. Hand, Polly was "a thin spare made bright mulatto tolerably strait brown hair—her teeth were tolerably wide and separated—[who] had a white child, a girl about two or three years of age and blue-eyed."[53] In sum, the plaintiff was contending that both Polly's light physical appearance and inconsistency with the certificate of her sale should void the sale because they vitiated the documentary evidence that had traveled with her and Mary when they were imported from Mississippi.

Most such cases are liberally sprinkled with descriptions of the social conduct and relations of mothers, for example, whether or not they were visited by or were received into the society of other "respectable white ladies."[54] However, in their clear avoidance of descriptions of the physical features of the father, these same cases show that the physicality of mothers was far more closely inscribed in physical constructions of racial identity based on descent and thus in the biological imagination of whiteness and blackness.

White Fathers and the Social Reproduction of Racial Identity

With the exception of one instance involving a white mother in our collection of records, white fathers played far more prominent roles in cases involving children acknowledged to be of mixed race.[55] However, in almost none of these cases did white paternity acquire a legal significance with respect to slave status or racial identity because the mixed-race children were already identified as black. Although it played little role in *defining* the color line, white paternity was frequently decisive when that line was crossed, determining when and how children of mixed race would be permitted to acquire some of the legal rights of whites. In these cases, judges and juries were effectively deciding when and how to assign "whiteness" by either encompassing or refusing to encompass these children within those rights. In all our cases, the social and public aspects of white paternity, not its biological influence on the features of the children, were the primary issues. The fact (or not) of white paternity was thus demonstrated by the public actions and attitudes of the ostensible father, not by the physical features he had transmitted to his ostensible children.

As in most slave states, Louisiana law both condoned interracial sexual relations and protected white men by either veiling their indiscretions or viewing their intimate relationships as matters of individual taste, however exploitative or distasteful to public morality they may be.[56] However, the offspring of such interracial connections, unlike the illegitimate children born to white parents, were always legally regarded as bastards, or "natural children." As such, they could not be legitimized by marriage and were also legally unable to prove paternal descent unless their white father acknowledged his paternity.[57]

Although the *Louisiana Civil Code* nullified marriage between whites and free people of color, "quadroon balls" regularly brought wealthy white men and upper-class women of color into intimate contact. In several cases, they subsequently entered into long-term domestic arrangements that included the formation of households in addition to the man's white family.[58] Cohabitation between white patriarchs and slave women and their children was also fairly common in New Orleans and Louisiana generally, and mulatto and black women also worked in the many brothels that flourished in New Orleans under accommodating city ordinances and law enforcement practices.[59]

Long-term unions between white men and black women, both free and enslaved, resulted in progeny to whom their white father occasionally became quite devoted.[60] In such cases, these white fathers went to great lengths to legally endow both the children and the mother with claims upon their property by recognizing their relations. Such white

Table 4.1 Legal Determination of Paternity under Antebellum Louisiana Law

		Race of the Father	
		White	Black
Race of the Child	White	The child may prove paternity.	Under the law, this is impossible since, by definition, no white child can have a black father.
	Black	Child cannot prove paternity unless the father acknowledges siring the child.	If the black child is free and his or her father is also black, he or she may prove paternity.

Source: Louisiana Civil Code, Book I, Title VII, Chapter III, Section II, Articles 226 and 230.

masters had both the financial resources to prosecute cases in the courts, and controlled assets (e.g., estates) that were worth adjudicating when disputed by the father's other white heirs.[61]

Louisiana law stipulated that white fathers could only recognize their mixed-race offspring in two ways: through a formal public declaration "executed before a notary public, in presence of two witnesses" or by permitting their paternity to be recorded "in the registering of birth or baptism of such children." The law also emphatically insisted that "no other proof of acknowledgement shall be admitted in favor of children of color" in the courts.[62]

Despite this injunction, litigants often offered less formal evidence of paternal acknowledgment in the form of open displays of affection and publicly announced intentions to provide for their children. The courts sometimes accepted this evidence as a legal representation of a social reality in which the father was emotionally committed to his children's well-being. In *MacArty v. Mandeville* (1847), for example, Eugene MacArty's white heirs claimed that the vast estate of his female companion of color, Eulalie Mandeville, had been illegally given to her.[63] Mandeville's defense was that the property in her possession (valued at that time at $155,000) was not a gift from MacArty but had been "honestly acquired [as] the result of her industry and economy during half a century," the same period of time during which she and MacArty had been cohabiting. Chief Justice George Eustis found that the property rightfully belonged to Eulalie Mandeville and was not a part of MacArty's estate. The diminished size of MacArty's estate was held instead to be the consequence of his natural paternal "affections" that led him to lavishly provide for his five mixed-race children:

> It seems to us, when . . . the education and position of the children of the deceased are considered, that the *tendency of his affections and the claims of his children would render them much more probably recipients of the bounty of their father than the defendant*, who it is conceded was provided for by her own means . . . Two of his children were established there, and remittances are proved to have been made to them at different times . . . amounting upwards of $30,000. And supposing that the *deceased bore the expenses of his own household and of the education and establishment of his own children, and the right to do this we do not understand to be drawn in question*, the smallness of these means at the time of his death is fairly accounted for.[64]

Contrary to statutory limitations on the inheritance claims of "natural children" of color,[65] the court upheld (and thus legitimated) Eugene MacArty's paternal "expenses on his own household and of the education and establishment of his own children" as a "right" not "drawn in question." Witnesses had testified that the father and one of his sons had closely and intimately cooperated as they invested their own and Eulalie's money. One of the witnesses, a notary named Philip Lacoste, recalled numerous occasions in which Eugene and his son came to his office for the purpose of passing acts (bonds) which were formally listed in the names "of Eulalie Mandeville or of the Son, but the father gave the directions." Lacoste noted that "the father and son generally came to witness together, and the son interested himself more about the acts than the father. MacArty Sr. sometimes came alone, but more often with his son."[66]

Other witnesses described the social intimacy of MacArty's mixed-race household in that "he kept a very good table and had always two or three persons at dinner." In conversations with friends and neighbors, MacArty made constant, affectionate references to his mixed-race children and on one occasion remarked to a witness that "he could not understand how his children could not become rich inasmuch as they had fine plantations."[67] Several witnesses also recalled that "MacArty received a letter from his children in Cuba" asking him to visit them "on the island."[68]

Although the petitions, testimony, and judgments in this case ran to almost three hundred pages, the ostensible immoral or unconventional nature of the MacArty mixed-race household was rarely mentioned by anyone other than the plaintiffs. Chief Justice Eustis did acknowledge their claim by stating that "we are not insensible to the appeal made to us in this case, in the interest of morals, religion and social order." However, Eustis also noted the social acceptability of the long-term union that had, among other things, "received consent of her [Mandeville's] family, which was one of the most distinguished in Louisiana," and that, everything considered, it was "the nearest approach to marriage which the law recognized, and in the days in which their union commenced it imposed serious moral obligations."[69] Judging these "moral obligations" to outweigh those imposed by the statutes, the chief justice found for Eulalie Mandeville and denied the claims of the white heirs.

In another case, *Compton, Heirs v. Executors* (1845), the verdict similarly turned on extensive evidence of a father's (Leonard B. Compton) acknowledgment of and affection for his natural children of color, Scipio and Loretta, and their mother, Fanchon Morres, a free woman of color. In a will written in his own hand, Compton had bequeathed his plantation of 545 acres, including all the slaves and improvements, along with $10,000, to his children. To Fanchon, he gave all the movable items in the household. In addition, he had also arranged to have various tracts of land given to both the mother and the children. The case file includes letters, almost fifty pages when totaled, in which the white father expresses deep affection and fond hopes for his son, Scipio. Leonard Compton often ended these letters to his son by asking him "to accept the well wishes of an affectionate father who wishes for nothing more in this life than your advancement in life," always signing off with "your father." He frequently referred in these letters to Scipio's mother, Fanchon, sometimes chiding his son for neglecting her and reminding him that "your mother is always anctious [*sic*] to hear from you." In the same vein, the father sternly declared in another letter that "there is a certain respect due from you to those who has [*sic*] been instrumental [*sic*] in your existence . . . your mother is very much displeased and I think she has a right to be as in your last two letters you have never even mentioned her name."

In a letter to Scipio's head teacher, Mr. Furman, Leonard first thanked him for his last letter and then writes that "nothing can be more gratifying to a parent than to hear of the health & good conduct of his child," and that he hoped "that Scipio will never depart from the principles that you will instill into his mind in his early youth." That hope, Leonard wrote, was the "principal cause" of his "parting with him [Scipio] at so early a time of life."[70] Leonard also made many trips to Ohio to visit Scipio at his school and to Missouri, where Loretta was being educated. He also made handsome payments to these schools for their training. In all these ways, the evidence in the case file amply documents the paternal affections and obligations of a white father for his natural children of color.

Upholding Compton's bequests to Fanchon and his children, the district court dismissed the claims of the white heirs to the estate. Upon appeal, Supreme Court Justice Florent Edouard Simon noted that Compton had acknowledged Scipio and Loretta as his children in his will and that "he always treated them as such." In addition, Compton "had caused one of them to be educated in Ohio at his own expense, and always showed them the affection of a father." Justice Simon's ruling declared that Compton's public acknowledgment of paternity allowed the two children to inherit one-fourth of his estate, a share similar to that allowed to white illegitimate children who had been publicly recognized. In so ruling, he stated, "the object of the law is to exclude illegitimate colored children from any right in their natural father's estate, *who has not acknowledged them*" (emphasis added). While confirming that Fanchon could not, as a "concubine," receive more than one-tenth of the movable property in Compton's estate, Justice Simon ruled that that legal limit did not apply to "duly acknowledged natural children" and their right to inherit immovable property because the "child has his own capacity . . . of receiving to the extent of one-fourth of the estate of the father, and they cannot be deprived of it." To deprive them of their rightful share "would amount to an absolute prohibition of the father's making [a bequest to them], during the lifetime of the mother."[71] In effect, the father's formal acknowledgment of paternity and his social display of affection allowed his mixed-race children, in the eyes of the law and for the purposes of inheritance, to become white.

Suits for Freedom

Although public acknowledgment of paternity could confer (albeit to a limited degree) whiteness upon children of color when the white father's estate was distributed, maternal descent was decisive in suits for freedom by mixed-race slaves. In the case of *Foster v. Mish* (1859), for example, Andy Foster sued for freedom on the grounds that he had been kidnapped and illegally sold into servitude, having been the son of John Foster, a white man (now deceased), and Nancy Foster, a free woman of color who was "still living in the State of Kentucky, and who was free previous to his birth." He claimed that his father "always recognized him as his son and as free" and had taken him "from Kentucky to Ohio . . . and there left him (as free) to attend school, and also to learn a trade."[72] James W. Cole, a white friend, testified that "John Foster told [him] often in his life time that he was the father of said Andy Foster," and that "John Foster fed and clothed the said Andy" and often "told his friends that Andy was his son."[73] Even the white son of John Foster, who would have been Andy's half-brother, testified on Andy's behalf, saying that "he [would] often hear his father say that Nancy and her son Andy were free and that Andy was his son."[74]

Despite the substantial body of evidence demonstrating both paternal affection and public recognition, the written opinion justifying the Supreme Court's decision to free Andy Foster never referred to the acknowledged paternity and emotional involvement of the white father. The court instead focused on the mother, noting that she had "been constantly recognized in the State of Kentucky as a free person of color, and has been continuously in the actual enjoyment of her freedom."[75] In this and other cases, the affection, public recognition, and material support of a white father could not have outweighed the status of the mother; if she were a slave, then her child was a slave, regardless of what the white father might say or do. This was especially so in the 1850s as the courts increasingly curbed white men's prerogatives in the quest to solidify the bonds of slavery, best exemplified in Louisiana's 1857 ban on manumission.[76]

The courts were similarly unwilling to assign legal significance to white paternity when adjudicating the property rights of mulatto children when the mother was a slave. Because fathering mulatto children with slave women undermined the assumed ethical foundations of the southern social order, the immorality of white paternity was frequently cited in cases involving slave mistresses and their mixed-race slave children. In these decisions, the courts viewed the sexual involvement of white masters with slave women as both private "sins" and as transgressions against "public decency" and "public morals."[77] When, for example, John Trumbull (1856) acknowledged in his will that he had fathered children with a slave woman and provided that they all be emancipated, his intimacy with the mother was denounced as "offensive to morality" and his fatherhood was "without operation in law" with respect to the children he had sired.[78] Regardless of how much affection and social recognition the white master had bestowed on the slave mother and their children, public acknowledgment of paternity in these cases was seen as serious fissure in the moral edifice of slavery.[79] While public recognition by a white father might on occasion "lift" free companions of color and their mixed-race children ever so slightly above the color line, that line granted no exceptions if the mother was a slave.

Conclusion

If white men had never become sexually involved with black women, slavery would have rested on a much firmer foundation. There would have been, for one thing, no conflict between the labor system and the color-delineated assumptions essential to the reproduction of the white patriarchal family. The unqualified commitments of Louisiana courts to the social orders of slavery and family would thus have required little or no reconciliation. However, many white men did become intimately involved with black women and in these instances the courts sometimes had to choose between respect for the emotional attachments of their fatherhood and an ideological and consistent imposition of the color line that could clearly distinguish whites from blacks.

In making these choices, the courts constructed racial status through family frames, sometimes favoring fatherhood (and paternal affective practices) and sometimes reinforcing the racial organization of slavery. There can be little doubt that wealthy white patriarchs could sway the courts. The cases we have studied here were the product of wealth and privilege both in the size of the property holdings at stake and the fact that litigation was expensive. These cases nonetheless illustrate the tension between respect for family as the pivotal social order through which values and identities were reproduced in society and the social order of slavery in which spontaneous practices required a doxic embrace of white supremacy. The family was a bundle of attachments only partially structured and organized by the law. As such, it was not an "industrial mechanism" for raising children created and regulated by the state. As an organization of labor, slavery perhaps more closely approximated such a mechanism, but there were also families in the slave quarters and the raising of slave children similarly depended upon the attachments of enslaved parents for their offspring. In a sense, these two social orders clashed because one was grounded in affective attachment and the other in the economic exploitation of a race. Through the 1850s as the Civil War drew near and the political stakes of securing the slave order considerably increased, the clash between family and slavery assumed heightened significance and the family frames of racial status, biological maternity, and public paternity, through which the courts reconciled "messy" family practice to the system of slavery, became even more legally important.

Notes

The authors would like to thank Carol Nackenoff, Ken Kersch, and Julie Novkov for their comments on earlier iterations as presented at the meetings of the Western Political Science Association, American Political Science Association, and Northeastern Political Science Association. We also thank Ed Quish, Nazli Konya, and other members of PBAC at Cornell University for their advice and criticism. The errors remain, of course, our responsibility.

1. For ways in which the color line divided the free population, see Henry A. Bullard and Thomas Curry, *A New Digest of the Statute Laws of the State of Louisiana* (New Orleans: E. Johns and Company, 1842), 66–67, 70, 158–163, 258–259 (hereafter "New Louisiana Digest"); U. B. Phillips, *The Revised Statutes of Louisiana* (New Orleans: John Claiborne, 1856), 13, 48–65, 112–113, 319 (hereafter: "Louisiana Statutes"). On the centrality of a "negro" racial identity to slave status, see Thomas Cobb, *An Inquiry into the Law of Negro Slavery in the United States of America* (Philadelphia: T. and J. W. Johnson and Company 1858), chap. 1.

2. By "social practice," we mean the commonly shared habits and routines through which people organize and conduct their lives. These rest upon unthinking reflexive judgments in which categories and alternatives are "taken for granted" so that other decisions can be consciously evaluated.

3. On the centrality of race and the color line as a means to obtain the loyalty of non-slave-holding white southerners (and those with only a few slaves) to the system of slavery, for example, see Ariela J. Gross, *What Blood Won't Tell: A History of Race on Trial in America* (Cambridge, MA: Harvard University Press, 2008), 28–29, 46–47.

4. See Carol Nackenoff and Julie Novkov, Introduction to this volume, pp. 2–5; our focus in this chapter is the significance of family to the construction and determination of race and racialized slavery in the antebellum period.

5. On the appropriation and legal recognition of family emotional bonds to further the interest of the state, see Chapter 8 in this volume.

6. Remarking in 1861 on the widespread existence of such relationships, Mary Boykin Chesnut remarked: "Like the patriarchs of old our men live all in one house with their wives and their concubines, and the mulattoes one sees in every family exactly resemble the white children—and every lady tells you who is the father of all the mulatto children in everybody's household, but those in her own she seems to think drop from the clouds." Mary Boykin Chesnut, *A Diary from Dixie*, ed. Ben Ames Williams (Cambridge, MA: Riverside Press, 1961 ed.), 21.

7. Mark Tushnet, for example, wrote that "it would have been hard [for southern courts] to suppress the natural inclination of white fathers to free their slave children." *The American Law of Slavery, 1810–1860: Considerations of Humanity and Interest* (Princeton, NJ: Princeton University Press, 1981), 155. Family sentiment and affective conceptions of marriage and child rearing were increasingly salient in nineteenth-century society and in family law cases, including those in antebellum southern courts; see Michael Grossberg, *Governing the Hearth: Law and the Family in Nineteenth-Century America* (Chapel Hill: University of North Carolina Press, 1985), 8–9; Peter Bardaglio, *Reconstructing the Household: Families, Sex, & the Law in the Nineteenth-Century South* (Chapel Hill: University of North Carolina Press, 1995), 26–27, 43.

8. By the late antebellum period, patriarchal (or domestic) paternalism was assembled and cited as the primary defense of the institution of slavery against the claims of northern abolitionists. See Lacy K. Ford, *Deliver Us from Evil: The Slavery Question in the Old South* (New York: Oxford University Press, 2009), 144–146.

9. In and of themselves, interracial sex and the mixed-race progeny that it produced undermined but did not fatally threaten the integrity of the legal color line upon which white supremacy was based. See, for example, Tushnet, *American Law of Slavery*, 140. However, judicial regulation of the color line was directly threatened when white patriarchs chose to recognize and thus accord "white" legal standing to their mixed-race children by bequeathing property to them and/or emancipating them. Bernie D. Jones, *Fathers of Conscience: Mixed-Race Inheritance in the Antebellum South* (Athens: University of Georgia Press, 2009), 2.

10. Any sampling of the vast literature on the history of the southern family, with reference to the antebellum period, should include the following: Martha Hodes, *White Women, Black Men: Illicit Sex in the Nineteenth-Century South* (New Haven, CT: Yale University Press, 1997); Victoria Bynum, *Unruly Women: The Politics of Social and Sexual Control in the Old South* (Chapel Hill: University of North Carolina Press, 1992); Anne Firor Scott, *The Southern Lady: From Pedestal to Politics, 1830–1930* (Chicago, IL: University of Chicago Press, 1970); Steven M. Stowe, *Intimacy and Power in the Old South: Ritual in the Lives of the Planters* (Baltimore, MD: Johns Hopkins University Press, 1987); Joan E. Cashin, "The Structure of

Antebellum Planter Families: 'The Ties That Bound Us Was Strong,'" *Journal of Southern History* 56 (1990): 55–70. A sampling of legal studies of the southern antebellum family should include Bardaglio, *Reconstructing the Household*, and Marylynn Salmon, *Women and the Law of Property in Early America* (Chapel Hill: University of North Carolina Press, 1986).

11. On the differences between northern and southern conceptions of family in the nineteenth century and/or the distinctive characteristics of the southern family, see Rebecca Edwards, *Angels in the Machinery: Gender in American Party Politics from the Civil War to the Progressive Era* (New York: Oxford University Press, 1997), 12–38; Laura F. Edwards, *The People and Their Peace: Legal Culture and the Transformation of Inequality in the Post-Revolutionary South* (Chapel Hill: University of North Carolina Press, 2009), 169–186; Bardaglio, *Reconstructing the Household*, 82, 84, 117–119.

12. See, in particular, Bardaglio, *Reconstructing the Household*; Jones, *Fathers of Conscience*; and Edwards, *The People and Their Peace*.

13. Such important works on the law and the construction of the color line in the antebellum period include Ariela J. Gross, "Litigating Whiteness: Trials of Racial Determination in the Nineteenth-Century South," *Yale Law Journal* 108, no. 1 (1998): 109–188; and *What Blood Won't Tell*, chapters 1 and 2, pp. 16–72; Ian Haney Lopez, *White by Law* (New York: New York University Press, 1996); Walter Johnson, "The Slave Trader, the White Slave, and the Politics of Racial Determination in the 1850s," *Journal of American History* 87 (2000): 13–38; Peggy Pascoe, *What Comes Naturally: Miscegenation Law and the Making of Race in America* (New York: Oxford University Press, 2009), 112–119.

14. Julie Novkov, *Racial Union* (Ann Arbor: University of Michigan Press, 2008), 4–5; Also see Pascoe, *What Comes Naturally*, 27–30.

15. Mark F. Fernandez, *From Chaos to Continuity: The Evolution of Louisiana's Judicial System, 1712–1862* (Baton Rouge: Louisiana State University Press, 2001), 1–15; A. N. Yiannopoulos, "The Civil Codes of Louisiana," *Civil Law Commentaries* 1, no. 1 (Winter 2008): 1–7.

16. Judith Kelleher Schafer, *Slavery, the Civil Law, and the Supreme Court of Louisiana* (Baton Rouge: Louisiana State University Press, 1994), 9.

17. For comparative analysis of the Black Code and the Spanish law that it replaced, see Schafer, *Slavery, the Civil Law, and the Supreme Court*, 6; Kenneth R. Aslakson, *Making Race in the Courtroom: The Legal Construction of Three Races in New Orleans, 1791–1812* (New York: New York University Press, 2014), 27–28, 97–99.

18. *Acts Passed at the First Session of the Second Legislature of the Territory of Orleans* (New Orleans: Bradford & Anderson, 1807), chap. 10, 82; *Louisiana Civil Code*, Book I, Title I.

19. Gwendoline Alphonso, "Public and Private Order: Law, Race, Morality and the Antebellum Courts of Louisiana, 1830–1860," *Journal of Southern Legal History* 23 (2015): 117–160.

20. Schafer, *Slavery, the Civil Law, and the Supreme Court*, 16.

21. Fernandez, *From Chaos to Continuity*, xv.

22. Sybil Ann Boudreaux, "The First Minute Book of the Supreme Court of the State of Louisiana, 1813 to May, 1818: An Annotated Edition" (PhD diss., University of New Orleans, 1983), 3–4.

23. Fernandez, *From Chaos to Continuity*, 17; Schafer, *Slavery, the Civil Law, and the Supreme Court*, 13.

24. Despite disagreement over the extent of the influence of American common law on the Louisiana legal system in this period, no one disputes that American common law principles were incorporated into legislation and court rulings. See Fernandez, *From Chaos to Continuity*, 17, 22, 25, 31–35, 39, 53–54, 57–73, 112–113; Ronald Fonseca, "Blackstone's Commentaries: Foothold or Footnote in Louisiana's Antebellum Legal History" (PhD diss., University of New Orleans, 2007); Shael Herman, "The Louisiana Code of Practice (1825): A Civilian Essai among Anglo-American Sources," *Electronic Journal of Comparative Law* 12, no. 1 (May 2008): 1–25.

25. Fernandez, *From Chaos to Continuity*, 87–88; Shael Herman, "The Louisiana Code of Practice," 14.

26. Emily West, *Family or Freedom: Free People of Color in the Antebellum South* (Lexington: University Press of Kentucky, 2012), 38.

27. Peter J. Kastor, *The Nation's Crucible: The Louisiana Purchase and the Creation of America* (New Haven, CT: Yale University Press, 2004), 13–14. Also see Thomas D. Morris, *Southern Slavery and the Law* (Chapel Hill: University of North Carolina Press, 1996), 8.

28. For a full citation for Gross, see note 13 in this chapter; for Schafer, see note 16; also see Catterall, *Judicial Cases Concerning American Slavery and the Negro* (Washington, DC: Carnegie Institution, 1926; reprinted by New York: Negro Universities Press, 1968); and *Louisiana Digest: 1809 to Date* (St. Paul, MN: West Publishing, 1959).

29. For a good summary of the literature on crossing the color line, see Aslakson, *Making Race*, 7–11.

30. For a descriptive history of racial distinctions in Louisiana during Spanish, French, and American rule, see Virginia R. Dominguez, *White by Definition: Social Classification in Creole Louisiana* (New Brunswick, NJ: Rutgers University Press, 1986), 23–36.

31. Jennifer L. Hochschild and Vesla Weaver, "Policies of Racial Classification and the Politics of Racial Inequality," in *Remaking America: Democracy and Public Policy in an Age of Inequality*, ed. Joe Soss, Jacob Hacker, and Suzanne Mettler (New York: Russell Sage Foundation: 2007), 159–182.

32. Morris, *Southern Slavery and the Law*, 22. Alabama adopted a blood quantum rule in 1852. See Peter Wallenstein, "Race, Marriage, and the Law of Free-

dom: Alabama and Virginia 1860s–1960," *Chicago-Kent Law Review* 70, no. 2 (1994): 371–437, 374.

33. Justin Desautels-Stein, "Race as a Legal Concept," *Columbia Journal of Race and Law* 1 (2012): 3–5.

34. On the origins of this legal principle in Roman law, see Judith Kelleher Schafer, "Roman Roots of the Louisiana Law of Slavery: Emancipation in American Louisiana, 1803–1857," *Louisiana Law Review* 56 (1996): 409–422. One of the major differences between Louisiana statutes and Roman law was that slave status in the latter was not based on race (because many slaves were captives taken in war), while race and slave status were inextricably intertwined in Louisiana and in the American South; see *Civil Code of the State of Louisiana* (privately published, 1825), Book I, Title I (henceforth *Louisiana Civil Code*).

35. Schafer, "Roman Roots," 410. The Supreme Court decision in *Ulzere v. Poeyfarre*, No. 468, 8 Mart. (o.s.) 155 (La. 1820), declared that Indians could not be enslaved in Louisiana and thus restricted slave status to people of African origin.

36. Answers to Interrogatories by Moses Morrison, Transcript of trial, *Morrison v. White*, No. 442, 34–35 (collection of Earl K. Long Library, Special Collections and Archives, University of New Orleans, Supreme Court Records [hereafter UNO-SCR]), La. New Orleans Dist. Ct. Sept. 1858 rev'd, 16 La. Ann. 100 (1861). For more on this case, see Gross, *What Blood Won't Tell*, 1–3, 39–40.

37. Johnson, "The Slave Trader," 16.

38. Johnson, 16.

39. Transcript of trial, *Boullemet v. Phillips*, 1–2, No. 4219, La. New Orleans Par. Ct. May 1836 (UNO-SCR) rev'd, 2 Rob. La. 365 (1842) (Petition of Stephen Boullemet).

40. Transcript of trial, *Boullemet*, 9–10 (Testimony of Francis Olroyo), 34 (Testimony of Ralpph Hubbard).

41. Transcript of trial, *Boullemet*, 65–66 (Testimony of Mrs. Lavigne).

42. Transcript of trial, *Boullemet*, 45 (Testimony of Norbert Vandry).

43. Transcript of trial, *Boullemet*, 109–111 (Opinion of the Court, Parish Court, New Orleans).

44. Transcript of trial, *Boullemet*, unnumbered pages (Appeal from the Parish Court).

45. Transcript of trial, *Boullemet*, 1 (Louisiana Supreme Court Opinion), 2 Rob. La. 365 (1842). A "menagerie" was a woman who ran the household for a man to whom she was not married.

46. Transcript of trial, *Boullemet*, 1 (Louisiana Supreme Court Opinion).

47. Such relationships, of course, did exist but they were more rare and far less likely to become the subjects of litigation. On maternity, racial identity,

and the legal presumption that white women would not willingly have sexual relations with black men, see Morris, *Southern Slavery and the Law*, 41–49, 314.

48. On the tolerance of southern antebellum law of white men who had sexual relations with black females, see Bardaglio, *Reconstructing the Household*, 49–50.

49. Transcript of trial, *Dobard v. Nunez*, No. 1944 (6 La. Ann. 294 (1851)) (UNO-SCR).

50. Transcript of trial, *Cauchoix v. Dupuy et al.*, 1, No. 425 (La. New Orleans Par. Ct. Jan 1831) (UNO-SCR), aff'd 3 La. Ann. 206 (1831).

51. *Cauchoix*, 3 La. Ann. 206 (1831) 208.

52. Transcript of trial, *Gottschalk v. DeLaRosa*, No. 2550, 3 (La. 1st Judicial District Court, April 1833) (UNO-SCR) aff'd 6 La. Ann. 219 (1834) (Defendant's Answer).

53. Transcript of trial, *Gottschalk*, 7–8 (Deposition of John Hand).

54. For example, Transcript of trial, *Boullemet*, 16–17 (Testimony of Mrs. Lavigne); and Transcript of trial, *Cauchoix*, unnumbered pages (Testimony of Honore Landreax).

55. The exception was the case of *Boyer v. Tassin*, No. 196 (La. 13th District Court, Par. Avoyelles April, 1854) (UNO-SCR), aff'd 9 La. Ann. 491. This case involved a white mother's request for retaining the custody of her children against the wishes of their grandfather. She claimed she had originally married a black man in Mississippi where, at the time, the union of a black man and a white woman was not illegal. They had since moved to Louisiana, where the marriage was null and void, the husband had died, and she remarried. She alleged that the second marriage was not a proper ground to vitiate her status as the children's guardian (as per the law), since the first marriage could not be considered legal in Louisiana. The court refused to consider the racial identity of the children's father.

56. Jones, *Fathers of Conscience*, 57–58. See, for example, a case involving a relationship between a deceased master and a slave concubine whom he attempted to free in his will. Transcript of trial, *Vail v. Bird*, No. 2129 (District Court E. Baton Rouge, April 1850) (UNO-SCR), rev'd 6 La. Ann. 223 (1851). For a brief description of this case, see Jones, *Fathers of Conscience*, 62 and Alphonso, "Public and Private Order," 144–145.

57. *Louisiana Civil Code*, Book I, Title VII, Chapter III, Section II, Article 226. Mixed-race children born of unions between white fathers and black mothers were usually unable to prove paternity throughout the South (Jones, *Fathers of Conscience*, 65–66). However, the law did provide that illegitimate children could prove descent from their mothers, even if their mothers were white and they were of mixed race: *Louisiana Civil Code*, Book I, Title VII, Chapter III, Section II, Article 230.

58. Although interracial households assumed various forms, many resulted

from formal domestic arrangements (commonly known as *plaçage*) between light-skinned Creoles and wealthy white men governed by written contracts, social norms, and publicly observed conventions. Joan M. Martin, "*Plaçage* and the Louisiana *Gens de Couleur Libre*: How Race and Sex Defined the Lifestyles of Free Women of Color," in *Creole: The History and Legacy of Louisiana's Free People of Color*, ed. Sybil Kein (Baton Rouge: Louisiana State University Press, 2000), 57–70; James Hugo Johnston, *Race Relations in Virginia & Miscegenation in the South, 1776–1860* (Amherst: University of Massachusetts Press, 1970), 309–311; Ira Berlin, *Slaves without Masters: The Free Negro in the Antebellum South* (New York: Oxford University Press, 1974), 267; Kenneth S. Aslakson, "The 'Quadroon-Placage' Myth of Antebellum New Orleans: Anglo-American (Mis)interpretations of a French-Caribbean Phenomenon," *Journal of Social History* 45, no. 3 (2012): 709–734.

59. Regarding cohabitation, see John Hope Franklin and Alfred A. Moss Jr., *From Slavery to Freedom: A History of African-Americans* (New York: Alfred A. Knopf, 1985), 35; regarding brothels, see Judith Kelleher Schafer, *Brothels, Depravity, and Abandoned Women: Illegal Sex in Antebellum New Orleans* (Baton Rouge: Louisiana State University Press, 2009), 12.

60. Interracial relationships were not uncommon in the antebellum South. Most of them occurred when white men coerced black women, both slave and free, into sex (Julie Novkov, *Racial Union*, 11). Mulatto children, many of whom were slaves following the condition of their mothers, were the outcome of the widespread incidence of such miscegenation (Franklin and Moss, *From Slavery to Freedom*, 140). On judicial recognition of emotional ties between masters and slaves generally, see Jenny Wahl, *The Bondsman's Burden: An Economic Analysis of the Common Law of Southern Slavery* (New York: Cambridge University Press, 1998), 45–47. On recognition of "emotional ties between slave mothers and their children," see 44–45.

61. For example, Tushnet notes that "disputes among heirs over who should inherit what" often raised issues of racial identity and paternity "because the stakes were large, and there were few continuing relations between the parties [e.g., the white father and the black mother] that would be strained by libelous charges." As a result, "miscegenation . . . could not be kept out of legal materials because it directly posed serious questions of property rights about which it was worth going to court" (Tushnet, *The American Law of Slavery*, 14).

62. *Louisiana Civil Code*, Book I, Title VII, Chapter III, Section II, Article 221.

63. The heirs cited the *Louisiana Civil Code*, Book III, Title 2, Chapter 2, Article 1468, prohibiting donations to "concubines" in death or life of any immovable property and not more than one-tenth of the movable property of the entire estate.

64. Emphasis added. *MacArty v. Mandeville* f.w.c., 3 La. Ann. 239, 239 (Supreme Court Opinion).

65. *Louisiana Civil Code*, Book I, Title VII, Chapter V, Section II, Article 259; Book III, Title 1, Chapter 3, Article 913.

66. Transcript of trial, *MacArty v. Mandeville f.w.c.*, No. 626 (Second District Court, New Orleans, 1847), 93–95 (UNO-SCR), aff'd 3 La. Ann. 239 (1848) (Testimony of Philip Lacoste).

67. Transcript of trial, *MacArty v. Mandeville f.w.c.*, 248 (Deposition of Mrs. Widow Chabenet).

68. Transcript of trial, *MacArty v. Mandeville f.w.c.*, 245.

69. *MacArty v. Mandeville*, 3 La. Ann. 239, 239 (Supreme Court Opinion). Also see Jones, *Fathers of Conscience*, 60–62.

70. Transcript of trial, *Compton, Heirs v. Executors*, No. 1059, 72–73, 79 (Court of Probates, Par. of Rapides, June 1862) (UNO-SCR), aff'd in part and rev'd in part, 12 Rob. La. 56 (1845), 72–73, 79. Leonard also consistently referred to Fanchon as "Mrs. Compton" in his conversation and correspondence.

71. *Compton*, 12 Rob. La. 56 (1845), 62, 64, 63.

72. Transcript of trial, *Foster v. Mish*, No. 6344, 1 (La. Fourth District Court of New Orleans, April 1859) (UNO-SCR), rev'd 15 La. Ann. 199 (1860) (Petition of Andy Foster). Foster claimed that he had been kidnapped and brought to New Orleans to be sold as a slave.

73. Transcript of trial, *Foster v. Mish*, 23 (Deposition of James W. Cole), also 31 (Deposition of Albert G. Collins).

74. Transcript of trial, *Foster v. Mish*, 35 (Testimony of James M. Foster).

75. *Foster v. Mish*, 15 La. Ann. 199 (1860), 199.

76. One of us has previously found that from the 1830s through the 1850s, the Supreme Court of Louisiana became increasingly reluctant to uphold the rights of the white patriarch in cases where the color of family dependents was a legal issue. The patriarch's wishes were upheld three out of four times in the 1830s and then three out of five times in 1840s, but by the 1850s the courts more often found *against* the patriarch, in sixteen out of thirty such cases. Alphonso, "Public and Private Order," 127.

77. Alphonso, "Public and Private Order," 146.

78. Transcript of trial, *Turner, Curator v. Smith, et al.*, No. 5076 (Dist. Ct. W. Feliciana, Dec. 1856) (UNO-SCR), rev'd 12 La. Ann. 417, 418. For a similar case, see Transcript of trial, *Vail v. Bird* (1851).

79. On shaming testators who fathered mixed-race children, see Jones, *Fathers of Conscience*, 66–67.

5 | A "Bridge to Our Daughters"
Title IX Fathers and Policy Development

Elizabeth Sharrow

What would it mean to place the family at the center of our analyses of policy development? Why is it important and illuminating to do so? What can we learn about the evolution of the gendered order from public policies that unintentionally invoke familial relationships at the same time as they target a core community? Although neither families nor fathers are targeted constituencies of Title IX of the Education Amendments of 1972 (a foundational sex non-discrimination policy in education), I argue in this chapter that an explanation for the durability of a policy aimed at women's rights in educational institutions is, unexpectedly, related to fathers. Looking at policy through a historical lens reveals that fathers have acted as policy advocates motivated to political action through their relationships with their daughters.

In 2002–2003, during public hearings of the US Department of Education's (DOE's) Commission on Opportunity in Athletics (a group tasked with evaluating the equal athletic opportunity standards at the heart of policy), this politicization of fathers was readily apparent. Their testimony, when traced throughout the policy history of Title IX, suggests the need for greater attention to the political engagement of men in that domain. Men's advocacy has at times operated to support feminist aims and at other times to subtly undermine them. In this chapter I examine, historicize, and theorize about fathers as policy advocates to demonstrate (1) how the effects of Title IX's implementation ripple through familial relationships, and therefore (2) how American families became imbricated in "policy feedback"[1] to illustrate (3) how "feedback effects" reshape both the politics of families and policy development.[2]

Examining the policy development of Title IX makes clear that policy has, over time, politically activated familial relationships. During periods of political threat, fathers have claimed the role of policy advocates, suggesting that policy has reshaped both targeted *and* "relational" constituencies (i.e., fathers related to policy by way of their daughters).[3] This operated in recursive ways. In the case of Title IX, the implementation of policy reshaped athletic opportunities for girls and women, which then altered the ways in which many American families spent their time. Increased opportunities for girls in youth athletics also expanded coaching and spectating opportunities for parents, which, in time, provided them with space to see the needs for and benefits from athletic opportunities for their daughters.

The archival records of the US Congress and the Department of Education show that fathers, in particular, have joined forces with the many feminist advocates at work in Title IX's policy domain to support women's activism and, in critical moments, to advocate directly for girls and women when other forms of exclusion meant that women weren't in the room to advocate for themselves. This chapter traces that history and illustrates the uneven consequences of policy feedback in developing fathers as stakeholders in Title IX. It echoes the findings by Eileen McDonagh in Chapter 6 of this volume that familial roles are often implicated in political gains that benefit women, though, as Gwendoline Alphonso and Richard Bensel observe in Chapter 4, paternity and androcentric roles can produce uneven outcomes. Paternalism remained central to the frameworks mobilized by advocate-fathers, and while fathers' support of sex equity policy in congressional testimony and statements to the 2002 DOE Commission provided cross-gender support to counteract critics of Title IX, fathers often expressed this support by mobilizing protectionist frames. As a result, the advocacy of fathers in the public politics of Title IX has bolstered support for certain feminist aims, while also at times operating at cross-purposes with broader feminist aims. Among these issues, activist fathers have not tackled some of the thorniest issues at the heart of Title IX, including the maintenance of sex-segregated structures and the lingering homophobia associated with homosocial spaces. Instead, their activism has served to naturalize these problematic facets of women's athletic advancement under Title IX. Thus, the alliance of fathers with the cause of Title IX should be met with some cautious optimism; family relationships were politically mobilized but not radically reordered under policy implementation.

This chapter begins with a theoretical account of how Title IX shaped familial relationships, before diving into the history that illustrates how this process took root. It demonstrates that fathers, during key moments of policy debate, provided important cross-gender support for equity policy. While doing so, they advanced two key frameworks for discussing their role: (1) fathers-as-caretakers, and (2) fathers-as-protectors. These frames culminated in the emergence of "fathers-as-advocates" during a key policy debate in 2002. I discuss these frameworks in turn, placing them in the broader conversation about evolving gender politics, in order to illustrate how paternalism and economic class remained surprisingly central to policy debate.

Policy, Families, Feedback, and Fathers: Policy Development and Title IX

Fathers unexpectedly emerged as policy advocates from the broader context of Title IX's policy history. Signed into law in June 1972, Title IX was the first piece of sex non-discrimination policy aimed at American educational institutions.[4] Although two congressional hearings on the topic of women's treatment in higher education were convened in 1970, the law itself received limited congressional debate. Lawmakers scarcely discussed the specific content of what became Title IX before it passed as part of the more expansive Education Amendments of 1972.[5] In the months leading up to the votes on the amendments, women members of Congress reportedly requested that feminist groups abstain from lobbying altogether in order to shield the proposed legislation from undue negative attention from potential foes.[6] Instead, the focus of education-related disputes among members of Congress converged around ongoing efforts to racially desegregate schools; Title IX was incorporated into the amendments with very limited discussion.[7] Although the legislation was primarily aimed at tackling the pervasive problems of sex-based exclusions, biases, and discrimination embedded in educational institutions generally, the most acute and contentious debate over its implementation subsequently converged on college and high school athletics.[8] Congress left limited guidance for policymakers in their efforts to execute the law; between the early 1970s and the first decade of the twenty-first century the implementation in athletics drew the preponderance of public and political consideration.[9] In the following years, sports continued to draw significant public attention.

Given that the storied policy and legal history of Title IX has centered on contested expansion of opportunities for women and girls in education and athletics, a chapter that focuses on *fathers* may seem surprising. The extent to which men became more engaged in their daughters' political futures was fundamentally conditioned on the public policy successes of the second-wave feminist movement. Since the early 1970s, when a small cadre of feminist activists first framed the paucity of women in higher education as "sex discrimination," Title IX's history has been directly tied to the actions of many feminist activists, most of them women, who have advocated for policy both within and beyond American political institutions.[10] Historians rightly point to the central role that women's *self*-interest has played in shaping the direction of policy as second-wave liberal feminists leveraged governmental institutions to secure and retain sex non-discrimination protections.[11]

However, during the same years of policy implementation and debate when the prospects for American girls and young women took on broader possibilities in athletics and higher education, the impacts of policy reverberated across the lives of those with whom they held the most intimate connections. Parents in particular saw prospects expanding for their daughters as sporting opportunities drastically improved for girls and women at the youth, high school, and collegiate levels.[12] Over the first four decades of policy implementation, opportunities for girls and women to participate in sports grew exponentially. Figure 5.1 traces the growth in athletic opportunities at the college level; high school sports for girls evolved along similar lines.[13]

During these years, family became an unlikely participant in policy implementation. Throughout the late twentieth century, and in increasingly large numbers as girls' participation in youth sports became more prevalent and normative, familial relationships co-evolved in tandem with more equitable opportunities for girls. As Donna Lopiano, women's sports activist and former women's athletic director at the University of Texas, speculated on the implications: "Dad was the one who took his daughter into the backyard to play catch. Mom would have, but because she'd never had the chance to play, she didn't understand how much it meant. And when his daughter became a surrogate son through sports, Dad saw her go from porcelain doll to athlete."[14]

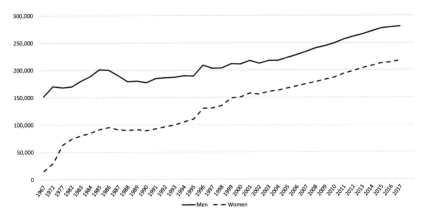

Figure 5.1. Annual College Athletics Participation Number, 1967–2017.
Source: NCAA Sports Sponsorship and Participation Rates Report, 2017.

Concurrently, American families adapted the ways in which they spent their time, dedicating more resources and energy to developing athleticism in their daughters as well as their sons,[15] a trend that co-evolved with the social and familial shifts toward children's increasing value within American families and transformed familial relationships.[16] Women's and girls' increased participation in sports necessitated a parallel growth in numbers of available coaches and team support staff, which often drew dedicated family members into such positions. Men regularly volunteered to coach, but women were often relegated to positions of team "support."[17] These gendered trends, in turn, reshaped the attitudes of many men toward their daughter's athleticism.[18]

Yet research on Title IX itself has most readily investigated how policy *directly* restructured the lives of girls and women, illustrating how implementation has impacted women's educational attainment, workforce participation, and economic independence in adulthood.[19] Less often theorized are these *secondary* impacts of policy on what might be thought of as *relational constituencies*, wherein policy also shapes familial relationships. Men's *relational* activism, on behalf of their daughters, on and around feminist causes illustrates what scholars of public policy elsewhere describe as a form of "policy feedback." This line of research examines how policy design can encourage or discourage political participation.[20] Feedback can take multiple forms, sometimes inspiring new forms of political participation in target populations (what scholars call "positive feedback")[21] and other times suppressing participation or engagement by key constituencies (known in the literature as "negative feedback").[22]

Policy design is often key in facilitating feedback, just as family plays an "important role in achieving policy aims."[23] Andrea Campbell points to the impacts of health care and disability policies on families, noting the many ways in which *families* of people with disabilities are permanently altered by policy gaps and design characteristics, among other salient examples.[24] Title IX's design was likely central to politicizing fathers as activists for their daughters. Sex-segregated athletics, nearly ubiquitous at the high school and college levels because of Title IX's implementation guidelines, ensure that the stark contrast between the treatment of females and males in school sports became visible to fathers with daughters.[25] Still, the feedback literature has yet to explore how policy implementation altered the politics of parents of young athletes.[26]

Studies that focus on the political dynamics of family document a variety of ways in which daughters can influence the political dispositions of their fathers, as political socialization may flow *from* children to their parents.[27] Political elites with daughters are more apt to support feminist issues in their roles as judges and lawmakers.[28] Corporate executives with daughters are more apt to provide women with higher wages and run more socially responsible companies.[29] Parents are more politically sensitized to and more likely to support gender equity when they are raising daughters, and fathers parenting a daughter are particularly apt to hold opinions that challenge "traditional" gender roles.[30] While some researchers conclude that fathering daughters makes men more conservative in their opinions toward abortion, on issues of feminism and gender egalitarianism studies suggest that fathering daughters leads men to express more liberal attitudes.[31] Two recent studies indicate that fathers of first daughters now express significant levels of support for Title IX and other sex equity policies, more so than fathers of first sons, and they are likely to vote for women candidates who campaign on issues that foreground their daughters' interests.[32] This work echoes contributions from gender and political history illustrating that gendered relationships and identities are central to the development of the American political order.[33] Such findings from multiple methodological perspectives hint at emergent politicized relationships among fathers, daughters, and feminist policy. However, research has yet to examine the political history that connects the dots between Title IX's interventions into athletic and educational institutions—domains that scholars widely acknowledge both affect and are affected by the family—and familial relationships or political engagement.[34]

Applying these findings complicates the more conventional political history of Title IX, which has focused on the activism of women and girls.[35] Although girls and women have undoubtedly been the leading advocates for their own opportunities in sports, examining the legislative and bureaucratic record demonstrates that they have, at multiple junctures, also relied on male sponsors to accomplish their aims.[36] Although Title IX's history has occasionally been marked by periods of gender conflict over the allocation of athletic opportunities and resources between women and men, self-proclaimed "Title IX dads" have offered cross-gender support by claiming a status as policy constituents invested in retaining athletic opportunities that they value for their daughters.[37] Policy design focused on imbuing girls and women with individual rights to athletic opportunity, and those rights required a cadre of dedicated protectors—among congressional elites, and the public—during periods of policy threat. Fathers became unlikely allies to late-twentieth-century century gender egalitarianism.

While fathers-as-advocates have generally supported feminist aims, their concerns did not differentiate the crosscutting inequalities of race, class, and physical ability that defined policy implementation. Further, men's relatively benevolent paternalistic impulses to support women's teams did not challenge the sex-segregated system, and stopped far short of advocating for women's participation on men's teams.[38] This provided instrumental support to liberal feminist aims at the same time as it centered male authority as the solution to the specter of homophobia that haunts women in sports.[39] Such unanticipated consequences of men's involvement in policy discussions would come to define the tensions and ironies of policy development in the early twentieth century.

Evidence of the culmination of relational feedback effects became most pronounced in 2002 when the George W. Bush presidential administration formalized a simmering public debate over sex equity practices that pitted men's athletics against the equity imperatives within Title IX. The world of athletics for girls and women had dramatically transformed since 1972.[40] At the high school level, sporting opportunities for American girls rose an astounding 970 percent (from 294,015 girls participating in 1971 to over 2.8 million in 2002);[41] in college, opportunities for women expanded from 16,000 in 1970 to over 160,000 in 2002.[42] The nationwide participation numbers in youth sports rates were even more dramatic, with 69 percent of girls reporting participation in organized and team sports in the early years of the decade.[43] These transformations derived from hard-fought legal and policy victories, most recently converging around the 1996 policy interpretation in which the DOE spelled out how to comply with the law.[44] The guidelines clarified the use of the "proportionality" standard for equity—in which the proportion of male to female student-athletes was to mirror the proportion of male to female students in the undergraduate population—as one of three means to demonstrate compliance with Title IX.[45]

But the transformation of athletic governance under the mandate of equity, designed to compel institutions to add women's teams, was not universally well received. In practice, schools around the country sought proportionality through many different means. Some added additional teams for women to lift the total number of athletes competing for their school; others cut men's teams to achieve proportionality; still others added both men's and women's opportunities, but only in some sports. At schools where football was increasingly well supported by significant growth in participation opportunities, some institutions elected to promote football while cutting other men's sports (in multiple cases the canceled men's programs were gymnastics and wrestling).[46] These implementation inconsistencies meant that by June 2002—the same month as Title IX's thirtieth anniversary—the law again became the topic of national political attention.

That month President Bush charged his secretary of education, Roderick Paige, to appoint a Commission on Opportunity in Athletics to reevaluate the "application of current Federal standards for measuring equal opportunity for men and women and boys and girls to participate in athletics under Title IX."[47] Tasked with collecting information and obtaining "broad public input directed at improving the application of current Federal standards for measuring equal opportunity . . . to participate in athletics under Title IX," the Commission subjected policy enforcement guidelines that had been in effect since 1979 to significant deliberation and public comment.[48] Fifteen members with educational and athletic backgrounds sat on the Commission, which was co-chaired by Cynthia Cooper-Dyke (a former player and coach for the Women's National Basketball Association) and Ted Leland (the Stanford University director of athletics).[49]

Over the course of eight months, the Commission convened eleven public meetings in six cities.[50] Some meetings featured invited expert and public testimony (in Atlanta, Chicago, Colorado Springs, and San Diego), while others involved deliberation among the commissioners (in Philadelphia and Washington, D.C.). On the days of invited testimony, the Commission hosted approximately fifty witnesses per day. Testimony came from both experts and laypeople, representing Title IX advocacy groups, higher education institutions, think tanks, and sports governing bodies. The Commission heard directly from "hundreds of parents, athletes, and administrators" from all levels of sports.[51] Within the testimony, an unanticipated set of stakeholders also took the stage. At the San Diego town hall meeting, one man addressed the crowd:

> I am Joe Kelly, Duluth, Minnesota. I have twin daughters, college seniors, and I'm Executive Director of Dads and Daughters, a national education advocacy nonprofit that works on strengthening father/daughter relationships, and I'm here to tell you that Title IX is one of the best things that ever happened to fathers . . . Why? Because Title IX has begun to make it unremarkable for girls to play sports, unlike in generations past. Because most men grow up seeped in sports and, as sports fans, thanks to Title IX, fathers and daughters now have a whole new playing field on which to connect. A father/daughter relationship can thrive on playing catch or on a jump shot or cheering on a team . . . I think that's in part because sports are a natural comfort zone for men, and Title IX makes it a bridge to their daughters.[52]

Kelly was a longtime advocate on women's issues, co-founding the nonprofit Dads and Daughters (DADs), which operated from 1999 to 2008.[53] Kelly's interest in women's sports came by way of his commitment to fathering his daughters and shepherding them through issues of self-esteem and body image, the topics around which he founded DADs.[54] By the fall of 2000, DADs' membership included 1,600 men.[55]

Strikingly, Kelly was one of many fathers who rose to speak in support of Title IX during the hearings and articulated similar stories: they claimed interest in the positive benefits secured by Title IX in light of their relationships with their daughters. These relationships inspired their mobilization to ensure that the law remained concordant with its long-standing policy guidelines after the Commission's review. Their testimony also signaled an under-acknowledged phenomenon: fathers of Title IX beneficiaries were taking public stances on policy, signaling a shift from an amorphous identity to a policy interest group.[56] However, the historical record illustrates that this trend had been developing for a long time. Political elites active in Title IX's policy domain had previously referenced relationships with their daughters as motivation for supporting the law, suggesting that familial relationships require closer scrutiny in understanding Title IX's policy development.

"Best" for Daughters? Paternalistic Politics in Title IX's First Thirty Years

As striking as the emergence of fathers in 2002 may seem, fathers have personalized the meanings of policy since the earliest debates about Title IX. Starting in the 1970s and extending though the Commission's work, the most salient narrative mobilized by male political elites relied upon the notion of fathers' caretaking role over their daughters' athletic opportunities, extending the reach of paternalism into realms often thought to be liberating for girls and women (e.g., sports), rather than carving out space free from it. Across the first three decades of policy implementation, three themes of mobilization among activists and political elites demonstrate how fathers articulated their roles in shaping what they thought was "best" for their daughters. Fathers played an important role in defending sex equity policy, but they did so by mobilizing paternalistic frameworks of (1) fathers-as-caretakers and (2) fathers-as-protectors, two identities that culminated in 2002 with the emergence of (3) fathers-as-advocates. Rather than upending traditional gender roles, this relational feedback emerged by mobilizing traditional paternalism as a dominant framework for policy activism. Daughters, some of whom also testified on their own behalf, benefited from gaining male allies, but only in ways that also advanced conservative gender ideologies.

Framework 1: Fathers-as-Caretakers

Although Title IX's legislative innovators and feminist advocates were primarily women, debate over policy implementation in the 1970s unfolded in the male-dominated context of Congress.[57] Thus, in the early years of policy debate and implementation, the voices of many men— from male congressional elites to athletes and coaches—occupied a dominant place in policy conversation. Debate in the 1970s cohered around the meanings of equity in athletics, and the extent to which historically empowered men would need to cede resources in order for colleges to comply with federal non-discrimination law.[58] Yet from the start, the status of some lawmakers as fathers of daughters made the gendered battle lines unclear. In the initial athletic policy implementation debates, several of the policy's erstwhile *critics* found it difficult to maintain strictly anti–Title IX stances in light of their relationships with their daughters. Members of Congress with daughters frequently suggested that, while they may quibble with the mechanics of implementation guidelines, their paternal relationship motivated them to work toward implementation. Even those who were most concerned with the prospects for dominant sports like men's football under an emerging equity regime articulated their desire for "reform" instead of repeal because of their daughters' fortunes.

Senator John Tower (R-TX) features in most accounts of Title IX's history as one such strong critic of policy.[59] When Tower introduced conservative legislation in 1974 to exclude so-called revenue-producing sports from proposed implementation guidelines, he joined cause with football coaches who aimed to ensure that they would not lose economic control over college athletics in light of equity law. However, Tower noted that his reasons for seeking "reform" were rooted in his family: "one of the prime reasons for my wanting to reserve the revenue base of intercollegiate activities is that it will provide the resources for expanding women's activities in intercollegiate sports. I have a vested interest because I have a daughter who is a potential varsity tennis player, and I would like to see that she gets the opportunity."[60]

Even those congressmen questioning the means of implementing policy found it difficult to reject wholesale the policy that was poised to provide new opportunities for their daughters. The Tower Amendment, introduced alongside Tower's statements about daughters, was contested by feminist interest groups because of its proposal that Title IX should not apply to any sports that garnered revenue from ticket sales.[61] Consideration of this amendment marked one of the first times that advocates for men's sports pursued strategies pitting the implementation of equity policy against "men's" interests, foreshadowing the ways in which lawmakers' interests as fathers sometimes operated against the grain of those activists poised to assert a unified interest among men. Equity policy became salient through familial relationships, even for male lawmakers who otherwise desired to promote the welfare of already empowered athletic interests (a cause led by football coaches in the 1970s). Tower's bill ultimately failed, replaced instead by another amendment that favored a more measured calculus for equity in spending across men's and women's programs.[62] Tower's desire to preserve Title IX for his daughter raises the question of what hard-line alternatives may have been pursued if not for his sense of paternal calling.

It was not only in Congress where fatherly identities emerged in policy debate. Throughout the 1970s and 1980s, Title IX's policy rules were contested in multiple court cases.[63] As Congress considered a legislative response to the US Supreme Court ruling in *Grove City College v. Bell*[64]—a case in which the US Supreme Court ruled that institutions that did not accept federal funds were not required to comply with Title IX outside of their financial aid departments—congressmen frequently characterized their relationships with their daughters as those that convinced them to push for broader congressional interpretation of policy to explicitly include athletics.[65] Although Congress would eventually pass the Civil Rights Restoration Act in 1987, establishing that all educational institutions enrolling students who accepted Pell Grants or federal student loan money were required to comply with policy, the 1980s again provided an opening for lawmakers and activists to articulate their vision for public policy. Again, paternal relationships were featured. In congressional testimony, for example, Chairman John Buchanan of People for the American Way argued, "We will be turning back the clock on intercollegiate athletic opportunities for our daughters" by failing to rearticulate a fulsome congressional vision for Title IX's application in the aftermath of *Grove City*.[66]

Daughters provided male policymakers with both a personal credential and an attachment to feminist legislation. Among American adults in the late 1980s, 87 percent of parents believed sports were equally important to boys and girls, and respondents expressed high support for the notion that "sports provided important benefits to girls who participate."[67] Political elite fathers made statements in concordance with such opinions, suggesting that athletic girls and women required lawmakers to act as caretakers of equitable opportunity policy. Mobilizing traditionally paternalistic notions, fathers utilized long-standing forms of male political privilege to safeguard for girls and women opportunities secured by policy that they, as fathers, thought were deserved. The aims expressed in congressional statements engaged themes of bringing women and girls into their own sporting world, but not into those venues that had been historically reserved for men. Fathers were not publicly advocating for women's participation on men's football teams, or on "men's teams" more generally. Instead, men mirrored the arguments made by many feminist activists, which suggested that equity would be best achieved not through integration, but through separate but equal teams.[68] In this sense, "caretaking" by fathers in the early years of Title IX's implementation meant ensuring *opportunity* for their daughters, but not full inclusion on the same teams as their sons.

The mobilization of this caretaking role by fathers was at once an early feminist success and further evidence of the consequences of women's political exclusion. On the one hand, familial relationships provided feminist outsiders with powerful allies within androcentric political institutions. This was less a success of sustained activism and more a consequence of parental relationships of care.[69] Paternal policymakers did not credit important feminist luminaries with convincing them that sex equity policy was necessary. Instead, they credited their daughters. Perhaps the gendered hierarchy embedded within families ensured that men could retain a heroic stance by advocating "for" daughters, without needing to stand "with" second-wave feminists.

With women's representation in Congress at extremely low levels, and despite the newly emerging network of interest groups active on athletic equity, fathers mobilized in support of Title IX in ways that replicated their personal, even self-serving, familial responsibilities in the private sphere.[70] However useful and even apparently benevolent this caretaker framework may have been to advancing feminist goals, it also carried with it a more insidious subtext. As explicit homophobic views found political voice during the AIDS crisis of the 1980s, caretaking narratives took a darker turn.

Framework 2: Fathers-as-Protectors

With many fathers taking public stances in support of policy, men began to publicly grapple with women's leadership in sporting spaces and to introduce an alternative paternal framework. Women leaders in sport have long faced a double bind: the homosociality of athletic teams has always carried the threat and fears of same-sex desire and lesbianism, just as sex-segregated athletics provided one of the few reliable "closets" for lesbian women to pursue careers in sports and physical education.[71] The threat of lesbianism in athletic domains became an implicit target of fathers invoking this alternative "fathers-as-protectors" frame.

By the early 1980s, homophobia directed at gay men coalesced around the AIDS epidemic.[72] Simultaneously, Title IX's implementation was under threat by the Reagan administration's explicit attempt to stop enforcing the policy it privately called the "lesbian bill of rights."[73] Tensions between increased public awareness about same-sex desire, the gay liberation movement, and the ascendance of the conservative Right brought increased scrutiny on homosocial spaces, including athletic teams for girls and women. Such homophobic anxieties, often sublimated through interlocking expressions of misogyny and sexism, were also manifested in paternal narratives just as readily as in the caretaker framework for fathers' advocacy.[74] Particularly among conservatives, the processes through which women's athletic involvement was rewriting the strictures of traditional femininity also aroused homophobia. The notion that men could "protect" women from potential athletic lesbians represented a distinct form of paternalism that materialized in fathers' statements about securing rights for their daughters.

A *Washington Star* opinion piece, republished in the *Congressional Record*, argued:

> Well, another kind of war is going on right here in America—the War of Women's Liberation—and it, too, is being won on playing fields. Of course, the more cynical think it is being won through lesbian lifestyles. A great many think it is being won at the abortionist's abattoir. Still more believe it is to be won by adopting the manners and morals of men . . . The truth is this: The war is being won by young girls in sweatsuits and Adidas. How comes this inspiration? By way of my five athletically inclined daughters, that's how—daughters who are quicker than I am, better coordinated than I am, and (worst of all) who can beat me one-on-one in basketball! Childless people don't really know what's going on. Why, without my daughters I wouldn't be into Women's Lib.[75]

This article illustrates the essence of the fathers-as-protectors framework, wherein men articulated desires to fill appropriately masculine roles in the lives of young girls participating in sports, thereby displacing women leaders who they feared might be queer. This framework hints at a normative and authoritative role for fathers in sporting spaces where athletics had the potential to "masculinize" women. Herein, fathers exist against the archetype of the masculine lesbian (or gym teacher) as a more appropriate male role model for athletic girls.[76]

This framework also motivated fathers to mobilize their relative economic privilege by bankrolling lawsuits against large institutions that were loath to comply with policy. Megan Hull, a named plaintiff in a Title IX class action case against Brown University and a congressional committee witness in the 1990s, testified that her father first suggested they pursue a lawsuit—one of the most high-profile Title IX cases of the era—to contest Brown's equity practices.[77] The economic power available to some families ensured that during an era in which policy enforcement was uneven across institutions, daughters from families of means were most likely to have their sex discrimination claims addressed under threat or pursuit of lawsuits.[78] Lawsuits at multiple institutions around the country brought the fight by women athletes to secure the rights afforded by policy into the legal system.[79] In the mid-1990s, Congress acted again in passing the Equity in Athletics Disclosure Act (EADA) to require institutions to publicly report their equity practices in athletics each year.[80]

Established activists also foresaw the power of parents in Title IX enforcement. In congressional testimony, Lopiano noted: "If Title IX complaints are going to be filed, they are not going to be filed by the powerless women in athletics. Rather, objections with inequities will be raised by the parents of daughters suffering inferior treatment compared to their male counterparts."[81] Lopiano was right. Lawsuits to force equitable treatment required parental and financial involvement. One father, Herb Dempsey, famously filed nearly 1,000 Title IX athletic complaints with the Office for Civil Rights throughout the 1990s and 2000s to contest enforcement practices at the high school level.[82] It was not merely that fathers of young female athletes were changing the qualitative experience of being socialized into sport by both protecting and caretaking for their daughters' opportunities to play sports and, increasingly, to claim athletic scholarships; they were also providing the means through which female athletes were able to contest the policy's enforcement.

During the first thirty years of Title IX's implementation, involvement by fathers asserting what was "best" for their daughters was ongoing. Rather than emerging for the first time during the Commission hearings, fathers came to testify in 2002 and 2003 in line with a long tradition of men's activism. The historical record demonstrates that girls and women were equally likely to find allies—however contingent on problematic heterosexist narratives—among men-as-fathers as they were to find opponents among men-as-athletes. This held true until the turn of the twenty-first century.

Frame 3: Fathers-as-Advocates

By the early 2000s, the political environment around Title IX had evolved substantially, as had fathers' investment in women's sports. Despite significant growth in women's athletic opportunities, attention was increasingly focused on the impact of Title IX's implementation on men's teams. During his campaign for the Iowa presidential caucus, then candidate Bush was heavily lobbied by a group of wrestlers and ex-wrestlers, Iowans Against Quotas.[83] The group, along with its partners Americans Against Quotas and the Independent Women's Forum, aimed to reframe the loss of men's wrestling programs (programs that had experienced decline in numbers at the college level during the 1990s while college football opportunities for men expanded) as a problem of "quotas." They claimed, both in communications with Republican presidential candidates and eventually in a formal lawsuit, that Title IX forced schools to cut men's programs to achieve equity. Even before Bush was the Republican nominee, he spoke against "quotas" of all kinds, thereby linking Title IX to the broader push from conservative forces to end affirmative action in college admissions.[84] Such framing was a political tactic, in response to courts' rulings indicating that policy guidelines on Title IX withstood legal scrutiny.[85]

Still, this argument by Title IX's critics gained traction when, in the 2000 Republican Party platform and under the guidance of presidential candidate George W. Bush, party leadership announced that a Bush administration would revisit Title IX's enforcement guidelines.[86] Bush made other ambiguous statements about his intentions for Title IX enforcement, noting, "I support Title IX. Title IX has opened up opportunities for young women in both academics and sports, and I think that's terrific. I do not support a system of quotas or strict proportionality that pits one group against another. We should support a reasonable approach to Title IX that seeks to expand opportunities for women rather than destroy existing men's teams."[87]

Both Bush's selection for DOE secretary, Roderick Paige—a former college football coach—and the assistant secretary of education for civil rights, Gerald Reynolds, expressed support for changing the law.[88] Their positions aligned with those of the speaker of the US House of Representatives, Dennis Hastert (R-IL), a former wrestling coach and outspoken critic of the law.[89] Under this partisan leadership, calls for reform gained traction. In January 2002, the National Wrestling Coaches Association (NWCA) filed suit against the DOE, charging "reverse discrimination" under Title IX in light of athletic departments' decisions to cut some men's teams. The reverse discrimination argument was part of a wider effort to undermine civil rights protections by advancing claims that non-discrimination law injured dominant groups (i.e., male athletes). This followed a 2001 US General Accounting Office (GAO) report that concluded that although men's collegiate athletic participation had increased overall from 1982 to 1999, participation opportunities in men's wrestling experienced a net decrease.[90] Wrestling advocates charged that Title IX's implementation harmed men, universalizing the plight of wrestling programs to "all men," and framing women athletes as the aggressors enacting reverse discrimination on men through their efforts seeking policy enforcement. This agenda pitted women against men in what became framed as a new "battle of the sexes."[91]

While the media focused on the NWCA claims, less attention was paid to the mass of men living around the country and engaging with the implications of Title IX in very different ways. The US Department of Labor reported that in 2002, 5.5 percent of adult men volunteered to coach sport teams.[92] The ability of fathers to devote leisure time to coaching and spectating was, of course, facilitated by other gendered labor trends like men's freedom from the demands of a "second shift" of housework.[93] For many men, particularly those middle-class fathers who enjoyed freedom from work in the evenings and on weekends, opportunities became more plentiful to engage in parenting their daughters "through sport,"[94] and families increasingly devoted monetary resources and time to their children's competitive athletic training.[95]

As the Bush administration took office and contemplated the means of enforcing Title IX, it did so during a time of increasing attention to the daughters of famous male athletes. Tamika Catchings, daughter of National Basketball Association star Harvey Catchings, famously led the Tennessee Lady Volunteers women's basketball team to an undefeated season and a national title in the 1997–1998 season. Candice Wiggins, daughter of Alan Wiggins, a former major league baseball player, became the Stanford University and Pac-10 Athletic Conference all-time leading scorer before she was drafted into the Minnesota Lynx franchise of the Women's National Basketball Association. Stanford basketball also recruited the daughter of John Elway, a highly visible Denver Broncos quarterback. Laila Ali, daughter of Muhammad Ali, became a high-profile professional boxer in the early years of the twenty-first century. Although Ali was reportedly ambivalent about his daughter boxing, many of these famous fathers openly supported their daughters' athletic careers, even speaking out on the role of Title IX in their daughters' development.[96] Increasingly, high-profile athletic fathers were recognized as being sympathetic to women's athletic equality.[97]

Such developments were both intended and unintended consequences of policy implementation. The policy intentionally put pressure on high school and college athletic departments, forcing them to adapt their age-old practices of focusing on teams for boys and men.[98] This then trickled down to youth sports, where teams for young girls expanded both because girls' athleticism became more normative and because the increasing volume of teams for girls and women in high school and college inspired the possibility that girls need not cease training and competition during adolescence merely because of the lack of teams. As the talent pool deepened, competition for college scholarships intensified.[99] These youth sports required coaches, most of whom were parents (and many of those, fathers) of participants. This explosion in youth sports for girls meant that—as a secondary effect of policy—institutional change forced lower-level cultural change, and those cultural changes altered families. In the years before the Commission began its work, not only were opportunities for girls and women significantly expanding, but also these shifting tides began reshaping familial relationships and, in time, political identities and advocacy patterns. Support for Title IX among famous fathers echoed majoritarian support for policy that had been noted in opinion polls since the mid-1990s.[100] During the 2000 US presidential campaign, one national poll found 79 percent of Americans supported "equal opportunities for girls and women in high school and college athletics."[101] With strong support for the ideological underpinnings of sex equity in athletics and growing attention to cross-gender allies for women athletes, those advocating for changes to Title IX faced narrowing options.

Men versus Women and Men versus Men:
Gendered Discord at Commission Hearings

Despite strong public support for the law, opponents (e.g., the NWCA) of the proportionality standard in Title IX's implementation openly suggested that women lacked "interest" in sports commensurate with expanding athletic opportunities.[102] As early as 1997, the *Congressional Quarterly Researcher* posed the provocative question on the cover of an issue devoted to gender concerns in sports, "Does federal law help female athletes by hurting men?"[103] In both the court case against the DOE and in public commentary in congressional hearings, the NWCA actively aimed to frame Title IX as a "problem" for men as the Commission began its work.[104]

In opening comments, Ted Leland, Commission co-chair, detailed the task of the Commission as primarily to "listen," naming parents as one of the primary stakeholders in the proceedings. Evaluating whether Title IX's standards for equal opportunity worked uniformly well for men and women was among the Commission's seven tasks.[105] Senator Birch Bayh (D-IN), a Title IX advocate since the 1970s, was called to testify. He drew attention to the congressional conversation regarding whether or not the standing policy guidelines on proportional athletic opportunity constituted "quotas." As many subsequent witnesses also noted, the decisions by some schools to gain policy compliance by cutting men's athletic teams instead of adding opportunities for women was of central concern.[106] However, even those interested in reform were inclined to suggest that the problem with the policy was not the intent of equity, but was instead the means of enforcement.[107] Those concerned with quotas aimed to move the conversation about Title IX away from addressing the long-standing domination of athletics governance within colleges and universities that, before the advent of Title IX, overwhelmingly favored male athletes, and back to ensuring that men retained both authority and the majority of competitive opportunities.[108]

Wrestlers, wrestling coaches, and wrestling proponents argued that policy regulations were disproportionately harming male athletes, particularly those competing in "non-revenue-producing" sports. But fathers, openly engaging in advocacy that supported both women athletes and marginalized men athletes, complicated any obvious gendered battle lines by advocating, instead, primarily for girls and women. Like fathers advocating for daughters in previous eras, Commission witnesses articulated the importance of parenting experiences in the formulation of their political beliefs surrounding Title IX. Fathers of basketball, baseball, softball, and tennis players—many of them coaches of their daughters' teams—gave testimony during the public forums, more frequently foregrounding their parental status than their occupation or personal athletic experiences.[109] Fathers of daughters in youth sports, high school sports, and college sports repeatedly communicated the belief that their daughters were equally deserving of sporting spaces as their male counterparts.

As testimony progressed, fathers articulated some of the mechanisms through which Title IX's implementation had exposed them to the sexist belief system that pervades girls' sports. Keith Keller, a father and coach to his three girls, stated:

> I'm an advocate of Title IX, and I want to talk about why it's important to me and more importantly, why it's important to my three girls . . . My youngest is the sports animal of the family. She's a good little basketball player and soccer, but also plays baseball and tennis. So she's an all-sports person . . . we were playing basketball and her coach said, "Dad, this is really more of a boy's sport." And comments like that certainly frustrate me as a father because I think she heard it from someone at her school. And I told her, I said, "You have a good opportunity. You have talent, and you should have the same opportunity as the boys to excel at sport and be successful in your career no matter what you do. If it's sports, that's great. If it's something else, that's great too."[110]

Such exasperation was palpable in testimony from many fathers. Men detailed the ways in which fathering daughters whose abilities challenged antiquated beliefs about girls' and women's physical potential then altered their policy beliefs about the type of opportunities that girls and women deserved. This, in turn, led men to see Title IX as a panacea against still-evolving social barriers that discouraged both girls' athleticism and the life lessons sports can offer.

The gendered battle lines of men versus women that pro-wrestling groups had attempted to draw became increasingly muddied. Fathers' paternalistic tendencies to nurture opportunities for their daughters made them less sympathetic allies to those hoping to frame Title IX as a policy that "hurt" men. As wrestlers and their supporters attempted to reframe the conversation about Title IX as one that needed to attend to what was best for men, fathers remained steadfast as advocates for girls and women rather than joining the cadre of voices framing Title IX as a policy pitting men against women. Lost in the shuffle was a more acute critique of the ascending status of college football. Despite the long-evolving trends of bloated spending, wherein budgets and rosters for football comprised the majority of spending in college athletics and drained resources and opportunities away from men's non-revenue-producing sports, wrestlers and advocates for Title IX did not find much common cause.[111]

Yet fathers openly embraced using their economic privilege to promote women's equality and to reject the battle-of-the-sexes narrative:

> My name is Blair Hull. My daughter, Megan, was a plaintiff in the lawsuit against Brown University in 1992. So it's in a very personal context that I'm here today. After 30 years of advocacy and controversy, it's important to remember that Title IX is not just a women's issue. It's an issue of basic fairness and equality . . . supporting our daughters and our sons is one of the most important things we can do as parents . . . encouraging them to stand up for their rights, whether it's on the field or off the field . . . On every possible level, it is as important for our daughters to participate in sports as it is for our sons. So I urge this Commission to do everything you can to ensure that these opportunities continue to exist.[112]

The deeper gendered conflict over whether men, as a group, were losing opportunities to girls and women at the same time as fathers were gaining new access to relating to their daughters did not fit a simple narrative. As Hull's quote suggests, some parents even saw *themselves* as policy beneficiaries and/or potential victims of policy reform. Such statements not only suggest the culmination of a feedback loop of policy implementation on fathers' as "relational constituents," they underscore the class-based privilege of families that had the means for both recreational sports participation and lawsuits to secure it for girls and women. However, although the most acute cases were led by families of financial means, their legal and political activism spilled over to help ensure that policy was not destabilized.

At the conclusion of the Commission's work, it declined to fully rewrite DOE policy for implementing sex equity in athletics.[113] The Commission's final report reached a complex decision that fell short of rewriting the proportionality standards and left the fundamental question regarding reform to college athletics unresolved; feminist activists were concerned.[114] As the Commission disbanded, two of Title IX's key supporters on the Commission, Donna deVarona and Julie Foudy, circulated a minority report about which several members of Congress agreed to hold future hearings.[115] In the courts, the NWCA lawsuit foundered when the judge ruled that the wrestlers failed to demonstrate appropriate legal standing to bring their case; within months the Office for Civil Rights instead published a guidelines clarification that reiterated the DOE's commitment to "aggressively enforce Title IX standards."[116] Despite the powerful allies that male wrestlers had in Speaker Hastert and President Bush, the willingness of fathers to testify along with direct policy beneficiaries served as a gendered bulwark against those conservative interests aimed at undermining Title IX. Political organizing within the American family and cross-gender, paternal advocates served as a vital player in policy maintenance.

Conclusions

This chapter suggests a number of inferences for scholars of the American family, policy feedback and development, and political identity and behavior. Placing family at the center of our analyses of the impacts of Title IX illustrates that feminist-inspired policy ramified in many unexpected ways, shaping opportunities for American girls and women, and generating allies through familial relationships. As political science pays increased attention to the politics of the family, scholars would be wise to bear in mind that policy feedback, used as a historical instrument, can help scholars place contemporary phenomena—like evidence of daughters' impacts on men's political behavior—"in time."[117] Doing so illustrates the co-evolving roles of policy, identity, and politics.[118]

The case of Title IX also suggests some discrete conclusions for scholars of gender and public policy. Familial relationships, evolving in light of feminist policy, have altered men's relationships to sex equity concerns; when public policy inadvertently creates cross-gender stakeholders via familial attachments, opposition forces have greater difficulty in contesting equity measures. Rather than pitting men against women, familial relationships give fathers a new understanding of the need for, and the potential consequences of, a future with greater equity for their daughters. The family can operate as an unlikely incubator for feminist allies.

Feedback of and from paternalistic aims helped to produce more durable policy, but with complicated consequences. Among these, the engagement of fathers did not counteract some core economic inequalities within Title IX's implementation. Activist fathers have emerged primarily from economically empowered communities and have pursued activism (and funded lawsuits) on behalf of mostly middle- and upperclass girls and women. To the extent that during these same decades gendered income inequality became more pronounced, and girls from low-income families were more likely to grow up in homes without fathers, the increased profile of fathers-as-advocates exacerbated instead of ameliorated the ways in which Title IX benefits already advantaged women and girls.[119] Thus, paternal activism most directly benefited economically privileged women and girls and, in so doing, reified other forms of class (and interlocking racial) biases in the implementation of policy.[120]

With family at the core of sex equity dynamics, Title IX's history demonstrates how men's gendered patterns of activism can evolve. However, it also demonstrates that as long as fatherhood remains the catalyzing political event, traditional forms of paternalism may haunt equity politics. In the absence of historical or quantitative evidence that men's other familial relationships with women (like sisters or female partners) exert similarly liberalizing political transformations, these lessons should be cautiously celebrated. Title IX's specific history also raises serious concerns about the unilateral value of fathers' activism that has carried paternalistic impulses, even a homophobic subtext, within calls for men's athletic leadership.[121] Fathers' activism can serve to reestablish male authority in yet another domain, which complicates its value to those concerned with unraveling the interlocking systems of gender, sex, and sexual oppressions.

There are also implications for scholars of American Political Development who explore whether and how gender (along with race and class) is at the very core of our political systems.[122] While this study demonstrates some ways in which gendered battles have evolved at the edges, it leaves open questions regarding what will be required for gendered hierarchies to be razed. Feminists, both scholars and activists, place significant weight on the impact of Title IX to lead the way in these efforts, but one policy alone has many limitations. In fact, this author joins a community of critics who argue that Title IX's impacts have been both positive and fraught.[123] The activism of fathers has pushed to reify policy design, including the problematic feature of sex-segregated athletics, rather than challenging it. Likewise, the class-based biases of fathers' activism (and their interlocking race-based and ableist concerns in sport) have ensured that Title IX is most fruitful in securing athletic opportunities for privileged women and girls.

Still, this chapter demonstrates the ways in which policies can expand the possibilities for creating allied interests within feminist causes, operating through intimate relationships to generate "relational feedback." At the same time, it suggests that the development of male allies to feminist causes can come at a cost, including subverting women's voices and supplanting them with those of already empowered men. On the one hand, the outcomes of fathers' activism have helped to promote sustained opportunities for girls and women. On the other hand, focusing on Title IX reminds us that unexpectedly relying on the family—a traditionally heterocentric institution in practice—may not produce all of the liberating outcomes that feminists otherwise desire. Now that a generation of adult women who were themselves direct policy beneficiaries have reached maturity, could a larger cadre of mothers emerge if (or when) Title IX's application to athletics next comes under threat? Research suggests that current female college athletes and male athletes who are aware of the persistence of sex discrimination in society are prepared to mobilize on behalf of Title IX.[124] This chapter suggests that they, as women and potentially as mothers of daughters, will likely continue to find allies in fathers of daughters. The implementation of policy has, by virtue of its impacts on the family, only become more entrenched. With the growth of intensity in youth athletics, the future of Title IX will likely be determined by the advocacy of these constellation groups.[125]

Notes

The author acknowledges financial support for the research and writing of this paper from the American Association of University Women, the Social Science Research Council, the Gerald Ford Presidential Library Foundation, the National Collegiate Athletic Association, and the Myra Sadker Foundation.

1. Andrea Campbell, "Policy Makes Mass Politics," *Annual Review of Political Science* 15, no. 1 (2012): 333–351.

2. The literature on "policy feedback" suggests that policy, in its implementation, can reshape the politics of affected constituencies. See Campbell, "Policy Makes Mass Politics."

3. Policy scholars have long acknowledged that policy can shape "target populations"; see Anne L. Schneider and Helen M. Ingram, "Social Construction of Target Populations: Implications for Politics and Policy," *American Political Science Review* 87, no. 2 (1993): 334–347.

4. Deondra Rose, "Regulating Opportunity: Title IX and the Birth of Gender-Conscious Higher Education Policy," *Journal of Policy History* 27, no. 1 (2015): 157–183.

5. US Congress, House of Representatives, Committee on Education and Labor, Special Subcommittee on Education, *Discrimination Against Women*, 91st Cong., 2nd sess. (Washington, DC: US Government Printing Office, 1970); US Congress, House of Representatives, Committee on Education and Labor, Special Subcommittee on Education, *Discrimination Against Women, Part 2* (Washington, DC: US Government Printing Office, 1970).

6. John David Skrentny, *The Minority Rights Revolution* (Cambridge, MA: Harvard University Press, 2002).

7. Elizabeth Sharrow, "'Female Athlete' Politic: Title IX and the Naturalization of Sex Difference in Public Policy," *Politics, Groups, and Identities* 5, no. 1 (2017): 46–66.

8. Amanda Ross Edwards, "Why Sport? The Development of Sport as a Policy Issue in Title IX of the Education Amendments of 1972," *Journal of Policy History* 22, no. 3 (2010): 300–336.

9. Welch Suggs, *A Place on the Team: The Triumph and Tragedy of Title IX* (Princeton, NJ: Princeton University Press, 2005).

10. See, on women's congressional activities, Rose, "Regulating Opportunity"; and Andrew Fishel and Janice Pottker, *National Politics and Sex Discrimination in Education* (Lexington, MA: Lexington Books, 1977). Women also pushed for enforcement within their colleges and universities; see Diane LeBlanc and Allys Swanson, *Playing for Equality: Oral Histories of Women Leaders in the Early Years of Title IX* (Jefferson, NC: McFarland & Company, 2016). Likewise, women's athletic organizations battled to maintain self-governance; see Ying Wushanley, *Playing Nice and Losing: The Struggle for Control of Women's Intercollegiate Athletics, 1960–2000* (Syracuse, NY: Syracuse University Press, 2004).

11. Sara Evans, *Tidal Wave: How Women Changed America at Century's End* (New York: Simon and Schuster, 2010); Anne Costain, "Representing Women: The Transition from Social Movement to Interest Group," *Western Political Quarterly* 34, no. 1 (1981): 100–113; Michael McCann, *Rights at Work: Pay Equity Reform and the Politics of Legal Mobilization* (Chicago, IL: University of Chicago Press, 1994); Katherine Turk, *Equality on Trial: Gender and Rights in the Modern American Workplace* (Philadelphia: University of Pennsylvania Press, 2016); Deondra Rose, *Citizens by Degree: Higher Education Policy and the Changing Gender Dynamics of American Citizenship* (New York: Oxford University Press, 2018); Serena Mayeri, *Reasoning from Race: Feminism, Law, and the Civil Rights Revolution* (Cambridge,

MA: Harvard University Press, 2011). Although this chapter focuses on Title IX's application to sports, see Celene Reynolds, "The Mobilization of Title IX across Colleges and Universities, 1994–2014," *Social Problems* 66, no. 2 (2019): 245–273, on the more recent evolution of policy toward addressing campus sexual assault.

12. Michael Messner and Michela Musto, *Child's Play: Sport in Kids' Worlds* (New Brunswick, NJ: Rutgers University Press, 2016); National Collegiate Athletic Association, "45 Years of Title IX: The Status of Women in Intercollegiate Athletics" (Indianapolis, IN: NCAA, 2017).

13. National Federation of High School Associations, "1969–2014 High School Athletics Participation Survey Results" (Indianapolis, IN: National Federation of State High School Associations, 2015).

14. Alexander Wolff, "Father Figures: A Girl's Best Friend in the Fight for Playing Time Was Often Her Dad," *Sports Illustrated*, May 7, 2012, http://sports illustrated.cnn.com/vault/article/magazine/MAG1197986/index.htm.

15. Hilary Levey Friedman, *Playing to Win: Raising Children in a Competitive Culture* (Berkeley: University of California Press, 2013); Michael Messner, *It's All for the Kids: Gender, Families, and Youth Sports* (Berkeley: University of California Press, 2009).

16. Viviana Zelizer, *Pricing the Priceless Child: The Changing Social Value of Children* (Princeton, NJ: Princeton University Press, 1994); Messner, *It's All for the Kids.*

17. Michael Messner and Suzel Bozada-Deas, "Separating the Men from the Moms: The Making of Adult Gender Segregation in Youth Sports," *Gender & Society* 23, no. 1 (2009): 49–71. Messner and Bozada-Deas describe and problematize this gendered trend.

18. Justin Heinze et al., "Gender Role Beliefs and Parents' Support for Athletic Participation," *Youth & Society* 49, no. 5 (2017): 634–657.

19. Betsey Stevenson, "Beyond the Classroom: Using Title IX to Measure the Return to High School Sports," *Review of Economics and Statistics* 92, no. 2 (2010): 284–301; Ellen J. Staurowsky et al., "Her Life Depends On It III: Sport, Physical Activity, and the Health and Well-Being of American Girls and Women" (East Meadow, NY: Women's Sports Foundation, 2015); Phoebe Clarke and Ian Ayres, "The Chastain Effect: Using Title IX to Measure the Causal Effect of Participating in High School Sports on Adult Women's Social Lives," *Journal of Socio-Economics* 48 (2014): 62–71. Despite the imbalance of policy benefits toward white, able-bodied women from economically advantaged families, many scholars regard the impacts of policy as largely positive. But see National Women's Law Center and the Poverty & Race Research Action Council, "Finishing Last: Girls of Color and School Sports Opportunities" (Washington, DC, 2015); Eileen McDonagh and Laura Pappano, *Playing with the Boys: Why Separate Is Not Equal in Sports* (New York: Oxford University Press, 2007); Elizabeth Shar-

row, "Sex Segregation as Policy Problem: A Gendered Policy Paradox," *Politics, Groups, and Identities*, 2019, doi:10.1080/21565503.2019.1568883.

20. Paul Pierson, "When Effect Becomes Cause: Policy Feedback and Political Change," *World Politics* 45, no. 4 (1993): 595–628; Suzanne Mettler and Joe Soss, "The Consequences of Public Policy for Democratic Citizenship: Bridging Policy Studies and Mass Politics," *Perspectives on Politics* 2, no. 1 (2004): 55–73.

21. Suzanne Mettler, *Soldiers to Citizens: The G.I. Bill and the Making of the Greatest Generation* (New York: Oxford University Press, 2005); Andrea Campbell, *How Policies Make Citizens: Senior Political Activism and the American Welfare State* (Princeton, NJ: Princeton University Press, 2003).

22. Joe Soss, *Unwanted Claims: The Politics of Participation in the U.S. Welfare System* (Ann Arbor: University of Michigan Press, 2000); Eric Patashnik and Julian Zelizer, "The Struggle to Remake Politics: Liberal Reform and the Limits of Policy Feedback in the Contemporary American State," *Perspectives on Politics* 11, no. 4 (2013): 1071–1087; Amy Lerman and Vesla Weaver, *Arresting Citizenship: The Democratic Consequences of American Crime Control* (Chicago, IL: University of Chicago Press, 2014).

23. Patricia Strach and Kathleen Sullivan, "The State's Relations: What the Institution of Family Tells Us about Governance," *Political Research Quarterly* 64, no. 1 (2011): 94–106. On policy design, see David J. Greenstone and Paul Peterson, *Race and Authority in Urban Politics* (New York: Russell Sage Foundation, 1974); Joe Soss, "Lessons of Welfare: Policy Design, Political Learning, and Political Action," *American Political Science Review* 93, no. 2 (1999): 363–380.

24. Andrea Campbell, *Trapped in America's Safety Net: One Family's Struggle* (Chicago, IL: University of Chicago Press, 2014).

25. Sharrow, "'Female Athlete' Politic"; Sharrow, "Sex Segregation as Policy Problem."

26. Mothers have famously mobilized around their identity to create interest groups like Mothers against Druck Driving, or to make statements about crime and violence through venues like the Million Mom March; see Kristin Goss, "Rethinking the Political Participation Paradigm: The Case of Women and Gun Control," *Women & Politics* 25, no. 4 (2003): 83–118; Kristin Goss and Michael Heaney, "Organizing Women as Women: Hybridity and Grassroots Collective Action in the Twenty-First Century," *Perspectives on Politics* 8, no. 1 (2010): 27–52. The Black Lives Matter movement has centered mothers as core to the movement, mobilized by their children's encounters with criminal justice policies and the police state; see Amy Chozick, "Mothers of Black Victims Emerge as a Force for Hillary Clinton," *New York Times*, 2016, https://www.nytimes.com/2016/04/14/us/politics/hillary-clinton-mothers.html. From "Promise Keepers" to "fathers' rights" groups, men's political mobilization as fathers also foregrounds their relationships with their children; see Jocelyn Crowley, *Defiant Dads: Fathers' Rights Activists in America* (Ithaca, NY: Cornell University Press,

2008); John Bartkowski, *The Promise Keepers: Servants, Soldiers, and Godly Men* (New Brunswick, NJ: Rutgers University Press, 2004).

27. Michael McDevitt and Steven Chaffee, "From Top-Down to Trickle-Up Influence: Revisiting Assumptions about the Family in Political Socialization," *Political Communication* 19, no. 3 (2002): 281–301; Janelle Wong and Vivian Tseng, "Political Socialisation in Immigrant Families: Challenging Top-Down Parental Socialisation Models," *Journal of Ethnic and Migration Studies* 34, no. 1 (2008): 151–168; Jill Greenlee, *The Political Consequences of Motherhood* (Ann Arbor: University of Michigan Press, 2014); Laurel Elder and Steven Greene, *The Politics of Parenthood: Causes and Consequences of the Politicization and Polarization of the American Family* (Albany, NY: State University of New York Press, 2012).

28. Adam Glynn and Maya Sen, "Identifying Judicial Empathy: Does Having Daughters Cause Judges to Rule for Women's Issues?" *American Journal of Political Science* 59, no. 1 (2015): 37–54; Ebonya Washington, "Female Socialization: How Daughters Affect Their Legislator Fathers' Voting on Women's Issues," *American Economic Review* 98, no. 1 (2008): 311–332.

29. Michael Dahl, Cristian Deznő, and David Ross, "Fatherhood and Managerial Style: How a Male CEO's Children Affect the Wages of His Employees," *Administrative Science Quarterly* 57, no. 4 (2012): 669–693; Henrik Cronqvist and Frank Yu, "Shaped by Their Daughters: Executives, Female Socialization, and Corporate Social Responsibility," *Journal of Financial Economics* 126, no. 3 (2017): 543–562.

30. Rebecca Warner and Brent Steel, "Does the Sex of Your Children Matter? Support for Feminism among Women and Men in the United States and Canada," *Gender & Society* 13, no. 4 (1999): 503–517; Emily Fitzgibbons Shafer and Neil Malhotra, "The Effect of a Child's Sex on Support for Traditional Gender Roles," *Social Forces* 90, no. 1 (2011): 209–222.

31. On fatherhood as a conservatizing force, see Dalton Conley and Emily Rauscher, "The Effect of Daughters on Partisanship and Social Attitudes toward Women," *Sociological Forum* 28, no. 4 (2013): 700–718; Anastasia Prokos, Chardie Baird, and Jennifer Keene, "Attitudes about Affirmative Action for Women: The Role of Children in Shaping Parents' Interests," *Sex Roles* 62, nos. 5–6 (2010): 347–360. On fatherhood as a liberalizing force, see Shafer and Malhotra, "The Effect of a Child's Sex on Support for Traditional Gender Roles"; Rebecca Warner and Brent Steel, "Child Rearing as a Mechanism for Social Change: The Relationship of Child Gender to Parents' Committment to Gender Equity," *Gender & Society* 13, no. 4 (1999): 503–517.

32. Elizabeth Sharrow et al., "The First Daughter Effect: The Impact of Fathering First Daughters on Men's Preferences on Gender Equality Issues," *Public Opinion Quarterly* 82, no. 3 (2018): 493–523; Jill Greenlee et al., "Helping to Break the Glass Ceiling? Fathers, First Daughters, and Presidential Vote Choice in 2016," *Political Behavior* (2018), https://doi.org/10.1007/s11109-018-9514-0.

33. Suzanne Mettler, *Dividing Citizens: Gender and Federalism in New Deal Public Policy* (Ithaca, NY: Cornell University Press, 1998); Gretchen Ritter, *The Constitution as Social Design: Gender and Civic Membership in the American Constitutional Order* (Palo Alto, CA: Stanford University Press, 2006); Julie Novkov, *Constituting Workers, Protecting Women: Gender, Law and Labor in the Progressive Era and New Deal Years* (Ann Arbor: University of Michigan Press, 2001); Eileen McDonagh and Carol Nackenoff, "Gender and the American State," in *The Oxford Handbook of American Political Development*, ed. Richard M. Valelly, Suzanne Mettler, and Robert C. Lieberman (New York: Oxford University Press, 2016), 112–131.

34. Lucas Gottzen and Tamar Kremer-Sadlik, "Fatherhood and Youth Sports: A Balancing Act between Care and Expectations," *Gender & Society* 26, no. 4 (2012): 639–664; Tess Kay, ed., *Fathering through Sport and Leisure* (New York: Routledge, 2009); Messner, *It's All for the Kids;* Heinze et al., "Gender Role Beliefs and Parents' Support for Athletic Participation."

35. See Sharrow, "'Female Athlete' Politic," for the history of how policy constituted the identity of the "female athlete"; and Susan Ware, *Game, Set, Match: Billie Jean King and the Revolution in Women's Sports* (Chapel Hill: University of North Carolina Press, 2011), for the history of high-profile sports activists. See also Deondra Rose, *Citizens by Degree: Higher Education Policy and the Changing Gender Dynamics of American Citizenship* (New York: Oxford University Press, 2018), which provides an account of the policy's impacts on women's degree attainment.

36. On women as advocates for women's rights, see, for example, Kelly Belanger, *Invisible Seasons: Title IX and the Fight for Equity in College Sports* (Syracuse, NY: Syracuse University Press, 2016). My broader research on Title IX indicates that "mothers" have rarely mobilized under their identity as such for Title IX, and additional research should explore the extent to which "Title IX moms" self-identify and advocate as policy beneficiaries.

37. This conflict is most pronounced in claims advanced by activists from relatively low-profile men's sports like wrestling and gymnastics who suggest that increased opportunities for women have come at their expense. See Theresa Walton and Michelle Helstein, "Triumph of Backlash: Wrestling Community and the 'Problem' of Title IX," *Sociology of Sport Journal* 25 (2008): 369–386. In fact, such claims are unfounded, as participation opportunities in athletics for boys and men have increased substantially in the years since the policy was passed. On "Title IX dads," see Mark Schmitt, "Title IX Dad," *American Prospect*, October 21, 2009, http://prospect.org/article/title-ix-dad-o.

38. For extant critiques of sex-segregated athletics, see McDonagh and Pappano, *Playing with the Boys*; Sharrow, "'Female Athlete' Politic."

39. Homophobia is a consistent concern among advocates for female athletes, and although fathers were certainly not the cause, neither were they the

cure. See Mary Jo Festle, *Playing Nice: Politics and Apologies in Women's Sports* (New York: Columbia University Press, 1996).

40. National Coalition for Women and Girls in Education, "Title IX at 30: Report Card on Gender Equity" (Washington, DC: American Association of University Women, 2002); National Collegiate Athletic Association, "NCAA Sports Sponsorship and Participation Rates Report, 1981–82—2016–17" (Indianapolis, IN: NCAA, 2017).

41. National Federation of High School Associations, "1969–2014 High School Athletics Participation Survey Results."

42. Vivian Acosta and Linda Carpenter, "Women in Intercollegiate Sport: A Longitudinal, National Study, Thirty-Seven-Year Update, 1977–2014," 2014, http://www.acostacarpenter.org/; NCAA, "NCAA Sports Sponsorship and Participation Rates Report, 1981–82—2016–17." Importantly, these participation numbers were tilted disproportionately toward white, able-bodied girls and women from middle-to-high-income families.

43. Don Sabo and Philip Veliz, "Go Out and Play: Youth Sports in America" (East Meadow, NY: Women's Sports Foundation, 2008). They also note that boys participated at only slightly higher rates (75 percent) than did girls. These numbers vary greatly by age, region, and sport; see Aspen Institute, "State of Play 2016: Trends and Development" (Washington, DC: Aspen Institute Sports & Society Program, Project Play, 2016).

44. Policy guidelines for intercollegiate athletics were first formalized in 1979. Debates over implementation were ongoing in the 1980s, but the 1979 guidelines were the most stable indication of bureaucratic enforcement efforts. The US Department of Education offered a "clarification" on policy interpretation in 1996. For a summary of legal cases, see Deborah Brake and Elizabeth Catlin, "The Path of Most Resistance: The Long Road toward Gender Equity in Intercollegiate Athletics," *Duke Journal of Gender Law & Policy* 3 (1996): 51–92. For formal guidelines, see US Department of Education, Office for Civil Rights, *Clarification of Intercollegiate Athletics Policy Guidance: The Three-Part Test* (Washington, DC, 1996), http://www2.ed.gov/about/offices/list/ocr/docs/clarific .html. See also US Department of Health, Education, and Welfare, Office for Civil Rights, *Title IX 1979 Policy Interpretation on Intercollegiate Athletics* (Washington, DC, 1979), http://www2.ed.gov/about/offices/list/ocr/docs/t9interp .html.

45. Lee Sigelman and P. J. Wahlbeck, "Gender Proportionality in Intercollegiate Athletics: The Mathematics of Title IX Compliance," *Social Science Quarterly* 80, no. 3 (1999): 518–538.

46. NCAA, "NCAA Sports Sponsorship and Participation Rates Report, 1981–82—2016–17."

47. US Department of Education, Secretary's Commission on Opportunity in Athletics, *Open to All: Title IX at Thirty* (Washington, DC, 2003), 2.

48. US Department of Education, *Open to All.*

49. The full list of commissioners is found in Appendix 5 of the final report; see US Department of Education, *Open to All,* 53–58.

50. Until 2015, the US Department of Education hosted hearing transcripts online, which serve as data for the development of this chapter.

51. US Department of Education, *Open to All,* 4.

52. US Department of Education, Secretary's Commission on Opportunity in Athletics, *Official Transcripts of Town Hall Meetings: San Diego, November 20, 2002* (Washington, DC, 2002), 233–235.

53. Kelly wrote five books on fatherhood, including one during the year of the commission's work. See Joe Kelly, *Dads and Daughters: How to Inspire, Understand, and Support Your Daughter When She's Growing Up So Fast* (New York: Broadway Books, 2002). The Women's Sports Foundation—the largest women's sports advocacy group in the country—named him Title IX Father of the Year in 2004.

54. Amy Dickinson, "Dads and Daughters: Strengthening This Special Relationship Can Strengthen a Girl's Self-Esteem Too," *Time* magazine, May 13, 2002.

55. Abby Ellin, "Dad, Do You Think I Look Too Fat?" *New York Times,* 2000, http://www.nytimes.com/2000/09/17/style/dad-do-you-think-i-look-too-fat .html.

56. At the time, many observers noted this evolution. See Deirdre Fulton, "Dads Lobby Bush for Title IX," *Newsday,* January 28, 2003, http://www.newsday.com/sports/dads-lobby-bush-for-title-ix-1.429195; Ruth Conniff, "Title IX: Political Football," *Nation,* March 2003, https://www.thenation.com/article /title-ix-political-football/; Christine Brennan, *Best Seat in the House: A Father, a Daughter, a Journey through Sports* (New York: Scribner, 2006); Harvey Araton, "Sports of the Times; Proud Fathers Cheering Title IX," *New York Times,* 2003, http://www.nytimes.com/2003/07/17/sports/sports-of-the-times-proud-fa thers-cheering-title-ix.html.

57. Throughout the 1970s, women held only 3 percent of congressional seats. See Center for American Women in Politics, "History of Women in the U.S. Congress," Eagleton Institute of Politics, Rutgers University (2017), http://www.cawp.rutgers.edu/history-women-us-congress. Famously, it was Senator Birch Bayh (D-IN), not legislative innovators Representatives Edith Green (D-OR) and Patsy Mink (D-HI), who provided the majority of the limited public statements on the bill that became Title IX to gain the votes of his male colleagues. See Rose, "Regulating Opportunity." Although women played important roles, the initial public face of advocacy in Congress was disproportionately male.

58. Edwards, "Why Sport?"; Elizabeth Sharrow, "Forty Years 'on the Basis of Sex': Title IX, the 'Female Athlete,' and the Political Construction of Sex and Gender" (PhD diss., University of Minnesota, 2013).

59. See, for example, Suggs, *A Place on the Team.*

60. Senator John Tower, speaking on the Senate floor on May 20, 1974, 93rd Cong., 2nd sess., *Congressional Record* 120, pt. 15323.

61. Sharrow, "'Female Athlete' Politic."

62. Equitable spending is *not* required under Title IX, a concession that was introduced and eventually passed by Congress after the Tower amendment failed.

63. Deborah Brake, *Getting in the Game: Title IX and the Women's Sports Revolution* (New York: New York University Press, 2010).

64. *Grove City College v. Bell*, 465 U.S. 555 (1984).

65. In a key moment of introducing an early version of the Civil Rights Restoration Act, Representative Paul Simon (D-IL) noted: "Nothing is more vital to the future of this Nation than that we provide opportunity and justice and see that it is done for those citizens who have not always had either the opportunity or justice. My daughter is one of those who benefitted directly from Title IX. She was the AIAW, Division III High Jump Champion in 1982." US Congress, House of Representatives, Committee on Education and Labor, *Civil Rights Act of 1984*, 98th Cong., 2nd sess., 1984, 13. See also US Congress, House of Representatives, Committee on Education and Labor, *Sex Discrimination Regulations*, 94th Cong., 1st sess., 1975; US Congress, Senate, Committee on Labor and Human Resources, *Civil Rights Act of 1984, Part I*, 98th Cong. 2nd sess., 1984.

66. US Congress, House of Representatives, *Civil Rights Act of 1984.*

67. Women's Sports Foundation, "The Wilson Report: Moms, Dads, Daughters and Sports" (New York: Wilson Sporting Goods Co. & the Women's Sports Foundation, 1988).

68. See Sharrow, "'Female Athlete' Politic."

69. This, echoing Tronto's observations that familial relationships of care are important for democratic citizenship. See Joan C. Tronto, *Moral Boundaries* (New York: Routledge, 1993); and Tronto's Foreword to this volume.

70. Wushanley, *Playing Nice and Losing*; Edwards, "Why Sport?"

71. I examine this pattern of displacement elsewhere, in Sharrow, "Forty Years 'on the Basis of Sex.'" See also on the topics of homophobia in sports, Pat Griffin, *Strong Women, Deep Closets: Lesbians and Homophobia in Sport* (Champaign, IL: Human Kinetics, 1998); Susan Cahn, *Coming on Strong: Gender and Sexuality in Twentieth-Century Women's Sport* (Cambridge, MA: Harvard University Press, 1995).

72. Jennifer Brier, *Infectious Ideas: U.S. Political Responses to the AIDS Crisis* (Chapel Hill: University of North Carolina Press, 2009).

73. See Terrel Howard Bell, *The Thirteenth Man: A Reagan Cabinet Memoir* (Glencoe, IL: Free Press, 1988).

74. For example, a representative from the American Association of Catholic Schools testifying to Congress on the content of the Civil Rights Restoration

Act (the legislation that eventually countered the decision in *Grove City College*), articulated concerns about protecting girls and women against homosexuality, stating: "I have a daughter. I have a wife. I want the best for them, but it is a perversion and a corruption of our system to redefine these moral issues into terms of civil rights in such a corrupted and perverted way that we stand accused of violation of civil rights." From US Congress, Senate, Committee on Labor and Human Resources, *Civil Rights Act of 1984, Part I*, 98th Cong, 2nd sess., 1984, 349. His references to "perversion" implied the fear that Title IX would be construed to include protections for "homosexuals" in civil rights policies.

75. US Congress, House of Representatives, *Sex Discrimination Regulations*, 94th Cong., 1st sess., 1975, 382. The use of the language of "women's liberation" was more common in the mid-1970s to refer to the second-wave feminist movement in the United States. See Jo Freeman, "The Origins of the Women's Liberation Movement," *American Journal of Sociology* 78, no. 4 (1973): 792–811.

76. Notably absent from Title IX discussions in this era was an awareness of the potential for sexual abuse by male coaches.

77. US Congress, House of Representatives, Committee on Energy and Commerce, *Intercollegiate Sports (Part 2)*, 103rd Cong., 1st sess., 1993, 18. See also *Cohen v. Brown Univ.*, 879 F. Supp. 185 (D.R.I. 1995).

78. Sarah L. Stafford, "Progress toward Title IX Compliance: The Effect of Formal and Informal Enforcement Mechanisms," *Social Science Quarterly* 85, no. 5 (2004): 1469–1486; Brake, *Getting in the Game*.

79. Brake, *Getting in the Game*.

80. The EADA numbers now mean that compliance with policy is more easily tracked; see Alixandra Yanus and Karen O'Connor, "To Comply or Not to Comply: Evaluating Compliance with Title IX of the Educational Amendments of 1972," *Journal of Women, Politics & Policy* 37, no. 3 (2016): 341–358.

81. US Congress, House of Representatives, Committee on Education and Labor, *Hearings on the Role of Athletics in College Life*, 101st Cong., 1st sess., 1989, 90.

82. His activism continued for decades. Sociologist Celene Reynolds documents that in 2013 and 2014 alone, Dempsey co-filed over 3,000 Title IX athletic complaints; see Celene Reynolds, "The Mobilization of Title IX." See also Wolff, "Father Figures."

83. The group achieved some success, collecting 4,500 signatures on a petition against Title IX, and securing campaign pledges to reform Title IX from several Republican candidates. See Welch Suggs, "Foes of Title IX Try to Make Equity in College Sports a Campaign Issue," *Chronicle of Higher Education*, February 4, 2000.

84. Terry Anderson, *The Pursuit of Fairness: A History of Affirmative Action* (New York: Oxford University Press, 2004).

85. Welch Suggs, "2 Appeals Courts Uphold Right of Universities to Reduce Number of Male Athletes," *Chronicle of Higher Education*, January 7, 2000.

86. Republican National Committee, "2000 Republican Party Platform," *The American Presidency Project*, Gerhard Peters and John T. Woolley, 2000, https://www.presidency.ucsb.edu/node/273446.

87. "Q&A: The Candidates on College Issues," *Chronicle of Higher Education*, February 25, 2000.

88. Stephen Burd, "Bush Nominates Houston Official to Be Secretary of Education," *Chronicle of Higher Education*, January 12, 2001.

89. In 1995, Speaker Hastert wrote a letter signed by 133 congressional colleagues that urged the US DOE to more aggressively ensure that men's sports were not unduly hurt by Title IX; see Stephen Burd and Douglas Lederman, "Next Speaker of the House Has Not Focused on Higher Education," *Chronicle of Higher Education*, January 8, 1999; Suggs, *A Place on the Team*.

90. US General Accounting Office, *Intercollegiate Athletics: Four-Year Colleges' Experiences Adding and Discontinuing Teams*, GAO-01-297 (Washington, DC, 2001), accessed March 26, 2018, https://www.gao.gov/new.items/d01297.pdf.

91. Sporting settings routinely invoke this dubious "battle of the sexes" narrative. From Billie Jean King's famous tennis match against Bobby Riggs in 1973, to the 2002–2003 Commission hearings, the common framing of a battle of the sexes inhering in Title IX problematically naturalizes both the sex-segregated structure of sporting competition, as well as the notion that women and girls may be unfairly demanding access to venues that are "naturally" those for men and boys. See McDonagh and Pappano, *Playing with the Boys*; Sharrow, "'Female Athlete' Politic."

92. US Department of Labor, Bureau of Labor Statistics, *Volunteering in the United States, 2003* (Washington, DC, 2003), http://www.bls.gov/news.release/archives/volun_12172003.pdf.

93. Arlie Hochschild, *The Second Shift* (New York: Viking Penguin, 1989).

94. A phenomenon that also gave rise to a genre of parenting memoir. See, for example, Brennan, *Best Seat in the House*; Robert Strauss, *Daddy's Little Goalie: A Father, His Daughters, and Sports* (Kansas City, MO: Andrews McMeel, 2011).

95. Friedman, *Playing to Win*.

96. Araton, "Sports of the Times; Proud Fathers Cheering Title IX."

97. ESPN, *Fathers & Daughters & Sports: Featuring Jim Craig, Chris Evert, Mike Golic, Doris Kearns Goodwin, Sally Jenkins, Steve Rushin, Bill Simmons, and Others* (New York: Random House, 2010); Wolff, "Father Figures"; Scott Cacciola, "The Rise of Wellborn Daughters: Many Top Women's Basketball Prospects Have Famous Athletes for Dads; a Societal Shift," *Wall Street Journal*, August 19, 2011, https://www.wsj.com/articles/SB10001424053111903639404576516691099307456.

98. Robert Pruter, *The Rise of American High School Sports and the Search for Control, 1880–1930* (Syracuse, NY: Syracuse University Press, 2013).

99. The Women's Sports Foundation, the leading advocacy group on athletic opportunities for girls and women, published the annual *College Athletic Scholarship Guide for Women* for the first several decades of policy implementation.

100. Lee Sigelman and Clyde Wilcox, "Public Support for Gender Equality in Athletics Programs," *Women & Politics* 22, no. 1 (2001): 85–96.

101. Hart-Teeter Research Companies, "NBC/Wall Street Journal Poll #6006," Roper Center, Cornell University (2000).

102. Michael Messner and Nancy Solomon, "Social Justice and Men's Interests: The Case of Title IX," *Journal of Sport & Social Issues* 31, no. 2 (2007): 162–178.

103. Richard Worsnop, "Gender Equity in Sports," *CQ Researcher* 7, no. 15 (1997): 337–360.

104. Walton and Helstein, "Triumph of Backlash." These critiques foreshadowed the conversation that would emerge later in the decade, which suggested that women's success in college (in both enrollment and graduation) came at the expense of men.

105. US Department of Education, Secretary's Commission on Opportunity in Athletics, *Official Transcripts of Town Hall Meetings: Atlanta, GA, August 27, 2002* (Washington, DC, 2002), 16–17.

106. Walton and Helstein, "Triumph of Backlash"; Cindy Simon Rosenthal, "Sports Talk: How Gender Shapes Discursive Framing of Title IX," *Politics & Gender* 4, no. 1 (2008): 65–92.

107. Bill Hansen, Bush's deputy secretary for education (and father of six children), proclaimed in opening remarks that the administration was "adamant in [their] support for Title IX." US Department of Education, *Official Transcripts: Atlanta, GA, August 27*, 3.

108. The "quota" argument was central to the NWCA case in which they argued that Title IX was forcing cuts to men's sports; see Brake, *Getting in the Game*. In May 2002, the US DOE filed a motion to dismiss on the grounds that the plaintiffs were unable to trace the harms directly to Title IX. This narrative of Title IX's threat to men's sports was salient during the hearings, and many male wrestlers and their advocates urged the Commission to reevaluate the enforcement provisions, regardless of the outcome of the lawsuit. Ultimately, the US District Court for the District of Columbia granted the DOE's motion to dismiss in June 2003. The NWCA's appeal was unsuccessful. An amicus brief filed by the National Women's Law Center, on behalf of multiple feminist organizations, provided much of the evidence that the court drew upon to reject the suit.

109. A limited number of fathers of wrestlers spoke on behalf of their sons. Although a small number of women spoke to the importance of their roles as

mothers to their advocacy work around Title IX, self-identified fathers advocating for maintaining the status quo were most numerous.

110. US Department of Education, *Official Transcripts: Atlanta, GA, August 27, 193–195*.

111. John R. Thelin, *Games Colleges Play: Scandal and Reform in Intercollegiate Athletics* (Baltimore, MD: Johns Hopkins University Press, 1994).

112. US Department of Education, Secretary's Commission on Opportunity in Athletics, *Official Transcripts of Town Hall Meetings: Chicago, IL, September 17, 2002* (Washington, DC, 2002), 206–207.

113. See Suggs, *A Place on the Team*, chap. 10.

114. The National Women's Law Center published a series of papers on the topic in the years that followed. See, for example, Jocelyn Samuels and Kristen Galles, "In Defense of Title IX: Why Current Policies Are Required to Ensure Equality of Opportunity," *Marquette Sports Law Review* 14, no. 1 (2004): 11–48.

115. Rita James Simon, ed., *Sporting Equality: Title IX Thirty Years Later* (Edison, NJ: Transaction Publishers, 2005); Donna de Varona and Julie Foudy, "Minority Views on the Report of the Commission on Opportunity in Athletics," *Marquette Sports Law Review* 14, no. 1 (2004): 1–20.

116. US Department of Education, Office for Civil Rights, *Further Clarification of Intercollegiate Athletics Policy Guidance Regarding Title IX Compliance* (Washington, DC, 2003), https://www2.ed.gov/about/offices/list/ocr/title9 guidanceFinal.pdf.

117. Paul Pierson, *Politics in Time: History, Institutions, and Social Analysis* (Princeton, NJ: Princeton University Press, 2004).

118. On this point see also Chapter 6 in this volume, "The Feudal Family and American Political Development" by Eileen McDonagh, for her discussion of the identity of motherhood and political empowerment.

119. On marriage and income inequality, see June Carbone and Naomi Cahn, *Marriage Markets: How Inequality Is Remaking the American Family* (New York: Oxford University Press, 2014).

120. See, for example, NWLC and PRRAC, "Finishing Last"; National Collegiate Athletic Association, "NCAA Student-Athlete Race/Ethnicity Report" (Indianapolis, IN, 2011).

121. The replacement of women coaches and athletic administrators with men has been well-documented over the past forty-five years. See National Collegiate Athletic Association, "Gender Equity in College Coaching and Administration: Perceived Barriers Report" (Indianapolis, IN, 2009).

122. See, for example, Ritter, *The Constitution as Social Design*; Julie Novkov, *Racial Union: Law, Intimacy, and the White State in Alabama, 1865–1954* (Ann Arbor: University of Michigan Press, 2008); Mettler, *Dividing Citizens*.

123. In brief, see McDonagh and Pappano, *Playing with the Boys*; Cheryl Cooky and Michael Messner, *No Slam Dunk: Gender, Sport and the Unevenness of So-*

cial Change (New Brunswick, NJ: Rutgers University Press, 2018); Jaime Schultz, *Qualifying Times: Points of Change in U.S. Women's Sport* (Champaign: University of Illinois Press, 2014).

124. James Druckman, Jacob Rothschild, and Elizabeth Sharrow, "Gender Policy Feedback: Perceptions of Sex Equity, Title IX, and Political Mobilization among College Athletes," *Political Research Quarterly* 71, no. 3 (2018): 642–653.

125. Sean Gregory, "How Kids' Sports Became a $15 Billion Industry," *Time* magazine, August 24, 2017.

6 | The Feudal Family versus American Political Development

From Separate Spheres to Woman Suffrage

Eileen McDonagh

Family and APD: The Problem with a Liberal Agenda

The American feudal heritage. American political development (APD) is in part the story of how reformers used liberal principles to abolish or reform feudal institutions, starting with the monarchical state. Feudal institutions are based on premises of *inequality* between groups, such as monarchs and their subjects; political rule based on *coercion*, such that those on the bottom have no right to consent to the rule of those on the top; and *hierarchal structures* based on ascriptive characteristics acquired at birth, such as membership in the royal family as a criterion for eligibility to be a political ruler.[1] The ideological and institutional legitimacy of these principles as a basis for the monarchical state was destroyed by the American Revolution.[2] In its place, the Founders proudly constructed a republican state based on liberal principles, which include the premise that all individuals are created *equal* with inalienable rights to self-ownership; all individuals have a right to *consent* to relationships with others, which can be formalized as a contract; and political rule is based on a *nonhierarchical structure* on the principle that everyone is eligible to be a political ruler.[3] As a result, though egregious flaws remained, directly or indirectly, it was the vote of the people that determined who would be the political rulers of the state.[4]

Though founders destroyed the monarchical state and replaced it with a liberal republic, American society remained saturated with additional feudal institutions, what Karen Orren refers to as "belated feudalism," and what Rogers Smith refers to as an "Americanist tradition" that mimics the feudal use of ascriptive inequalities to structure coercive relationships of dominance. Most notably, the nefarious institution of *slavery*[5] violated liberal principles, but also *coverture marriage* conveyed authority to husbands over wives simply because of an ascriptive sex difference, and American courts maintained the feudal, common law *master-servant household institution* as applied to the relationship between employers and their employees.[6] To establish congruence between the new liberal state and American society, therefore, reformers continued a project of institutional development that drove political change. They abolished those institutions that could not be reformed to be liberal, such as slavery, and they reformed other institutions to be based on liberal principles of equal individualism and consent, such as marriage between adults and economic relationships between employers and employees.

The family: Permanently feudal. One feudal institution, however, was, and, still is, a roadblock to APD's liberal agenda: the family. Defined by the relationship between *parents* and *children*, the family is intractably based on feudal principles of inequality, coercion, and hierarchical structure. To become a parent, for example, requires biological *parental inequality* because only women are socially (if not actually) constructed to have the parental maternal capacity to be pregnant and to bear children. If at least some women do not exercise this capacity, no child will ever be born, and, consequently, no one will ever be a biological parent.

What is more, a fertilized ovum is conceived on the basis of *coercion*, since it obviously cannot consent to its existence, prior to that existence. Thus, a *pregnancy contract* between a woman and a fertilized ovum, an embryo, and a fetus, as based on consent, is impossible.[7] In addition, the family is structured *hierarchically* based on ascriptive birth status. Parents are the rulers of the family who exercise dominance over their children by providing authority for rules of behavior and care work. Thus, presumably, it is ludicrous to conceptualize the family as a liberal institution composed of equal, autonomous individuals in which both men and women become pregnant and bear children and in which infants have a right to consent to a contract to be conceived (prior to being conceived) and then consent to an election to determine who will be the rulers of the family. Thus, the family is a permanently feudal institution, even within a liberal state, and there is no way to make the feudal family congruent with the liberal state.

The liberal solution: Separate spheres. As feudal institutions, both the family and the monarchical state violate liberal principles. However, while Americans could destroy their monarchical heritage, they could not abolish or liberalize the feudal family. The solution, as proposed by John Locke, was simply to put the feudal family in a private sphere separated from the public sphere of the liberal state. He did not argue that the family and the liberal state do not affect one another. Rather, he argued *correctly* that the family and the liberal state are necessarily ruled on opposite principles, namely, *parental rule of the family*, which is feudal, and *political rule of the state*, which is liberal.

A little recognized principle of feudal institutions, however, is that those at the top of an ascriptive hierarchy not only had authority over their subordinates but also responsibility for their care. This is obvious in the family. Parents as the rulers of the family have authority over their subordinates, their children, but also bear responsibility for their care. This dual combination, however, applied not only to the feudal family, but to all feudal institutions, including coverture marriage, household relationships between masters and servants, and the monarchical state.[8] Monarchs, therefore, had authority over their subjects, but also responsibility for their care.

Notably in western European history, therefore, the public and political elites commonly viewed monarchs as the "parents of the people," as James I put it.[9] In addition we find evidence throughout the centuries that the *office of kingship/queenship* itself is defined in terms of parental roles of care for the well-being of the people or metaphorical care-work equivalents, such as shepherds who are responsible for the care of their sheep. As the Dutch Declaration of Independence stated, in 1581, the first such declaration in modern times, "a prince is constituted by God to be ruler of a people, to defend them from oppression . . . as the shepherd his sheep; and . . . to love and support them as a father his children or a shepherd his flock."[10]

Abolishing or reforming feudal institutions to be based on liberal principles destroys the premise that rulers have legitimate dominance over others based on coercive, ascriptive hierarchies and inequalities. However, so, too, is the feudal complement lost, namely, that rulers have responsibility for the care of their subordinates. Once everyone is equal, as is necessitated by liberal theory, in principle, there are no subordinates any longer, much less legitimate, ascriptive rulers over subordinates.

Separate spheres ideology, therefore, by separating the feudal family from the liberal state, renders the family as the only site where *parental rulers* are responsible *for providing to people what they need but do not have,* particularly children, but also the elderly and the ill, such as providing shelter, food, education, health care, and so on. By contrast, in the new, public sphere of the liberal state, *political rulers* are responsible only *for protecting what people already have,* namely, their property and their person, from nonconsensual intrusion by other people or by the state itself. As Seyla Benhabib puts it, "An entire domain of human activity, namely nurture, reproduction, love, and care . . . [is now] excluded from . . . political considerations."[11]

Bringing the family back in to the state. Many feminists view separating the family and the state as not good for women. As Catharine Mac-Kinnon argues, separate spheres ideology strands women in the private sphere of the family without the protection of the state from abusive husbands, marital rape, and other atrocities, as if women were still in the state of nature.[12] In addition, scholars have established that the *political meaning* of women's maternal identities in a separate spheres configuration of the state locates women in the family as the sole site of caregiving rather than positing the family and the state as dual sites of caregiving. Thus, many feminist theorists have long argued that separating the family from the state keeps women out of politics, while connecting the family and the state as analogous institutions promotes women's political inclusion.

Yet how can a feudal family be considered similar to a liberal state when each institution is founded on opposite principles? The answer is, since the family cannot be abolished or reformed to be a liberal institution, to establish congruence between both institutions, the liberal state must be reformed to be more like a family. The latter may sound impossible, but that is exactly what happened in the United States in the early decades of the Progressive Era, when women finally achieved a constitutional guarantee prohibiting the use of sex as a voting criterion. And this is exactly the template that characterizes most western European democracies, which typically combine liberal principles based on equal individualism with familial principles that it is the responsibility of the state to provide care to those in need. The term usually applied to this template is the "welfare state," and that is what the American state became, at least to some degree, in the Progressive Era. An analysis of woman suffrage in the United States illustrates that it is the welfare state formula, which combines the family and the state as similar institutions with the principles of a liberal democratic state, that promotes women's political citizenship rather than the liberal state alone.

APD and the Family

Notably, APD attention to the family is very recent. The word "family," for example, did not even appear in the index of the anthology, *Democratization in America*, published in 2009.[13] However, more recently, "family" occupies an entire chapter written by notable political science scholar Patricia Strach in the *Oxford Handbook of American Political Development*, published in 2016.[14] Similarly, the journal *Polity* recently published a special issue focusing on the family and the American state.[15]

Understanding separate spheres. Analyzing the family in the context of APD inevitably raises questions about the separate spheres doctrine that locates the family in the private sphere and the state in the public sphere.[16] Recently, a great deal of innovative research argues that the family and the state are anything but separate institutions. Rather, each influences the other. Other scholars point to the way in which the family as an institution enables the state's governance of the people in the transference of inheritance and property.[17]

Scholars such as Larry Bartels and Jacqueline Stevens, for example, study inheritance and tax rules, finding that they allow families to accumulate wealth unequally in a way that results in significant consequences for future generations.[18] The work of Peggy Pascoe, who argues that miscegenation laws prohibiting interracial marriages emerged at the end of the Civil War as a materialization of the fear that white property interests were at risk, is a related examination of the way in which the institutional nature of the family enabled the furthering of certain political agendas.[19]

Strach identifies a shift in the kinds of organizations policymakers identify as key actors in the manifestation of their policies. During the Progressive Era, New Deal, and Great Society, she argues that the state most often created federal agencies when implementing new policies. From the 1970s on, however, she identifies a shift away from such federal agencies and instead toward market actors, who then correspondingly shift the responsibility and burden of taking part in public programs to the individual family. For example, school vouchers are not implemented by the state but rather by "family members who must learn about vouchers, enroll their children in the school of their choice, and arrange for transportation."[20] In other words, the family as a private organization of citizens has become increasingly identified by the state as a means for realizing public policy.

Opposite principles of rule. Missing from these analyses of the connections between the family and the state, however, is recognition that liberal theory does not assert that these two institutions have no effect on one another. Rather, the liberal argument is that the family and the liberal state are ruled on opposite principles, parental and political, respectively. These features of the family and the state make the family incongruent with APD, which configures development as abolishing or reforming feudal institutions so that societal institutions are congruent with the liberal state. What is more, it is the idea that the family is not a liberal institution that most affects women's identities as being suitable for political participation, such as voting. When women's maternal identities link them only to feudalism, it becomes more difficult to argue that women should be participants in the liberal state.

The family precedes the state. Others contend that the family is an institution created and defined by the state.[21] Missing from this view of the family-state relationship, however, is the recognition that before there were states, there had to be families, defined by the relationship between parents and children. Before the state can regulate the family, there have to be people to regulate in the first place. And to have people available for state regulation as a family requires that at least some women who have the capacity to be pregnant and to bear children do so. The family, defined narrowly as the relationship between parents and children in general and mothers and children in particular, therefore, is an institution that historically preceded the state as an institution. Or, as liberal theorists would say (and did) the family exists initially in a state of nature prior to the existence of the state.[22]

Anthropologists agree with liberal theorists. On the basis of recent fossil discoveries in Morocco, for example, researchers now date the emergence of our species, *Homo sapiens*, to 300,000–200,000 years BCE.[23] The first communities of *Homo sapiens* that anthropologists analyze as including government or a state, however, do not occur until as late as 5,000 BCE. Clearly, there is a big—really big—time gap of hundreds of thousands of years between the emergence of *Homo sapiens* as a species and the emergence of the state as an institution, however the latter is defined. Yet presumably, prior to 5,000 BCE, there were families, defined narrowly as the relationship between parents and children. If not, there would be no people to constitute a nation, much less a state, at any point in history.

The family, household, and home. Other scholars focus on the distinction between two often conflated terms, the "household" and the "family," suggesting that it is only by fitting the state's designations of who and what a family looks like that a mere household transforms into a family.[24] In addition, however, it is important to recognize that the relationship between the family and the home is a connection that most likely does not depend upon legal recognition by the state, but rather upon the subjective attitudes of family members. Broadly, a household can be legally and socially defined in terms of a dwelling consisting of one or more people (usually a nuclear family) sharing accommodation, space, and resources. Modern governmental definitions of households for countries like the United States and United Kingdom define a household as "a single person or group of people living at the same address who either share one meal a day or shared the living accommodation, e.g., a kitchen or living room."[25] Conversely, while "household" applies to the economic and utilitarian aspects of the family as a nuclear resource organization, the term "home" occupies a realm characterized by emotion and symbolism in the collective minds of societies.[26]

From an archaeological standpoint, the origin of the home as a familial conception that is distinctly different from that of a household dates to a very early period in human civilization, the Neolithic, beginning in 8,250–8,000 BCE in the Near East.[27] Excavations conducted at Qermez Dere in Iraq illuminated important architectural developments occurring at the beginning of the Neolithic period, which signify the progression of the conception of households as homes where familial relationships had ideological significance.[28] The changes altered the view of "the house as shelter, the centre of certain everyday activities, to the house as home, the centre of the family and the focus for the representation of appropriate symbolic values."[29]

Furthermore, evidence of daily practices of cleaning and waste disposal suggests the houses were intentionally kept very clean, and debris or waste material was not found within the houses.[30] This type of cleaning and daily practice is associated with the construction of habits that create identity and memory within households, thus possibly enforcing an ideology of the home as a site of familial, emotional, and social principles as distinct from economic or production-related activities that define a household unit.[31]

In addition, each house was constructed with one or more non-structural clay pillars.[32] This suggests that society purposefully incorporated and found value in non-utilitarian or more decorative elements in the design of houses.[33] One could say that this mirrors somewhat the behavior of modern society, in the sense that scores of families and homeowners enjoy and strive to decorate houses in functional and non-functional ways to mark their individual or family identities. These values and practices have so permeated modern society that society itself has become very aware of this desire to achieve a site for nurture, warmth, care, familiarity, and contentment and, thus, render a house a home.[34] This demonstrates and reinforces the strong connection between concepts of "home," as opposed to "household," and the ideals and values of familial unity, protection, and nurture.[35]

Analyzing the family in the context of APD, therefore, entails analyzing the *home*. Of course, the subjective feelings of comfort and security can be felt by individuals who find their "home on the range." However, for most people, home as a subjective state is equated with the family as an institution. An individual who poses a threat to the ideological, symbolic, or emotional health or unity of a household that contains a family, therefore, typically is known as a "home-wrecker" and possibly a "family-wrecker," not a "house-wrecker" or a "household-wrecker."

The family, therefore, is not only a necessary institution, but one that is subjectively valued by its members, including the subordinates in the family, the children, and in patriarchal familial structures, sometimes, even subordinate wives and mothers. Reform activities that are interpreted as a threat to the family as an institution, therefore, often generate severe backlash, not only from those who are dominant in a patriarchal family, such as husbands and fathers, but also from those who are subordinate in a family, such as wives and mothers. This backlash is unique to the family as an institution in the United States, whether it involves women who formed anti–woman suffrage organizations in the Progressive Era or the legacy of Phyllis Schlafly's Eagle Forum in contemporary times.

The family: An identity-based institution. Intersectionality scholars analyze how individuals are a mixture of many ascriptive identities: age, sex, race, class, and so on.[36] However, as Julie Novkov notes, some institutions intersect with one primary ascriptive identity.[37] Slavery, for example, intersects with race. And the feudal family intersects with women's biological maternalism because it only originates or can exist when women give birth.[38] It is important, therefore, to understand the family as a unique institution that most often also constitutes the home. In addition, as many point out, historically the family and the home have been gendered by patriarchal norms that traditionally identify a male as head of household. What is more important, however, for the very existence of the family, throughout all historical eras as well as today, is that when defined by the relationship between parents and children, the family is an institution that becomes socially constructed as dependent upon women's biological maternal capacities to be pregnant and give birth. Hence, although the patriarchal structure of a family can be liberalized to confer equal status on parents, women's maternal identities as the source of the family in the first place necessarily remain a constant throughout time and place.

There is only one solution, therefore, to achieve congruence between the feudal family and the liberal state. Namely, since the feudal family cannot be abolished or reformed to be liberal, the liberal state must be reformed to be more familial. The result of this configuration, usually termed the "welfare state," confers upon the government a "parental" responsibility for providing care work to those in need of food, shelter, education, and health care, among other things. In addition, a familial state provides a gender boost to women's political citizenship by abolishing separate spheres ideology. The family and the state are now congruent institutions, thereby linking women's maternal identities not only to the family, but also to the state itself. The result promotes women's inclusion in the state as political citizens. And this is exactly what happened in the United States in the Progressive Era, when women finally obtained a constitutional guarantee prohibiting the use of sex as a criterion for voting rights.

Woman Suffrage in the United States

A vast scholarship provides myriad explanations as to how and why the woman suffrage movement failed and succeeded when and where it did. Some scholars argue that enfranchisement was achieved due to changing ideologies, specifically about gender roles and the capacity of women, within society at large. "In essence," Corrine McConnaughy writes, "the argument is that women were granted voting rights when and where the idea of their enfranchisement was no longer a radical one."[39] For example, some say that the frontier experience, with its roots in the expansion into the American West, led to changes in gender roles that facilitated woman suffrage in western states earlier than in other regions of the United States.[40] Another example is scholarship about changes in women's levels of education and their increased participation in the workplace and, more broadly, in the public sphere. Especially in the later years of the movement, woman suffrage activists were able to leverage these changes and the resulting shift in conceptions of the capacity of women to further the movement for the vote.[41]

Other scholars credit the organizational and political tactics of suffrage activists for the overall success of the movement: "success came when suffragists dropped principled arguments for extending voting rights to women—that is, appeals to issues of republican ideals and legal justice—and instead turned to arguments defined by political expediency."[42] The movement was successful because, such scholars argue, woman suffrage leaders were able to find a way to fit the debate over suffrage rights into ongoing political debates, "promising that enfranchising women might contribute to the victory of one side over another."[43]

Still others have turned their attention not to the work of suffrage activists themselves but rather to that of their opponents, arguing that the suffrage movement succeeded in moments and locations where organizers were able to disable their major opponents. Finally, some explanations of the success of suffrage movements at both the state and federal levels emphasize specific political conditions of the moment. One notable example is the significant literature that links woman suffrage to parties in general and to third parties in particular. As a political issue, woman suffrage was often welcome on the platform of minor political parties—such as the Populists, Socialists, and Progressives—and suffrage was adopted in a number of states during times when such third parties were experiencing electoral success.[44] McConnaughy summarizes this last type of interpretation of the woman suffrage movement's success as being "ultimately explanations about political opportunities—cracks in the system of politics as usual that might make space for the admission of new voters."[45]

In *The Woman Suffrage Movement in America: A Reassessment*, McConnaughy argues that the kinds of explanations summarized above derive primarily from the vantage point of the movement itself. While these explanations can function as a list of possible influences on the decisions made with regard to woman suffrage, she argues that they do not serve as "clear answers to questions about how, when, and why each translated into the political behavior that produced voting rights policy outcomes."[46] McConnaughy instead asserts that in order to understand how, when, and why the suffrage movement succeeded, it is necessary to focus not only on suffragists but on the lawmakers who ultimately passed legislation enfranchising women. She provides two models of enfranchisement: strategic enfranchisement and programmatic enfranchisement. Strategic enfranchisement, according to McConnaughy, is the extension of suffrage that stems from a political party's expectation that they will benefit electorally by enfranchising new voters. For this form of enfranchisement to succeed, the new voters in question must have some sort of clear and distinct political identity that can make it possible to predict how they will vote as a collective group.

Gendered arguments about "the woman vote"—for example, superficial assumptions that women "oppose prohibition, are in favor of education (presumably because of their love of children), vote morally (referring in a vague way to their attitude toward prostitution) and voted for [Woodrow] Wilson rather than [Charles Evans] Hughes (because the West voted for Wilson)"[47]—certainly proliferated in the public imagination. McConnaughy argues, however, that "real *political* essentialism of the category 'women'" did not exist among policy makers of the time. William Ogburn and Inez Goltra supported this claim in 1919, describing such gendered voting predictions as "speculation," for which "no evidence . . . has been adduced."[48] McConnaughy points out the irony of how both the common attitudes toward gender roles held by male politicians of the time (male dominance and women's subservience) *as well as* the feminist arguments of woman suffrage activists effectively made strategic enfranchisement an impossibility for women seeking the right to vote. Male politicians saw women as doubling the existing vote by only voting in line with their husbands or fathers (often referred to as the "family vote"). Therefore, no one political party had any more to gain or lose by enfranchising women. Suffrage activists, however, emphasized factors other than gender that would influence how women voted. In doing so, "their implication for the expectation of the partisan outcome of women's voting behavior was essentially the same: women promised no new voting bloc on account of their sex."[49]

Because strategic enfranchisement depends upon a cohesive voting bloc, which could not be identified in the case of woman suffrage, McConnaughy asserts that the success of the movement came about instead through programmatic enfranchisement, the extension of suffrage as an "accommodation of the interests of existing voters in these new voting rights."[50] In other words, "where and when voting rights for women were actually delivered, it was through the coalitional politics of the programmatic enfranchisement model."[51] In order for it to work, politicians needed to be electorally beholden to organized constituent groups, specifically groups engaged in the suffrage cause.[52] Key to this strategy is the existence of both political partners skilled at movement work, *and* overlapping interests and social networks between suffrage activists and interest groups with electoral power or leverage.

In practice, this played out within the woman suffrage movement in a number of ways. Third parties were key in the eyes of McConnaughy due to their unique applicability to the programmatic enfranchisement model specifically, and other scholars also credit their contributions. Third parties not only increased political competition, an important motivating factor for policy makers, but they also offered "an unmatched level of certainty about the electoral cost of failing to meet the demand of its electoral constituents."[53] McConnaughy focuses on the motivations and actions of policymakers that made woman suffrage possible and, perhaps as a result, does not significantly touch upon the way in which dominant understandings of women's role in society, particularly in relation to the home, factored into the suffrage movement.

Aileen S. Kraditor's *The Ideas of the Woman Suffrage Movement,* in contrast, primarily considers the dialogue between suffrage activists and anti-suffragists to better understand how women engaged with the question of suffrage articulated their understandings of the home and the family. Kraditor posits that a foundational component of the anti-suffragist movement was the argument that the enfranchisement of women would "contradict the inherent nature of woman and destroy the home."[54] Exactly how "the home" and even "woman" were to be defined became one of the main points of friction between those in favor of and those opposed to woman suffrage.

Beginning in the 1890s, Kraditor traces a shift within suffragist arguments toward emphasizing, rather than brushing aside, differences between men and women. Suffragists began to highlight key differences between men and women in both the private and public spheres that could be used to make the case that women's participation in politics would be beneficial to the country as a whole. For example, they argued that the woman's role in the home, where her chief duty was to bear children and care for them, naturally endowed her with a superior capacity to love, serve, and promote peace, qualities "sorely needed in government."[55] In the public domain, women were, "whether inherently or by training," the more moral, temperate, and law-abiding half of the population and could bring these qualities to the electorate. This shift can be considered a return to the strategic enfranchisement strategy.[56]

It was difficult for many to reconcile the suffragist movement's invocation of motherhood as the primary function of women with its equally strong argument that women possessed inherent strength and independence, particularly because contemporary dominant beliefs about motherhood were strongly linked to a state of dependence.[57] Woman suffrage activists also argued with regard to the home and family that the political status of men and women did not accurately reflect their respective economic statuses with the home.[58] Wives did *not* depend on their husbands, they argued. In fact, it was because of the woman's ability to transform the money that her husband brought home into food, clothing, and a comfortable home that the family could subsist on the husband's income. In other words, neither husband nor wife depended on one another—suffragists saw men and women as instead taking part in an equal distribution of labor within the home, and argued that therefore this equality must be reflected in the public, political status afforded to the genders.

In *The Rise of Public Woman: Woman's Power and Woman's Place in the United States, 1630-1970*, Glenna Matthews explores how "public womanhood" both contributed to, and was further developed by, the woman suffrage movement. For example, Matthews takes a historical analytical approach to understanding the construction of private and public womanhood during the Gilded Age, and argues that nineteenth-century woman's culture, especially its strong emphasis on "service" by women, limited the possibility of public womanhood. "Women needed to be able to conceive of themselves as having interests as well as duties," Matthews writes, in order to be able to advocate actively for access to higher education and a full range of employment opportunities.[59] The growth of a class of independent wage earners during the Gilded Age, as more women began to seek employment outside the home, laid the groundwork necessary for women's successes during the twentieth century, including enfranchisement.

Matthews articulates two ways in which the success of the suffrage movement positively contributed to public womanhood. For one, during the movement itself, women began to take to the streets in unprecedented numbers, participating in movement parades and demonstrations as well as putting on plays, pageants, and tableaux.[60] "In short, there had never been a time in American history when so many women had participated in ritualized public behavior, especially public behavior designed to advance female self-interest."[61] Women also began to participate in politicking in a bolder and more forceful manner than previously. Carrie Chapman Catt, for example, went so far as to lobby Woodrow Wilson personally for advice and support.[62]

Woman Suffrage and the American Congress

Women and the state. As is clear from the summary above, scholars studying woman suffrage in the United States focus on a wide range of explanations for why women finally achieved a constitutional guarantee in the early decades of the twentieth century that prohibited the use of sex as a criterion for voting. Most analyses, however, focus on how advocates or opponents of woman suffrage depicted women as individuals who are the same as or different from men, and how women's roles in the private sphere of the family as an institution affected the public's perception of women's suitability as political participants in the public sphere of the state. Missing from these perspectives, however, is attention to how the identity of the state itself changed in the Progressive Era to include attributes that made the liberal state similar to a family and how this transformation of the liberal state intersected with women's identities as both equal to and maternally different from men.

The Progressive Era is a remarkable period in the history of American political development because for the first time, at both the state and national levels, legislative branches of government attempted to protect people suffering from the consequences of unregulated industrial capitalism. State legislatures passed bills regulating the hours of work, mothers' pensions, child labor restrictions, vocational education opportunities, and other safeguards for the vulnerable in society. At the national level, Congress passed similar legislation, including bills permitting workers to organize into unions. All this was accomplished in a context void of an economic emergency or a war. Rather, it was recognition by the public and political elites, as Robert Fogel puts it, that people were suffering from maladies outside their own control, needing government assistance to deal with multifaceted problems. Thus, as Fogel notes, it is in the Progressive Era that the word "poverty" came to replace "pauperism," signifying recognition that economic distress was a systemic condition requiring the resources and authority of government to address.[63]

In the United States, members of Congress accepted arguments that women were equal to men and at the same time maternally different from them, while supporting the view that the family was a site of women's contributions to society and to the state. However, an additional argument stands out, namely, the argument that the liberal American state is also like a family. This argument is astounding. It defies John Locke's and other liberal theorists' analysis that the family is a feudal institution ruled according to a principle of parental authority while the state is a liberal institution ruled according to a principle of political authority. Yet it is precisely this new conception of the liberal state as also embodying a familial component, defined by the responsibility of the government to provide care work to those in need, that was used by members of Congress who supported women's political citizenship.

As historian Nancy Cott avows, by the 1910s the male and female reformers were working to establish new government policies for the "regulation of housing, factory conditions, and community health and safety," facilitating suffragists' arguments that "modern conditions bridged the chasm between the realm of politics and woman's conventional realm of the home." Consequently, the mid-nineteenth-century fear that female enfranchisement would profoundly threaten the home gave way to the contention in the Progressive Era that there was a "need as well as the right to vote in order to ensure domestic welfare . . . [as] part of women's duties as wives, mothers, and community members."[64]

We can follow how this happens during the Progressive Era by looking at arguments that members of Congress advanced, either against or supportive of women's suffrage. Specifically, I am interested in the relationship between the depiction of women as individuals who are the same as or maternally different from men in relation to the depiction of the American state as a liberal institution, a familial institution, or both.

Coding the Congressional Record. With research assistants, I analyzed a digital version of the *Congressional Record* for the Twenty-Ninth to the Sixty-Sixth Congresses (1846 to 1919). I searched for words related to the family (family, home, mother, father, child, household), the state (state, welfare provision, protective labor legislation, child labor, unions, education, states' rights), and woman suffrage (woman suffrage, women's suffrage, women's rights, right to vote). I coded 1849 arguments asserted by members of Congress in this designated time period related to the family, the state, and woman suffrage.

I also coded the party affiliation of members, whether they were in the House or Senate, the congressional session, their state affiliation, the type of argument they advanced, and whether the argument was used to support or oppose a national constitutional amendment prohibiting the use of sex as a criterion for voting rights. Legislation barring the use of sex as a qualification for voting rights passed the House and Senate in 1919 to become the Nineteenth Amendment to the US Constitution.[65]

In so doing, I identified sixty frames that constituted arguments for why women should or should not have the right to vote, including frames such as the home is like slavery, or women are captured in the home; sarcastic comments, such as that women voting is laughable; racial arguments, such as if we were to enfranchise women, that would include African American women, which some argued would be a disaster; dismissive comments that woman suffrage is a fad, and it will blow over; and religious arguments citing Scripture as evidence for or against woman suffrage.[66] I have omitted arguments that are sarcastic, racially oriented, and in other ways outside the scope of arguments about women's identities as individuals who are equal to or maternally different from men and about the state's identity as a welfare institution similar to a family. The result is four major frames:

1. The Liberal Individual Frame: Equal Individuals. Men and women are equal individuals and equally deserve the right to vote.

   An example of this frame is the statement: "My position in reference [to equal suffrage] has been, and I think always will be, that the question is not whether any particular benefit will result from the establishment of woman suffrage, but whether one-half of the citizens of the United States are not, as a matter of rights . . . entitled to the franchise with the other half of the citizenship."[67]

2. The Maternal Individual Frame: Maternally Different Individuals. Men and women are different individuals on the grounds of women's maternal identities as mothers and wives. Women contribute

to the public sphere of the state by rearing children to be good citizens.

An example of this frame is the statement: "I regard the home as the realm over which woman is best fitted to reign. I think motherhood the supreme function of woman. In that realm and the performance of that function she does her greatest work, because her influence there begins with infancy and ends only in eternity. If you will give me the influence of mothers, I will write the laws of the land, I will preserve our institutions in all their pristine vigor, and I will transmit them unimpaired in their usefulness to posterity."[68]

3. The Maternal Liberal State Frame. Women cannot be good mothers without the state's assistance in the form of benefits, such as mothers' pensions, educational programs, and labor legislation that protect women from working excessively long hours.

An example of this frame is the statement: "It has been strenuously contended that woman's place is in the home. Yes; we may all agree to that generous sentiment . . . [but the] law vitally affect[s] the woman's home and her happiness and her children and her health and her protection from crime . . . [so] the law and its administration become of vital concern to her when in its hand is the safety, the health, and the welfare of her home."[69]

4. The Familial Liberal State Frame. The American liberal state is based on a principle of equal individuals, but it is also similar to a family because government is or should be responsible for providing to people what they need.

An example of this frame is the statement: "In the evolution of government, the State has been gradually taking onto itself . . . the care and education of the child and the preservation of the purity of the home. Therefore, it is [appropriate] that the woman of today is demanding a voice and a place in the political household."[70]

As is apparent, the Liberal Individual Frame and the Maternal Individual Frame focus on the identity of women as individuals who are either the same or maternally different from men, respectively. And two frames, the Maternal Liberal State and the Familial Liberal State, focus on the identity of the American liberal state as *also* being a welfare-based institution responsible for providing care to those in need, and thus analogous to the family as an institution.[71]

Table 6.1 Frames over Historical Time, US Congress

Frames	Post–Civil War Reconstruction Era	Progressive Era	Total
	Women as Individuals: Equal/Different		
Liberal Individual Frame: Women are the same as men.	47.2% (42)	55.2% (689)	54.6% (731)
Maternal Individual Frame: Women are different from men.	36.0% (32)	19.5% (243)	20.6% (275)
	Liberal State as a Welfare State		
Maternal Liberal State Frame: Subverted Maternalism	3.4% (3)	3.9% (49)	3.9% (52)
Familial Liberal State Frame: Subverted Liberalism	13.5% (12)	21.5% (268)	20.9% (280)
Total	6.7% (89)	93.3% (1,249)	100.0% (1,338)

Note: Numbers in parentheses refer to number of arguments asserted by members of Congress; percentages may not add up exactly to 100 percent due to rounding.

Frame usage over time. The Liberal Individual Frame that defines women's identities as individuals who are the same as men is the dominant frame in both the post–Civil War Reconstruction Era and the Progressive Era, as reported in Table 6.1. However, contrary to what we might expect based on Kraditor's analysis, this frame is used more often in the Progressive Era. As we can see from Table 6.1, over half the statements offered by members of Congress rely on this argument. What is interesting is that the Familial Liberal State Frame dramatically increases, from 13.5 percent in the post–Civil War era to 21.5 percent in the Progressive Era. So, in the Progressive Era, it was not so much that members of Congress were arguing that women were maternally different from men as individuals as it was that they were arguing that the liberal state is similar to a family.

Women as individuals and suffrage support. When we consider how frames about women's identities as individuals who are the same as or different from men link to support or opposition to woman suffrage, we see overwhelming evidence, as reported in Table 6.2, that liberal argu-

Table 6.2 US Congress: Support for Woman Suffrage by Time Period and Argument Frames

Frames		Woman Suffrage	Post–Civil War Reconstruction Era	Progressive Era	Total
Women as Individuals: Equal to/Different from Men					
Liberal Individual Frame	Yes		100.0% (40)	100.0% (683)	100.0% (723)
	No		—	—	—
Maternal Individual Frame	Yes		3.3% (1)	6.3% (14)	6.0% (15)
	No		96.7% (29)	93.7% (208)	94.0% (237)
The Liberal State as Maternal/Familial					
Maternal Liberal State Frame	Yes		100.0% (3)	100.0% (49)	100.0% (52)
	No		—	—	—
Familial Liberal State Frame	Yes		100.0% (7)	100.0% (266)	100.0% (273)
	No		—	—	—
Total			6.2% (80)	93.8% (1,220)	100.0% (1,300)

Note: Numbers in parentheses refer to number of arguments asserted by members of Congress; percentages may not add up exactly to 100 percent due to rounding.

ments that women are the same as men increase support for women's right to vote. No member of Congress who argues that women are the same as men in either the post–Civil War or Progressive Eras was opposed to woman suffrage. However, when we turn to the Maternal Individual Frame, based on the assumption that women are maternally different from men, we see the opposite effect. Namely, members of Congress who viewed women as maternally different from men were almost 100 percent opposed to woman suffrage in both the post–Civil War and Progressive Eras, as reported in Table 6.2.

The state as a family and suffrage support. Equally significant, arguments that the American liberal state is also a welfare state similar to the family as an institution were 100 percent connected to arguments supportive of woman suffrage in both the post–Civil War and Progressive Eras, and in both the Maternal Liberal State Frame and the Familial Liberal State Frame, as noted in Table 6.2. Here we have evidence, therefore, that it is not simply women's identities as liberal individuals who are the same as men that promote women's political citizenship as voters, but also the view of political elites in Congress who see the liberal state as constituting a welfare state similar to the family. This view turns Locke upside down. Rather than the family and the state being ruled on opposite principles, the family and the familial liberal state are ruled on the same parental principle, namely, that institutional rulers (parents and the government, respectively) have a responsibility to provide care to those in need.

Additional influences. Additional influences associated with support or opposition to woman suffrage are political parties and regions of the country.[72] Republicans are more associated with support for women suffrage than are Democrats, and the West is associated with more support for woman suffrage than are other regions of the country.[73] Party identification in this period in Congress includes not only Democrats and Republicans but also the Progressive Party, Free Soil, Independent Party, Socialist Party, Whigs, States' Rights, and Unionist Party. However, Democrats and Republicans make up 94 percent of the party membership during this time, and I limit the analysis of parties to these two.

When we consider the relative importance of the type of frame used to support woman suffrage compared to the impact of party and region, as in Table 6.3, we see that particular frames matter. The Liberal Individual Frame and the Familial Liberal State Frame have positive impacts on woman suffrage support, as indicated by the unstandardized regression coefficients of .349 and .313, respectively. However, the Maternal Individual Frame has a negative impact on support for women's voting rights.

It is no surprise that being a Democrat has a negative influence on support for woman suffrage, as does being a member of Congress from the East or the South, as indicated in Table 6.3 by unstandardized regression coefficients of −.041, −.143, and −.148, respectively. Also not surprising, being a member of Congress from the West indicates support for women's voting rights. What is significant about the findings reported in Table 6.3, however, is the way in which arguments about the Familial Liberal State overshadow the traditional characteristics thought to explain support for women's rights: party and region. The most powerful source of negative influence on support for woman suffrage is the Maternal Individual Frame, with an unstandardized regression coeffi-

Table 6.3 US Congress: Support for Woman Suffrage by Frames, Parties, and Regions, 1866–1919

Frames, Parties, and Regions	Support for Woman Suffrage
Frames	
Liberal Individual Frame	.349 (.405)***
Maternal Individual Frame	−.472 (−.397)***
Familial Liberal State Frame	.313 (.272)***
Party	
Democrat	−.041 (−.047)***
Region	
West	.074 (.086)***
East	−.143 (−.118)***
South	−.148 (−.157)***
Constant	1.684***
Adjusted R Square	.677

*** $p \leq .001$.

Notes: Unstandardized regression coefficients with standardized regression coefficients in parentheses; omitted dummy variables are: Maternal Liberal State, Republican, and Midwest; constant includes the influence of those variables.

cient of −.472. Equally noteworthy, however, is the non-Lockean finding that the Liberal Individual Frame and the Familial Liberal State Frame are both stronger positive influences for generating support for woman suffrage than is being from the West.

Combining frames. Of course, members of Congress often use combinations of frames to argue for or against woman suffrage. These combinations are important because they reflect how political elites, if not the public as well, view women as being equal to or maternally different from men, and how that meshes with their views about the liberal American state—whether it is also a familial state, that is, a welfare state. Clearly, it is the individual frame that is most asserted by members of Congress. Namely, 68 percent of congressional assertions are that women are individuals equal to men, 6 percent claim women are maternally different from men, and 26 percent avow that women are both equal to men and maternally different from men, as reported in Table 6.4. What is striking, however, is that the vast majority of congressional statements, 78 percent, *combine* the view of women's equality with men with views of the state as similar to a family, as reported in Table 6.4. This is an important finding because it underscores that to promote women's

Table 6.4 US Congress: Frames and Combinations of Frames Referenced in Support of Woman Suffrage, 1866–1919

	Equal Individual Frame: Men and women are equal individuals.	Maternal Individual Frame: Women are maternally different from men.	Equal Individual Frame and Maternal Individual Frame: Women are both equal to and maternally different from men.	Total
Liberal State Frame	21% (183)	13% (10)	—	15% (193)
Familial Liberal (Welfare) State Frame	79% (669)	87% (68)	100% (318)	85% (1005)
Percent of Total	68% (852)	6% (78)	26% (318)	100% (1,198)

Note: When there is no argument asserted about the form of the state, Liberal State is the default; numbers in parentheses refer to number of arguments asserted by members of Congress; percentages may not add up exactly to 100 percent due to rounding.

political citizenship, political elites did not rely on the premise of liberal individualism alone. Rather, they combined that liberal premise with a view antithetical to liberal theory and practice, namely, that the liberal state incorporates a familial governing principle, thereby rejecting separate spheres ideology.

When we consider the frame that women are maternally different from men as individuals, we find that it is also used most often in conjunction with a familial view of the liberal state, 87 percent, which is not surprising, perhaps. Equally important, however, is the finding that members of Congress articulating the view that women are both equal to men and are maternally different from them always, 100 percent of the time, combined this dual view of women with a view of the state that also had a dual identity as being both liberal and familial, that is, as being a liberal welfare state, as reported in Table 6.4.

We find evidence, therefore, that members of Congress did more than argue about women as individuals in relation to woman suffrage. They did, of course, advance arguments that women were equal to men and that women were maternally different from men. What is astounding, however, is the way in which members of Congress combined both versions of women's identities as individuals and as maternally different with arguments that the liberal state is also like a family. Either the state must provide benefits to those in need, such as education, housing, and workers' protection, in order for women to be good mothers in the family (Maternal Liberal State), or the state must do so because it is responsible for the welfare of the people (Familial Liberal State).

It is apparent, therefore, that the key to arguments about women's political citizenship is not based on their individual identities or on making the family into a liberal institution congruent with a liberal state. Rather, to achieve congruence between the family and the liberal state requires modifying the liberal state to include familial responsibilities.

Conclusion

Separate Spheres: A new flaw. Gordon Wood emphasizes that, of course, there were serious flaws at the founding of the American state, but no "new" flaws.[74] Slavery as an institution had been present virtually since the beginning of recorded history, and at the time of the American founding, slavery was present around the world. So as egregious as slavery was, as an institution, it was nothing new. What is more, the use of property qualifications for determining political inclusion, such as voting rights, which virtually every state initially did in 1789, was not a policy invented by American founders but was common to most political systems prior to the founding of the American state. Similarly, coverture marriage was inherited from English common law rather than invented by Americans.

What Wood does credit as new and radical, however, in the founding of the American state, was the shift from a feudal monarchy based on ascriptive status to a liberal republic based on consensual contract. Yes, the American state was elitist, but it was no longer aristocratic. No one could have titles of nobility or other forms of inherited ascriptive status that conveyed more access to political rule to some people than others. This anti-aristocratic principle was incorporated into the Constitution in Article I, Section 9.[75] The liberal state's promise is that it will open up more political access to more people, even if it takes centuries to correct founding flaws that initially exclude people because of their ascriptive characteristics.

When we turn to women's political rights, however, there is a completely opposite pattern—the American state, in fact, was a *regressive* new nation. In the monarchical state from which the American founders rebelled, women in the dynastic family had access to political rule as queens, duchesses, and countesses and in other family-based political institutions. Yes, men were preferred as political rulers, but women were not excluded because of an ascriptive characteristic, their sex. Rather, sex was only one of many attributes considered relevant for political rulership. Age, soundness of mind, family heritage, and religion were more important than a person's sex.[76]

Women not only failed to share in the political expansion of voting rights for working-class white men and newly freed African American men, but women's political rights regressed at every period of reform marking the expansion of political rights for men. Prior to the twentieth century, every reform period that marks the progressive inclusion of men discriminated against on the basis of their class or race, marks the regression of women's political rights. At the founding of the country, for example, women came from a monarchical heritage where some women could be queens, but by 1808, every state prohibited all women from voting solely because they were female, and until 1920, no woman had a federal guarantee of voting equivalent to the Fifteenth Amendment's guarantee with regard to race, which was added to the Constitution in the aftermath of the Civil War. What is more, with the passage of the Fourteenth Amendment, the word "male" was added to the Constitution to make it clear that the guarantees in place for race would not be applied to women.[77]

The problem was not that reformers failed to argue that women were equal to men, much as reformers had argued that people are equal in spite of racial differences or economic differences. Rather, the problem was separate spheres ideology. It located women solely in the feudal family, an institution based on maternal identity, in a private sphere separated from and founded on principles opposite to those of the liberal state located in the public sphere. It was not until the Progressive Era in the United States that the liberal state was reformed to be more like a family. The new congruence between the feudal family and the liberal state now located women's maternal identities in both the family and the state as an important condition for promoting women's political inclusion.

Sex versus pregnancy/motherhood. Analyzing women's political incorporation in the context of the relationship between the family and the state illuminates new contours of APD. This analysis identifies not only belated elements of feudal institutions but also the family as an institution of intractable feudalism. It highlights that it is not merely the challenge of establishing that all individuals are equal in spite of their ascriptive identities that promotes political inclusion, but also how those identities intersect with institutions. A problem, however, is that many feminists and others fail to make a distinction between how women's sexual identities traditionally intersect with the institution of marriage while their pregnancy identities intersect with the institution of the family. Women's sexual identities specifically connect them in relationships with *born people,* whether it be men, women, transgender people, or others, and whether or not women's sexual activities are institutionalized as a marriage.

Women's pregnancy (biological maternal) identities, however, connect them with *unborn "potential life"/unborn "people"*—that is, fertilized ova, embryos, and fetuses.[78] In order to become pregnant, of course, male sperm first must be placed in a proximate location to female ova, by means of sexual intercourse, in vitro fertilization, or artificial insemination, and, second, a fertilized ovum must implant itself in a woman's uterus. However, once pregnant, women's biological maternal identities no longer directly connect them with born people, including even the biological father. Rather, a pregnancy relationship directly connects women as mothers only with unborn entities.

In contemporary times in the United States, courts recognize that women's maternal identities when pregnant are independent from any relationship with a born man, even if that man is the woman's spouse and/or the biological father of her unborn entity.[79] Rather, when pregnant, the woman has the sole right to decide whether to continue a pregnancy or not, that is, whether to continue a relationship with unborn life.[80] Why is this important? Because when people argue about the family, feminists often talk about the relative authority of the father and mother in relation to each other and in relation to their relative authority over children in a family, particularly when these relationships are structured on patriarchal principles. However, social and political relationships within the family are dependent upon an initial pregnancy relationship between women and unborn "potential life"/unborn "people," without which a family cannot come into being in the first place.

Marriage (sex) versus family (pregnancy/motherhood). Too often, however, feminist critics of the liberal state conflate marriage (a relationship between adults) and the family (a relationship between parents and children that originates with women's pregnancy relationship with unborn life). Carole Pateman, for example, is well known for identifying the sexual contract as the basis for the liberal state and women's oppression in that state. She argues that men and women have unequal relationships in terms of the sexual contract that becomes the marriage contract.[81] However, marriage as an institution can be reformed to constitute an equal relationship between married partners, thereby making the sexual contract an equal contract between partners.

The same is not true, however, for the family as an institution, defined by the relationship between parents and children in general and pregnant mothers in relation to unborn life in particular. There can be no pregnancy contract as a complement to a sexual contract because there can be no pregnancy contract between a woman and a fertilized ovum in the first place. It is not, therefore, patriarchy as an unequal sexual contract that stands in the way of women's political incorporation into the liberal state. Rather, it is the impossibility of a pregnancy contract in the feudal family that prompts the invention of the liberal solution of separate spheres ideology.

Others argue, however, that there is nothing in liberalism that disadvantages women because women can be equal to men. That is true, but individualism, like patriarchy, is not the problem. The problem is that liberal theory and practice separate the family and the state, a separation that strands women and their maternal identities in the private sphere of the feudal family, defined as opposite in principle to the liberal state. The result of separate spheres ideology is to identify women in terms of their maternal identities as being in the private sphere of the home, but not in the public sphere of the state, thereby depressing women's access to political rule.

Motherhood and the state. Liberal principles of individualism, therefore, are *not* the sole solution for advancing women's political citizenship. And maternal identities *alone* are not the problem that blocks women's political citizenship. Rather, it is the relationship between the family and the state that crucially affects women's political citizenship. Specifically, women's political inclusion expands in a state where the public and political elites view the family and the state as similar, if not analogous, institutions, such that both are associated with care work. When the family and the state merge as institutions, women's maternal identities then locate them not only in the family, but also in the state, which bolsters women's access to political rule as voters and as office-holders.[82]

Prior to the invention of the liberal state, it was the norm for centuries in European monarchies to view the family and the state as analogous institutions. Of course, it was radical to declare that all individuals are equal in spite of their ascriptive differences. However, from the point of view of political development, it was also radical—after centuries of fusion—to declare that the family and the state are opposite institutions. And it is this latter feature of liberalism that affects women's acquisition of political citizenship, as is illustrated by this study of woman suffrage in the United States.

In the contest between separate spheres versus woman suffrage, therefore, the key for promoting women's political inclusion rests not only on the question of whether men and women are equal or different as individuals. It also rests on the question of whether the family and the state are modeled on congruent or incongruent principles as institutions.

Notes

The author thanks Linda McClain, Carol Nackenoff, Julie Novkov, Ruth O'Brien, Karen Orren, and Patricia Strach for their crucial advice and critiques. For their superb research assistance, the author thanks Alla Baranovsky, Eriko Kay, Katherine Rose, and Sparsha Saha.

1. *The Oxford English Dictionary* (Oxford: Oxford University Press, 2019) defines the word "feudal" as a "system of polity which prevailed in Europe during the Middle Ages, and which was based on the relation of superior and vassal arising out of the holding of lands in feud." It defines the word "feudally" as "in a feudal manner or spirit." It defines the word "feudalism" as the "feudal system, *or its principles*" (emphasis added). My use of these words refers to principles that govern unequal relationships based on ascriptive hierarchies.

2. Peter H. Schuck and Rogers M. Smith, *Citizenship without Consent: Illegal Aliens in the American Policy* (New Haven, CT: Yale University Press, 1985), 42; James Kettner, *The Development of American Citizenship, 1608–1870* (Chapel Hill: University of North Carolina Press, 1978).

3. Rogers M. Smith, *Civic Ideals: Conflicting Visions of Citizenship in U.S. History* (New Haven, CT: Yale University Press, 1997), 120.

4. Gordon G. Wood, *The Radicalism of the American Revolution* (New York: Knopf Doubleday, 1993), 7–8.

5. Slavery might not be considered a feudal institution inherited from England at the time of the founding of the American state because England had banned serfdom in the 1600s. However, slavery is based on the feudal principles of hierarchical inequality and relationships based on coercion rather than consent.

6. Karen Orren, *Belated Feudalism: Labor, the Law, and Liberal Development in the United States* (Cambridge: Cambridge University Press, 1991).

7. Locke asserted that children tacitly consented to be born, but provided no evidence to support that claim. See Locke, "Of Paternal Power," *Second Treatise*, chap. 6, http://www.let.rug.nl/usa/documents/1651-1700/john-locke-essay-on-government/chapter-6-of-paternal-power.php.

8. Eileen McDonagh, "Ripples from the First Wave: The Monarchical Origins of the Welfare State," *Perspectives on Politics* 13, no. 4 (December 2015): 992–1016.

9. James I, for example, viewed a king "as a loving father and careful watchman, caring for them [the people] more than for himself . . . [and] his fatherly duty is bound to care for the nourishing, education, and virtutous gouervnment of his children . . . As a kindly father [he] ought to foresee all inconuenients and dangers that may arise towards his children . . . so ought the King towards his people . . . as the Fathers [*sic*] chief joy ought to be in procuring his children's welfare . . . so ought a good prince think of his people . . . for a King is trewly *Parens Patriae*, the politique father of his people." Johann P. Sommerville, ed., *King James VI and I: Political Writings* (Cambridge: Cambridge University Press, 1995), 65, 181, 195.

10. Dutch Declaration of Independence, 1581, https://sourcebooks.fordham.edu/mod/1581dutch.asp.

11. Seyla Benhabib, "The Generalised and the Concrete Other: The Kohlberg-Gilligan Controversy and Moral Theory," *Women and Moral Theory*, ed. E. F. Kittay and D. T. Meyers (Totowa, NJ: Rowman and Littlefield, 1987), 160. This is not to say, however, that the family in the form of politicized kinship groups is excluded from the state. To the contrary, even in countries with the most liberal of historical legacies, such as the United States, kinship groups are often entrenched in politics and in the election to political office, as is evident with the Kennedy and Bush "dynasties." And some scholars, such as Julia Adams, attribute the very building of state capacity to kinship networks, as she argues was the case in the Netherlands in the seventeenth century; see Adams, *The Familial State: Ruling Families and Merchant Capitalism in Early Modern Europe* (Ithaca, NY: Cornell University Press, 2007). However, this research distinguishes a familial

state defined in terms of how kinship networks interact with political rulers from a familial state defined as a form of government in which political rulers have a responsibility to attend to people's basic needs for food, shelter, education, health care, etc., as do parents in a family. The latter is what many would term a welfare state.

12. Catharine A. MacKinnon, *Toward a Feminist Theory of the State* (Cambridge, MA: Harvard University Press, 1989); Barbara Garlick, Suzanne Dixon, and Pauline Allen, eds., *Stereotypes of Women in Power: Historical Perspectives and Revisionist Views* (New York: Greenwood Press, 1992).

13. Desmond King et al., eds., *Democratization in America: A Comparative-Historical Analysis* (Baltimore, MD: John Hopkins University Press, 2009).

14. Richard Valelly, Suzanne Mettler, and Robert Lieberman, eds., *The Oxford Handbook of American Political Development* (Oxford: Oxford University Press, 2016).

15. Linda C. McClain, "The Family, the State, and American Political Development as a Big Tent: Asking Basic Questions about Basic Institutions," *Polity*, 48, no. 2 (April 2016): 224–242; Susan Burgess, "Introduction: Family, State, and Difference in Political Time," *Polity* 48, no. 2 (April 2016): 140–145.

16. Some APD scholars define the family as an institution, an organization, and a status defined by the state; see Patricia Strach, "The Family," in *The Oxford Handbook of American Political Development*, ed. Richard Valelly, Suzanne Mettler, and Robert Lieberman (Oxford: Oxford University Press, 2016), 707.

17. Carol Nackenoff, "Borrowing and Building State Capacity: The Immigrants' Protective League's Friendly and Sympathetic Touch, 1908–1924," *Studies in American Political Development* 28, no. 2 (2014): 129–160.

18. Larry M. Bartels, *Unequal Democracy: The Political Economy of the New Gilded Age* (New York: Russell Sage, 2008); Jacqueline Stevens, *States without Nations: Citizenship for Mortals* (New York: Columbia University Press, 2010), paraphrased from Strach, "The Family," 707.

19. Peggy Pascoe, "Miscegenation Law, Court Cases, and Ideologies of 'Race' in Twentieth-Century America," *Journal of American History* 83, no. 1 (June 1996): 44–69.

20. Strach, "The Family," 708.

21. Alison Gash and Priscilla Yamin, "State, Status, and the American Family," *Polity* 48, no. 2 (2016): 147.

22. Gordon J. Schochet, "Thomas Hobbes on the Family and the State of Nature," *Political Science Quarterly* 82, no. 3 (September 1967): 427–445.

23. Ewen Callaway, "Oldest *Homo sapiens* Fossil Claim Rewrites Our Species' History," *Nature*, June 8, 2017, https://www.nature.com/news/oldest-homo-sapiens-fossil-claim-rewrites-our-species-history-1.22114.

24. Gash and Yamin, "State, Status, and the American Family," 147.

25. M. Rowland and R. Gatward, "Family Resources Survey: Annual Techni-

cal Report," (2001–2002), Prepared for the Department for Work and Pensions, Office for National Statistics, London. A household is often considered the basic unit of microeconomics and other models of social and governmental analysis; see Arthur O. Sullivan and Steven M. Sheffrin, *Economics: Principles in Action* (Upper Saddle River, NJ: Pearson Prentice Hall, 2003).

26. Trevor Watkins, "The Origins of House and Home?" *World Archaeology* 21, no. 3 (1990): 336–347; Michael Dorris, "Home," *The Threepenny Review*, no. 54 (Summer 1993): 16–17.

27. In this period, major changes occurred, such as the shift from hunter-gatherer practices to farming, which then spurred the development of villages, towns, and the settlements of diverse groups. See Juan José Ibáñez et al., "The Emergence of the Neolithic in the Near East: A Protracted and Multi-regional Model," *Quaternary International* 470, Part B (2018): 266–252.

28. Watkins, "The Origins," 1990.

29. Watkins, 337.

30. Watkins.

31. Ian Hodder and Craig Cessford, "Daily Practice and Social Memory at Çatalhöyük," *American Antiquity* 69, no. 1 (2004): 17–40.

32. Watkins, "The Origins."

33. Watkins.

34. For example, one of the runners-up for the Oxford Dictionaries' 2016 "word of the year" was "hygge," a Danish word referring to a quality or feeling of coziness, contentment, charm, or well-being that can stem from time spent with friends and family, but especially from the "home." See Anna Altman, "The Year of Hygge: The Danish Obsession with Getting Cozy," *New Yorker*, December 18, 2016, https://www.newyorker.com/culture/culture-desk/the-year-of-hygge-the-danish-obsession-with-getting-cozy (accessed June 1, 2017).

35. Lastly, the evidence at Qermez Dere suggests that when these houses were abandoned, six weathered human crania were placed on the floor of the last house as it was purposefully demolished or closed; see Watkins, "The Origins." This arguably further demonstrates a measure to claim, or to imbue the houses with, a memory or connection to a specific familial line or kinship.

36. Ange-Marie Hancock, *Intersectionality: An Intellectual History* (New York: Oxford University Press, 2016).

37. Julie Novkov, "Identity and Law in American Political Development," in *The Oxford Handbook of American Political Development*, ed. Richard Valelly, Suzanne Mettler, and Robert Lieberman (Oxford: Oxford University Press, 2016), 1.

38. No amount of sexual activity per se produces a child. Rather, the family, defined as the relationship between parents and children, originates only on the basis of women's maternal capacity to become pregnant and to give birth.

39. Corrine M. McConnaughy, *The Woman Suffrage Movement in America: A Reassessment* (New York: Cambridge University Press, 2013), 5.

40. Holly J. McCammon and Karen E. Campbell, "Winning the Vote in the West: The Political Successes of the Women's Suffrage Movements, 1866-1919," *Gender and Society* 15, no. 1 (February 2001): 55–82.

41. Steven M. Buechler, "Elizabeth Boynton Harbert and the Woman Suffrage Movement, 1870–1896," *Signs* 13, no. 1 (Autumn 1987): 78–97.

42. McConnaughy, *The Woman Suffrage Movement*, 6.

43. McConnaughy, 6. Others, however, emphasize that woman suffragists also dropped principled arguments about equality by using racist and anti-immigration language to bolster their arguments for women's right to vote. Rosalyn Treborg Penn, *African American Women in the Struggle for the Vote, 1850–1920* (Bloomington: Indiana University Press, 1998).

44. McConnaughy, *The Woman Suffrage Movement*, 7.

45. McConnaughy, 7.

46. McConnaughy, 5.

47. William F. Ogburn and Inez Goltra, "How Women Vote," *Political Science Quarterly* 69, no. 1 (September 1919): 413–433, 413. For a recent and cross-national analysis of the partisan foundation of campaigns for women's right to vote, see Dawn Langan Teele, *Forging the Franchise: The Political Origins of the Women's Vote* (Princeton, NJ: Princeton University Press, 2018).

48. Ogburn and Goltra, "How Women Vote," 413.

49. McConnaughy, *The Woman Suffrage Movement*, 11.

50. McConnaughy, 10.

51. McConnaughy, 10.

52. McConnaughy, 12.

53. McConnaughy, 12.

54. Aileen S. Kraditor, *The Ideas of the Woman Suffrage Movement, 1890–1920* (New York: Columbia University Press, 1965), 96.

55. Kraditor, 110.

56. Kraditor, 111.

57. Kraditor, 111–112.

58. Kraditor, 120.

59. Glenna Matthews, *The Rise of Public Woman: Woman's Power and Woman's Place in the United States, 1630–1970* (New York: Oxford University Press, 1992), 156.

60. Matthews, 173.

61. Matthews, 173.

62. Matthews, 174. Recent scholarship focuses on women's voting activities after the Nineteenth Amendment was added to the Constitution; see J. Kevin Corder and Christina Wolbrecht, *Counting Women's Ballots: Female Voters from Suffrage through the New Deal* (New York: Cambridge University Press, 2016).

63. Robert Fogel, "Discussion Comments," *Panel: Culture, History, and Social Theory*, Social Science History Association, 1992.

64. Nancy F. Cott, *The Grounding of Modern Feminism* (New Haven, CT: Yale University Press, 1987).

65. Only a small percentage of such arguments (3.2 percent) come from the pre–Civil War era, so I omit that era from the analysis.

66. The intersection of racism and woman suffrage has a long and complicated history. See Rosalyn Terborg-Penn, *African American Women in the Struggle for the Vote* (Bloomington: Indiana University Press, 1998); Bernadette Cahill, *No Vote for Women: The Denial of Suffrage in Reconstruction America* (Jefferson, NC: McFarland Press, 2019).

67. *Congressional Record*, 63rd Congress, 1913–1914, S5096, statement of Sen. Thomas, Democrat, Colorado.

68. *Congressional Record*, 63rd Congress, 1913–1914, S4338, statement of Sen. Vaardaman, Democrat, Mississippi.

69. *Congressional Record*, 63rd Congress, 1913–1914, S4275, statement by Sen. Owen, Democrat, Oklahoma.

70. *Congressional Record*, 63rd Congress, 1913–1914, S4335, statement by Sen. Works, Republican, California.

71. Some scholars describe the Maternal Liberal State as the "maternalist welfare state" and define it as a set of politics that specifically target women's needs, such as mothers' pensions. See Elisabeth S. Clemens, "Organizational Repertoires and Institutional Change: Women's Groups and the Transformation of U.S. Politics, 1890–1920," *American Journal of Sociology* 98, no. 4 (January 1993): 755–798; Theda Skocpol, *Protecting Soldiers and Mothers: The Political Origins of Social Policy in the United States* (Cambridge, MA: Harvard University Press, 1992).

72. For a cross-national analysis of the influence of political parties for woman suffrage, see Teele, *Forging the Franchise.*

73. For analyses of the impact of regional influences on support for woman suffrage, see Jean H. Baker, ed., *Votes for Women: The Struggle for Suffrage Revisited* (Oxford: Oxford University Press, 2002); Sara Egge, *Woman Suffrage and Citizenship in the Midwest, 1870–1920* (Iowa City: University of Iowa Press, 2018).

74. Gordon S. Wood, *The Creation of the American Republic, 1776–1787* (Chapel Hill: University of North Carolina Press, 1969).

75. "No Title of Nobility shall be granted by the United States: And no Person holding any Office of Profit or Trust under them, shall, without the Consent of the Congress, accept of any present, Emolument, Office, or Title, of any kind whatever, from any King, Prince, or foreign State."

76. Eileen McDonagh, *The Motherless State: American Democracy and Women's Political Leadership* (Chicago: University of Chicago Press, 2009); Eileen McDonagh, "The Family-State Nexus in American Political Development: Explaining Women's Political Citizenship," *Polity* 48, no. 2 (April 2016): 186–204.

77. Eileen McDonagh, "Gender Politics and Political Change," in *New Per-*

spectives on American Politics, ed. Lawrence C. Dodd and Calvin Jillson (Washington, DC: Congressional Quarterly, 1994). If we turn to cross-national patterns, we also see that the United States is in no way a pioneer when it comes to women's political inclusion. While it was the first nation to include unpropertied men in the right to vote, it was the thirty-fifth nation to include any women in the right to vote. In addition, as of 2019, it is not even close to being ranked as one of the top nations to elect women to its national legislature, as are Sweden, Finland, Spain and Norway. Rather, the United States is ranked as the seventy-sixth nation in the world in terms of the percentage of women in its national legislature, thereby tied with Afghanistan and Cabo Verde with 23.6 percent. In addition, although there was an opportunity to do so in 2016, the United States as of 2019 has yet to elect a woman as president, which is in stark contrast to many other industrial democracies that have elected at least one woman to be president or prime minister, such as Canada, Finland, Germany, the United Kingdom, Australia, New Zealand, Iceland, and Norway.

78. In *Roe v. Wade*, the Supreme Court referred to embryos and fetuses as "potential life," though many people view embryos and fetuses as "unborn people."

79. In *Planned Parenthood v. Casey*, in 1992, the Supreme Court struck down as unconstitutional the requirement that a pregnant woman even *inform* her spouse that she was seeking an abortion, much less obtain the consent of her spouse.

80. For an analysis of the distinction between sex and pregnancy in the context of abortion rights, see Eileen McDonagh, "The Next Step after Roe: Using Fundamental Rights, Equal Protection Analysis to Nullify Restrictive State-Level Abortion Legislation," *Emory Law Journal* 56 (2007): 1173.

81. Carole Pateman, *The Sexual Contract* (Stanford, CA: Stanford University Press, 1988).

82. Jeremy Waldron, "'The Mother Too Hath Her Title': John Locke on Motherhood and Equality," New York School of Law, Public Law Research Paper Series (working paper no. 10-74, October 2010, https://papers.ssrn.com/sol3/papers.cfm?abstract_id=1687776.

7 | Building the Administrative State

Courts and the Admission of Chinese Persons to the United States, 1870s–1920s

Carol Nackenoff and Julie Novkov

Introduction

Controversies about which Chinese persons were entitled to enter or remain in the United States between the 1870s and the 1920s highlight a clash between strong sentiment for Chinese exclusion and time-honored state investment in acknowledging and supporting familial ties. The tension between these competing purposes helped open up space within which the courts preserved their authority to oversee and legitimate administrative processes. In the dynamic engagement between courts and emerging institutions of the administrative state, ever-more-restrictive laws still left enough matters unspecified to maintain federal courts' authoritative influence. In the course of addressing these controversies, courts determined how and when to recognize family ties and who had the authority to discern them.

The Chinese, who began arriving in significant numbers in the United States in the mid-nineteenth century to work in the mines, on railroads, and on farms, provoked the first wave of restrictive national immigration legislation after the Supreme Court in 1876 thwarted state-level efforts undertaken on the eve of the Civil War to restrict their entry.[1] When the Court held immigration to be a federal matter, Congress began to restrict immigration, passing the Page Act in 1875 and the Chinese Exclusion Act of 1882, barring the entry of Chinese prostitutes, coolie labor, and, by 1882, all laborers, and denying naturalization to the Chinese generally.[2] Subsequent acts attempted to choke off new

Chinese immigration and expel a number of others from the United States; exclusion would subsequently be extended to Asians from several nations.[3] While Chinese merchants and diplomats who advanced national economic and political interests were tolerated, suspicion and hostility dogged the overwhelming majority of Chinese seeking to enter or stay in the United States. States were permitted to prevent land purchases, restrict occupational choices, and prevent intermarriage between Asians and whites.[4] These policies shaped Chinese marriage practices, requiring men of Chinese origin residing in the United States (including birthright citizens) to find brides from China if they were to form families.[5]

Chinese litigants and state agents contesting deportation and exclusion orders faced structural questions such as who had access to courts, which institutions would make status determinations, and who had rights that courts recognized and would require administrative agencies to respect. In disputes over civic membership and family status, federal courts engaged these questions, helping to shape the development of the administrative state. Courts both influenced the practices of the administrative state and contributed to its legalization and legitimation. And in overseeing the administrative management of Chinese residency and migration, the courts sometimes reinforced abstract guarantees and rights that tempered or occasionally challenged administrators' imperatives to limit the Chinese presence in the United States. They thereby helped to establish the framework through which administrators would either recognize family ties or dismiss evidence concerning these ties as insufficient to trigger serious review.

The courts, whose currency was case-by-case adjudication, drew distinctions that would determine whether a person of Chinese ancestry could enter or stay in the United States. In the process, they reconciled statutory imperatives, common law principles about family relations, and the appropriate scope of administrative decision-making. Despite repeated legislative attempts to strip courts of discretion and to close the door to most Chinese, problems of family involving citizens and sojourners invited the courts' continued oversight. This chapter examines the courts' management of the relationship between the national agenda of Chinese exclusion and the emerging principles of post–Civil War citizenship. It is a story about who had the right to family ties. Understanding the relationship between exclusion and emerging principles of citizenship requires understanding the significance of family status and gendered family relations, a theme that resonates across this volume. Our narrative also illustrates how the layering of family on top of administrative agendas complicated these agendas. These complications at times invited judicial oversight, generating some modest independent governing authority on the part of the courts.

Gender and family relationships influenced the developing configuration of authority between courts and bureaucrats. Not only did immigration policy *writ large* help configure these relationships in the late nineteenth and early twentieth centuries, but gender and family were central factors in the contestation of authority. We contribute to the literature on state building by emphasizing how matters specifically involving Chinese women, children, and families influenced development. The meaning of familial relationships becomes a driver of political development, underscoring the vital importance of attending to gender and identity in studying American political development.[6] This foundational moment integrating immigration management with state recognition and use of family relationships reverberates through law and political development to the present day, as we readily observe in Alison Gash and Priscilla Yamin's work on contemporary immigration policy (see Chapter 8 in this volume).

A dominant narrative in political development scholarship posits that the rising American administrative state in the late nineteenth and early twentieth centuries increasingly wrested power from the courts.[7] In many accounts, enterprising bureaucrats carved out areas of discretion as they forged bureaucratic legitimacy.[8] Our review of cases from the Supreme Court and the Ninth Circuit of the US Courts of Appeals between the late 1800s and the early 1920s reveals a more complex relationship between branches of the federal government.

Our study resonates with recent findings by Daniel Ernst, who contends that "the standard of review of findings of fact was the most contested issue of administrative law in the early twentieth century."[9] Federal courts, rather than ceding the terrain, maintained authority over what decisions administrators could make, what procedures administrators had to use, and what evidence had to be considered to constitute the legitimate exercise of administrative discretion, often addressing these questions when common law principles of familial relations clashed with the statutory imperative of administratively managed exclusion. They scrutinized agencies and insisted on "seeing what administrators had done and understand why they had done it."[10] Despite repeated congressional efforts to stop courts from intervening in administrative decisions barring entry or ordering deportations of ethnic Chinese, "judges readily assumed that norms of due process that had been worked out in the courts ought also to govern the 'quasi-adjudication' of administrative agencies, and they condemned administrators who violated these norms."[11] As Anna Law notes, neither federal appeals courts nor the Supreme Court considered plenary power (the power of Congress to regulate entry of aliens) and due process to be mutually exclusive. When courts invoked procedural due process, they made clear they were invoking a constitutional requirement that enabled them to supersede administrative control.[12] The district and circuit courts also developed grounded interpretations of the Supreme Court's mandates, at times carving out room for additional oversight and control.

The courts' considerations of Chinese asserting rights to enter or remain in the United States based on family ties provide a useful site for untangling the relationship between courts and administrative authority. The tension between administrative management and judicial oversight was amplified as the courts navigated a legal environment that placed two imperatives in conflict. They grappled with an increasingly restrictive statutory regime, as Congress explicitly sought to trim back judicial intervention, while maintaining their repeatedly expressed interpretation of constitutional mandates regarding citizenship, statutory protections for certain classes of Chinese sojourners, and due process that required judicial intervention to ensure that minimal standards had been met.

The courts' role was particularly visible in familial status controversies, since familial relations and birthrights both conferred rights and posed particularly thorny evidentiary concerns. Citizens and merchants ostensibly had the right to form families, based either in long-standing common law principles or through treaty. The logic of citizens' rights and the need to preserve proper access to due process for them contradicted the perceived need for a streamlined and legitimate administrative process for removing or denying entrance to the Chinese, a process designed to discount the kinds of intra-ethnic testimony and evidence most likely to be used to prove parentage or birthplace. Courts eventually insisted that persons claiming birthright citizenship had constitutional rights that administrators could not capriciously disregard.[13]

As recent scholars note, the so-called private sphere involving marriage and the family was decidedly the subject of extensive public intervention throughout much of American history.[14] And as Chapters 2, 4, and 7 in this volume highlight, family relationships are both objects and tools of state regulatory authority, with the state's capacity to acknowledge such relationships creating a means of assigning status and rights. Marriage and the family have been shaped by the American state; have been the object of federal and state policy; and have been specified by race, class, and sexual orientation—including during the period under investigation here. Our investigation into Chinese immigration illustrates how struggles involving gender and family relations *helped shape* the American state. Women identified by the state as Chinese were wives, intended wives, and daughters of merchants, laborers, diplomats; they were natural-born citizens or wives and daughters of the same. They were, if single, deemed prostitutes, and some were.[15] Some were seeking entry or reentry into the country, and others had resided here for some time before being legally challenged. These classifications, some specified in laws, mattered for the "contest among possible visions of the relationship between law and administration."[16]

Given policy objectives that included keeping Chinese out and preventing the resident Chinese population from expanding, those Chinese legally within the United States struggled to form and maintain families that were safe from legal challenge, especially with so few marriageable Chinese women present in America's Chinese communities. Securing entry for wives, or for children born in China, was a major challenge.

The Legal Framework and Habeas Challenges

From 1875 at least to the Johnson-Reed Act of 1924, policy makers increasingly regulated entry and questioned the residence of Chinese seeking to come to, return to, or remain in the United States.[17] The Burlingame Treaty of 1868, promising the Chinese free immigration and travel in the United States and protection of Chinese citizens within the United States under the most-favored-nation principle, was succeeded by more restrictive treaties and at least twenty-five laws (culminating in the Johnson-Reed Act of 1924) that tightened access to American shores, restricted naturalization, stripped women of US citizenship when they married foreigners or foreigners ineligible for naturalization, and enabled deportations. Many of these measures specifically targeted the Chinese and later, other Asians. The appendix to this chapter summarizes this legislative activity.

The process began with the Page Act in 1875. Aimed at prostitutes and coolie labor, it targeted the Chinese. The first national comprehensive regulation of immigration in 1882 placed a ten-year moratorium, later extended and made permanent, on the entry of Chinese laborers. The 1892 Geary Act required Chinese to acquire and carry certificates of residence at all times, and authorized the arrest and deportation of those lacking documentation. The Immigration Act of 1891 centralized administration of immigration laws in the federal government, created the office of Superintendent of Immigration, and lodged the 1882 Chinese Exclusion Act's administration in the Treasury Department. Collectors of customs became the decision-makers admitting or denying Chinese arrivals in the United States.[18] While the Bureau of Immigration, created in 1895, shifted from the Treasury Department to the new Department of Commerce and Labor in 1903, this basic system prevailed until the passage of the Johnson-Reed Act in 1924, which barred immigration of Asians and Pacific Islanders.[19]

Our Study

Legislative history alone tells us little about struggles over implementation, or about what actually happened regarding familial ties. Even highly restrictive laws often left important questions unresolved. Federal court records reveal how often immigration officials' discretionary authority was challenged by those seeking to overturn decisions that would bar or remove them. The mechanism challengers overwhelmingly used was the petition for a writ of habeas corpus, which enabled review of administrative or judicial determinations that they were not permitted to enter or remain in the United States. Frequent appeals from administrative decisions pressed courts to clarify what constitutional and common law principles applied when persons of Chinese heritage, born in the United States, made rights claims; when wives of those Chinese legitimately within the United States sought to enter or remain; and when offspring of such persons sought to enter (if born abroad) or return to, the United States. The judiciary was continuously involved in governing Chinese immigration, in deciding when family status claims warranted judicial intervention, and in establishing the boundary conditions within which administrative discretion could be exercised.

We have collected reported opinions in Chinese habeas corpus cases from the 1870s through the 1920s from California federal courts and Ninth Circuit and Supreme Court cases originating there, as well landmark Supreme Court rulings in this legal arena. Many additional dispositions appear only in docket records.[20] Since the vast majority of ethnic Chinese seeking to enter or return to the United States entered through West Coast ports, this choice gave us the best sample. In addition, "the Ninth Circuit may have had a greater impact on the enforcement of anti-Chinese legislation than any other court, arguably including the Supreme Court itself."[21] The fate of those ethnic Chinese who claimed rights to enter or remain in the United States because they were wives or children of US citizens, even if born abroad (see the discussion of *jus sanguinis* later in this chapter), linked norms about the status of women and children and the question of who had legally cognizable rights to the struggle for control over immigration and deportation policy and practices.

As immigration laws tightened, entering the United States as wives and daughters offered practically the only means of access for Chinese women. As historian Martha Mabie Gardner explains, "Negotiating within the shadow of the law, Chinese and Japanese immigrant women saw access in marriage and family status."[22]

Contesting Chinese Exclusion

The Supreme Court established the parameters within which the lower federal courts addressed the dilemmas posed by the wave of habeas cases and, after 1888, appeared to collaborate with Congress. This left a broad scope for administrative authority and narrowed the avenues for direct judicial determinations of status. Prior to 1900, the Supreme Court seemed willing to accord the other branches full authority over the means by which they excluded or expelled aliens, though not all justices agreed.

Court Deference under the Geary Act—and Its Limits

The majority laid the groundwork for Congress to direct immigration management in the 1893 *Fong Yue Ting* decision upholding the previous year's Geary Act. Finding the right to exclude or expel all or any class of aliens, either absolutely or on certain conditions, "an inherent and alienable right of every sovereign and independent nation," Justice Horace Gray, writing for the Court, thought that if the end was within the constitutional powers of government, the means were as well.[23] Gray cited the majority opinion he had crafted just prior to the passage of the Geary Act in *Nishimura Ekiu v. United States* (1892), holding that while the courts could still interpret the statutory principles allowing aliens to enter, "yet Congress might intrust the final determination of those facts to an executive officer." With this duty granted to an executive officer, orders that person issued constituted due process, "and no other tribunal, unless expressly authorized by law to do so, was at liberty to reexamine the evidence on which he acted, or to controvert its sufficiency."[24]

For *Fong Yue Ting* dissenters, by contrast, the power to exclude had to be distinguished from the power to expel. Justice Stephen Field noted that Chinese who entered the country by governmental consent—implied when not explicitly withheld—could not subsequently be denied constitutional protections. Exclusion under these circumstances constituted punishment that was "beyond all reason in its severity," passing the threshold of cruel and unusual punishment. Justice Melville Fuller insisted that the Fifth and Fourteenth Amendments applied universally to those within the territorial jurisdiction of the United States.[25] Justice David Brewer asserted that aliens within the United States were entitled to some constitutional protections, and portions of the Geary Act that violated the most-favored-nation protections in the Burlingame Treaty as amended in 1880 were invalid.[26]

Congress did not trust the federal courts to defer to the political branches; fierce political pressure encouraged reforming the system by closing loopholes.[27] While part of the problem was a simple lack of management and control capacity, critics also objected to independent judicial review of orders and resented the courts' willingness to hear habeas cases and sometimes grant relief. J. Thomas Scharf, a Chinese inspector for the port of New York, blamed the courts: "From the passage of the first Chinese Exclusion Act . . . to the present . . . , there have been in the matter of hearings on habeas corpus in Chinese cases serious and radical conflicts of opinion between the judges of the Federal courts and the executive officers of the government, which have been the cause of a great many admissions."[28]

Congress emphatically lodged final determinations of alien exclusion decisions in the executive branch in the Sundry Civil Appropriations Act of August 1894. A provision in the act stipulated, "In every case where an alien is excluded from admission into the United States under any law or treaty now existing or hereafter made, the decision of the appropriate immigration or customs officers, if adverse to the admission of such alien, shall be final, unless reversed on appeal to the Secretary of the Treasury."[29] This would not be Congress's only attempt to keep the judiciary from reviewing administrative decisions.

However, the Supreme Court outlined constitutional limits to this authority. Picking up on themes established by *Fong Yue Ting* dissenters, the Court distinguished between stopping aliens at the border and treatment properly accorded those within the United States. The Geary Act included a provision (§ 4) that aliens found unlawfully within the United States could be subject to sixty days' hard labor and imprisonment prior to deportation. When this section was challenged in *Wong Wing v. United States* (1896), the Court invalidated Section 4, finding that it violated the Fifth and Sixth Amendments by imposing infamous punishment without an indictment and criminal punishment absent a jury trial, the Thirteenth Amendment's bar against involuntary servitude, and the Court's previous ruling in *Yick Wo v. Hopkins* (1886) extending the Fourteenth Amendment to non-citizens.[30] Legislation that provided for punishment at hard labor or confiscation of property could only be valid if it provided for a formal trial before a judge or jury to establish the accused's guilt. Gerald Neuman underscores the importance of *Wong Wing*: "For the first time in its history, the Court expressly invalidated a federal statute for violating the constitutional rights of an alien."[31]

Nonetheless, the Court would later cite the aforementioned 1894 congressional appropriations measure to reaffirm the political branches' power: "Congress may exclude aliens of a particular race from the United States; prescribe the terms and conditions upon which certain classes of aliens may come to this country; establish regulations for sending out of the country such aliens as come here in violation of law; and commit the enforcement of such provisions, conditions, and regulations exclusively to executive officers, without judicial intervention."[32] It also declared that "Congressional action has placed the final determination of the right of admission in executive officers, without judicial intervention, and this has been for many years the recognized and declared policy of the country."[33] However, in *Yamataya v. Fisher* (1903) the Court held that executive officers could not summarily deport aliens who had entered the country, even if they were alleged to be in the country illegally, without enabling them to assert their rights to remain: "No such arbitrary power can exist where the principles involved in due process of law are recognized."[34]

These cases set up a tension between Congress's efforts to shift decision-making to administrative agencies and the courts' responsibility to ensure a basic level of procedural due process. While this theme resonated across the entire body of habeas corpus claims and appeals filed by Chinese, it arose directly in the cases in which the fundamental rights of citizens ran up against the paramount policy goal of restricting Chinese immigration and residence.

Birthright Citizenship Litigation

Claims of US citizenship by ethnic Chinese proved to be particularly successful routes for gaining access to the courts, which were known not to be vigorous gatekeepers in the exclusion battle.[35] Buoyed by early, positive results, attorneys representing the Chinese kept taking admission applications by Chinese alleging US citizenship directly to courts, circumventing investigation by the collector of customs until Congress responded by centralizing administrative control of Chinese cases in the new Bureau of Immigration at the beginning of the twentieth century. Congress kept attempting to curtail access to federal courts, adding finality-of-review clauses to legislation on immigration and deportation. The Justice Department (in conjunction with the Supreme Court) also insisted that the Chinese had to first exhaust all administrative remedies before turning to the courts—even in cases involving claims of birthright citizenship.[36] Policy makers won victories against the courts, as we will demonstrate below, but they were incomplete victories. The legislative branch was still trying to exclude the courts from reviewing birthright citizenship when the 1917 Immigration Act declared that "In every case where any person is ordered deported from the United States under the provisions of this Act, or of any law or treaty, the decision of the Secretary of Labor shall be final."[37] Yet even afterward, the Supreme Court allowed limited judicial review of birthright citizenship claims.

We look here at claims for entry or for the right to remain in the United States based on *jus sanguinis*, or citizenship by descent. Jus sanguinis citizenship required proof of parentage, and for some children, proof of the parent's status as a citizen.

Birthright citizenship rested on long-standing common law principles incorporated into constitutional and statutory law. In the cases on both *jus soli* and jus sanguinis citizenship, courts wrestled with how to square the connection of full access to the legal process linked to citizenship with the streamlined administrative process increasingly endorsed for managing immigrants and their descendants. This struggle between long-standing common law principles of respecting family ties on the one hand and the state's racial imperatives on the other generated tensions that, as with the antebellum interracial families described in Chapter 4, were best resolved through judicial proceedings. While the courts largely continued to support and legitimize administrative decision-making, in both types of cases, they reserved some latitude for their own policy oversight. The legal developments in this period responded to the rapidly shifting legislative efforts to curb Chinese migration, but Congress intervened only minimally to change rules regarding citizenship and access to it. Most legislative changes came in the form of increasingly tighter restrictions that affected individuals suspected of not being citizens or presumed not to be citizens, but these suspicions and presumptions readily swept birthright citizens within their ambit. While the Supreme Court interpreted the Fourteenth Amendment in 1898 to extend citizenship to individuals born in the United States, our focus here is on jus sanguinis. The cases involving individuals who claimed citizenship via parentage raised additional questions about familial relationships, what kinds of relationships the courts would acknowledge, and how these relationships could be properly proven. These questions demanded judicial resolution to provide appropriate guidance for the administrators making the determinations on the ground.

Jus Sanguinis, the Consolidation of Discretion,
and the Fear of Fraud

Statutory law governed transmission of citizenship via parentage.[38] The basic rule applied in these years stemmed from the 1855 version of the 1802 act that established naturalization. In 1855, Congress extended citizenship without naturalization to individuals born outside the

United States if they were born to citizen-fathers who had resided in the United States.[39] Until 1934, this rule granted immediate citizenship to foreign-born children of American fathers, but not mothers.[40] An 1864 case from the Maryland Court of Appeals, *Guyer v. Smith*, distinguished between children of married and unmarried couples, weaving gendered bastardy laws into the determination of citizenship.[41] But bastardy alone could not resolve the problems arising from greater American engagement with the world. Citizenship by descent counterposed two ideological minefields. First were the patriarchal assumptions behind attributing citizenship to paternal, not maternal, descent. Second were the racialized dilemmas posed both by white male citizens' fathering of racially questionable children abroad and Asian American citizens' fathering of Asian American children abroad.[42] "Not until 1934 did naturalization law allow *either* citizen parent to transmit birthright citizenship to a legitimate child if the parent could show some prior residence in the United States."[43] Jus sanguinis thus incorporated gender, race, and marital status in its operation; for the Chinese, the primary effect was to generate and institutionalize particular suspicion about jus sanguinis claims of citizenship by children of Chinese men.

In the mid-1910s, the bulk of reported cases shifted to claims of citizenship based on descent rather than birthplace, although a few jus soli cases reached appellate resolutions into the 1920s. By the time these cases took center stage, the principle of deference was established, and these litigants' claims of citizenship based on the statutory grant to children born abroad to American fathers provoked no fundamental jurisdictional concerns. The statutory framework of exclusion clearly came first, and it was up to the litigants in administrative proceedings to produce the necessary evidence to reverse the presumption that they were not entitled to entry or continued residence.

Ancestrally based citizenship had a significant history in common law, but unlike jus soli citizenship, jus sanguinis citizenship was not constitutionally incorporated through the Fourteenth Amendment. Since the 1907 Expatriation Act provided that any American woman who married a foreign male took the nationality of her husband, the only pathway to citizenship was to claim it through a citizen-father.[44] For children of unmarried parents, gendered assumptions pulled in different directions. The nonmarital foreign-born child of an American mother was much more likely to be viewed as a citizen than the nonmarital foreign-born child of an American citizen-father; this was the default rule of the Bureau of Immigration and the Department of State.[45] While these rules were based on gender bias, ethnicity and race also specified their application and administration.[46]

American immigration officials generally presumed the illegitimacy or fraudulency of individuals claiming to be foreign-born children of American citizen-fathers of Chinese heritage. They also suspected that many Chinese merchants who were properly residents of the United States lied about their marital situation when trying to bring in children from China. Attempting to ferret out false citizenship claims, officials frequently challenged the Chinese-born children of such men when they tried to enter or reenter the country. Officials were convinced that many non-relatives sought to land while claiming to be the Chinese children of a legally domiciled "parent."

Even if the children were genuinely linked by blood, if the marriage in China was not exclusive (if there were children by another mother), then the landing was likely to be challenged and denied. Polygamy was a major concern across multiple policy fronts. Chinese men might have plural wives, and the children of second wives and concubines were considered legitimate heirs in China, but this practice meant that the children of Chinese men—especially when they tried to enter or reenter the United States—were suspected of possibly not being the fruit of a legitimate marriage. Just as the exclusiveness of the marriage mattered in determining the status of foreign-born children of American fathers,[47] the exclusiveness of the marriage mattered for these foreign-born children of legal residents, of those who naturalized prior to the 1882 ban on naturalization, or of natural-born citizens.

Nonetheless, the courts maintained oversight and demanded that basic procedural fairness be respected, granting some habeas claims on procedural appeals in the 1910s. The Ninth Circuit explained that in these cases, the "primary question would be, not whether there was an abuse of discretion on the part of the immigration authorities, nor whether the weight of the testimony purporting to have been given is for or against admission, nor whether he understood the import of the questions propounded to him, but . . . whether the applicant has been examined fairly at all as to his right to admission in the United States."[48]

This framework could sometimes produce modifications affecting multiple cases. In 1918, the Ninth Circuit held discriminatory the separate procedures that minors of Chinese heritage faced under Department of Labor guidelines when they claimed to be sons or daughters of US citizens, stating: "We know of no law making a race distinction in American citizenship, and by reason of such distinction excluding the sons of citizens of the United States of Chinese birth."[49] In several instances in 1916, the Northern District of California considered attempts by the commissioner of immigration to exclude adult children of citizens. The commissioner claimed that these adults had shown no interest in the United States as minors and that the citizen-parents themselves were insufficiently attached.[50] The courts rebuffed this line of attack by immigration officials. In reviewing these cases in 1919, the Ninth Circuit summarized their rule as requiring the proper appearance of these proceedings: "it should distinctly appear that the department was not influenced in its decision by considerations not authorized by law."[51] The Ninth Circuit additionally determined that regulations allowing for expedited management of exclusion for Chinese could not trump the general immigration statute's process for dealing with individuals claiming birthright citizenship, and reinforced the principle mandating a hearing before a board of special inquiry for individuals claiming citizenship.[52]

The tide turned drastically on the Ninth Circuit after 1919, though few judicial seats changed hands.[53] Almost all foreign-born children of US citizens of Chinese origin in our later reported cases were denied entry and/or deported. Nonetheless, the Supreme Court hinted at greater concern for procedural violations in both types of appeals.

The courts also resurrected the difference between those barred at the border and those detained within the United States. Those outside the borders of the United States who were denied entry despite claims of birthright citizenship were not constitutionally entitled to a judicial hearing (as per *Ju Toy*). Petitioner Ng Fung Ho (and his son) were afforded no judicial recourse, since violators of the Chinese Exclusion Acts could be deported upon executive order, and they had not claimed citizenship.[54] However, for those within the United States who had not entered surreptitiously, the Court posed this question: "May a resident of the United States who claims to be a citizen be arrested and deported on executive order?"[55] Ging Sang Get and Gin Sang Mo, both claiming to be foreign-born sons of a native-born citizen, prevailed. The Supreme Court, in an opinion written by Justice Louis Brandeis, unanimously granted habeas relief to these two individuals, allowing them to proceed to trial on the question of citizenship, because a claim of citizenship functioned as "a denial of an essential jurisdictional fact."[56] Brandeis grounded his analysis in due process, finding that "To deport one who so claims to be a citizen obviously deprives him of liberty. . . . It may result also in loss of both property and life, or of all that makes life worth living," and asserting judicial proceedings as the appropriate remedy. Without the protection of habeas, an executive officer could order deportation independently "whatever his race or place of birth," which would deny due process.[57]

Despite these rulings, in thirteen appellate cases the Ninth Circuit found the evidence below to be sufficient and properly enough weighed to support deportation, upholding rulings based on findings that the father's own previous admission was irrelevant,[58] that the relationship to an alleged citizen-father had not been adequately established because of age discrepancies,[59] that the father's polygamous marriage called the son's legitimate parentage into question,[60] and other concerns. In only one case did the Ninth Circuit overturn a deportation order, finding in *In re Kwock Seu Lum* that the adopted son of a citizen-father was entitled to jus sanguinis citizenship.[61]

Wives of Citizens and Merchants

Examining the competing logic of race-based restrictions and gender-based claims for exemption, Todd Stevens observes that Chinese husbands "sought exemptions from existing immigration laws based on their right to the company of their wives," and that this common law argument had surprising traction with the courts into the early years of the 1900s.[62] Despite the courts' agreement that Congress had the power to exclude certain types of immigrants, a "Chinese woman's marital status trumped her racial classification" quite frequently during these same years. A nineteenth-century husband was entitled to the "care and comfort" of his wife. Immigration laws sometimes explicitly conceded the right of some husbands (except laborers) to bring a wife to the United States. And since their children were also admissible, male citizens and merchants could adopt minors when visiting China and return with them to the United States.[63] However, deep suspicion of and hostility toward the Chinese led immigration officials to challenge familial claims. This then set the stage for legal appeals, in which a merchant's wife or the wife of a birthright citizen would often prevail, even as Congress tightened requirements for Chinese entry and residence.

The argument for care and comfort to which some litigants appealed was derived from coverture and common law. While various aspects of coverture (e.g., married women's property laws) were being dismantled, Chinese men invoked traditional male prerogatives and rights and traditional understandings of the home. As Kathleen Sullivan has observed, "The liberal appreciation of individual rights ended at the home, for unsettling the home would risk affecting larger social structures."[64] Full personhood developed when a woman's presence in a man's life tempered his harshness and deficiencies; home made a man more fully human.[65] While denying a male of Chinese ancestry the company of a spouse made him less fit for citizenship, being denied the comforts of the home—wife and children—arguably unmanned him.

Denying men the comforts of family in order to stem immigration and the growth of the Chinese American population clashed with other public policy objectives: using policy to support monogamous morality and to encourage elite Chinese men to contribute to American economy and diplomacy.[66] Untethered men were more likely to turn to prostitution or unsanctioned unions or perhaps become dissatisfied enough to depart; thus law on the books and legal constructions gave elite men the privilege of legitimate familial relationships. Nancy Cott notes, "Prostitution and marriage were opposites: where marriage implied mutual love and consent, legality and formality, willing bonds for a good bargain, prostitution signified sordid monetary exchange and desperation or coercion on the part of the woman involved."[67] This contradiction played out directly in the common binary identification problem facing every Chinese woman: was she a wife or a prostitute? American religious organization Mission Homes tried to rescue Chinese women from exploitative situations while introducing them to Victorian gender systems that emphasized marriage and facilitated and arranged marriages with Chinese men.[68]

However, many wives came through arranged marriages, having had little if any acquaintance with their US spouses, and immigration officials often presumed their claims fraudulent because they suspected unaccompanied females of being prostitutes. Questions designed to test a supposed spouse's knowledge of her mate, his kin, and his ancestral home kept out many of those sent for by males with legal residence in the United States. Immigration officials matched answers to prior testimony collected from husbands, relatives, and neighbors in the United States.[69] Even when a man obtained necessary reentry certification before traveling to China to obtain a bride and traveling back with her, inconsistent answers to questions posed to both parties often led immi-gration officials to conclude the relationship was fraudulent.

Although Asian women who married birthright citizens took on the class status of their husband (merchant, laborer), they did not acquire US citizenship when they married a birthright citizen.[70] This left them vulnerable in a number of ways. If a husband died, abandoned his wife, took up with another woman in the United States, or acquired another wife or concubine in China, the wife's status changed and she could be deported. A wife deprived of a husband and means of support who became a laborer was vulnerable to deportation. If a laborer who was in the country prior to the 1882 Chinese Exclusion Act or a merchant who visited China was barred upon reentry (as a number were), his wife was made vulnerable to deportation. A merchant adjudged no longer to be a legitimate merchant jeopardized not only his own status but that of his wife. Chinese women married to birthright citizens and merchants were thus in legally precarious positions, even if they had lived for many years in the United States.

At least in principle, "prior to the passage of the Cable and Johnson-Reed Acts, the Labor and State Departments had permitted Chinese wives of American citizens into the country despite the Chinese exclu-sion laws." The law dictated that even "women of full Chinese blood" were subject to men's right to have their wives' comfort and company, regardless of their wives' race.[71] Yet the strong suspicion that sham mar-riages allowed women destined for prostitution and others evading ex-clusion laws into the country meant that women faced challenges when claiming spousal status. The Commerce and Labor Department was unconvinced that federal judges would support a decision to exclude or expel citizens' wives. The 1907 Expatriation Act left the matter of non-resident, foreign-born wives of citizens in a gray zone, passing the question to judges, who issued rulings that failed to produce clear stan-dards for the disposition of later cases. Nevertheless, a number of fed-eral judges had shown "they could be more combative than cooperative when dealing with immigration issues."[72]

The Cable Act of 1922 gave immigration officials occasion to chal-lenge the "privileging of husbands and their rights." As Candice Bred-benner notes, "the Bureau [of Immigration] used the Cable Act as a strip of statutory ground from which to launch an assault on the notion that a husband's credentials for residence and citizenship transferred fully to his alien wife." It is not clear whether the architects of Johnson-

Reed anticipated the exclusion of Chinese wives of Americans—they were not on the list of nonquota immigrants. "Once again, it fell initially to the federal judiciary to grapple with the problem."[73]

While the Emergency Quota Law of 1921 made clear that alien minor children of US citizens, under eighteen years of age, were excluded from the quota, neither the 1921 quota law nor the 1924 Johnson-Reed Act specifically provided for wives of residents or citizens to be admitted as nonquota immigrants.[74] Thus, Gardner says, "The immigration bureau faced the unsavory task of balancing a historic belief in the importance of families to American national identity with laws requiring drastic restrictions on new racialized arrivals and the separation of husband and wife as a legal entity."[75] These kinds of silences also dealt courts in.

Wives of Citizens in the Courts

The appellate cases of citizens' wives, especially in the 1910s, often involved efforts to deport women already in the United States suspected of having entered into sham marriages but whom officials believed were really prostitutes and thus subject to exclusion on that basis.

The Ninth Circuit first dealt directly with the question of how to classify citizens' wives in 1902. Tsoi Sim had come to the United States with her parents as a three-year-old child in 1882; after passage of the Geary Act of 1892, she had failed to obtain the requisite certificate of residence. At the age of twenty-one, she married a birthright citizen. Arrested and held for deportation in 1901, the young woman was adjudged deportable as an unregistered manual laborer by both the commissioner of immigration and the district court for the Northern District of California.[76]

The circuit court reviewing the order conceded that, had the order been entered prior to her marriage, it would be proper. Both sides agreed that she had entered the United States lawfully and lacked a laborer's certificate, but her presence as the wife of a citizen raised a new interpretive problem. Relying primarily on cases involving the families of merchants, the court endorsed "the principle that the domicile of the parents is the domicile of the children, and . . . the status of the wife is fixed by the status of the husband."[77] While she could have been deported at any time after the adoption of the certificate requirement and before her marriage, Tsoi Sim's marriage changed her status. The judge elaborated, outlining points that would arise in later controversies:

> Appellant did not come to this country fraudulently, or in violation of any law. She did not get married in order to evade deportation. Her marriage was not fraudulent, but lawful, and in accordance with the usages and customs of our law. . . . By this act, her status was changed from that of a Chinese laborer to that of a wife of a nativeborn American. Her husband is not before the court, but his rights, as well as hers, are involved.[78]

The citation of the husband's rights nodded to the common law principle of coverture, confirming that the courts would require administrative agents to incorporate this idea into their handling of Chinese exclusion if a marriage was proven. The principle could cut both ways, as *In re Tang Tun* illustrated in 1909: while his wife was also a party in his habeas plea seeking entrance as a citizen, her claim received no consideration from the court, as her status was tied entirely to his. The Ninth Circuit's finding that the inspector had not erred in determining that he was a non-citizen likewise excluded her, with no controversy or even discussion.[79]

Appellate courts often refused to question the evidentiary basis for administrators' determinations that women purportedly married to citizens were not entitled to enter or stay in the country. Looe Shee entered the United States legally as the wife of citizen Lew Chow in 1906 but was arrested and ordered to be deported in 1907. Her deportation order was based on the allegation that she was in fact a prostitute, and that no meaningful marriage still existed between her and Lew Chow, if it ever had.[80] She resisted deportation, arguing that the harsher 1907 Immigration Act[81] did not apply to her because her status followed that of her citizen-husband, entitling her to fuller process. Quoting a dissent by Justice Oliver Wendell Holmes, the Ninth Circuit rejected this argument: "For the purpose of excluding those who unlawfully enter this country, Congress has power to retain control over aliens long enough to make sure of the facts . . . If a woman were found living in a house of prostitution within a week after her arrival, no one . . . would doubt that it tended to show that she was in the business when she arrived."[82] In a Ninth Circuit case adjudicated a year later, identification as a prostitute also placed the wife of Wong Heung outside the protection afforded through habeas; the couple married after she was already under a deportation order, and her marriage to a citizen was administratively deemed to be a sham.[83]

Two cases in 1914 did discover procedural errors sufficiently serious to warrant the granting of habeas. Ung King Ieng, who entered the United States as a wife in 1909 and was ordered deported as a prostitute in 1913, was forbidden to call witnesses because it would have been too much of a nuisance. The district court judge remarked caustically, "Perhaps it would, but to the petitioner the whole proceeding was probably a nuisance. The rights of the petitioner may not be wholly measured by the convenience or inconvenience to the immigration officers in affording her a fair hearing . . . They have vast powers accorded them by the law, and these powers should be fairly exercised."[84] Tsuie Shee and her infant son, detained upon an attempt to enter, were conditionally released because the wrong administrative official had handled their case, leaving them with no clear route of administrative appeal.[85] Likewise, in 1916, a wife achieved relief because the commissioner improperly authorized an immigration official to determine that she was a prostitute.[86] And in a 1917 case, although the Ninth Circuit did not find the original weighing of the evidence against Mah Shee to be problematic, the opinion found that she had been denied the "right to submit evidence and to defend herself," warranting a reversal and remand.[87]

As in the cases involving children, however, securing reversals of orders became more difficult. Many of the appeals raised by wives of citizens involved women who had resided in the United States but were suspected of being prostitutes. If the administrative process resulting in these determinations had functioned properly, even at a fairly minimal level, courts upheld them.[88] Dear Shee, for instance, accused of being a prostitute, objected on several procedural grounds—she had not being informed of a right to counsel at her preliminary examination, partial testimony from an entirely different case was admitted against her, and her purported husband was forbidden to testify on her behalf.[89] An unsympathetic Ninth Circuit denied relief.

Of five cases decided in 1924 and 1925, only one resulted in the granting of a habeas corpus petition. *Halsey v. Ho Ah Keau* surprisingly allowed the entry of Ho Ah Keau (also known as Ho Shee) on the basis of her 1891 marriage to Lau Ah Leong, despite the fact that all parties conceded that he had an additional wife.[90] Ho Shee had departed for China in 1910 with several of her children and returned around 1922. The central question for the Ninth Circuit "turns upon the finding that Ho Shee was entitled to admission as the wife of a citizen of the United States," and that determination, ruled the court, had to be based in prevailing Hawaiian law at the time of their marriage.[91] Because the original marriage was valid according to territorial law, even her husband's polygamous relationship did not undermine her status as a wife.

The circuit court, however, increasingly foreclosed relief. Wong Wing Sing and his unnamed wife were denied entry after a temporary visit to China despite their plea that Wong Wing Sing had previously entered the United States regularly, established a residence that he had not abandoned, and presented solid proof that his claim was "not frivolous."[92] The couple demanded a judicial hearing, but because they had been stopped at the border rather than detained within the United States, the Ninth Circuit held that they were not entitled to one.[93] Leong Shee claimed that she was a legitimately married wife, but the administrative process found that she was an unmarried concubine, and the Ninth Circuit refused to consider her claim that this determination had been made in error.[94] Chun Shee entered the United States in 1921 as a wife, but was identified as a prostitute in 1924 and faced deportation; the Ninth Circuit did not accept her contention that the refusal to allow her to call a witness was unfair.[95]

When the Johnson-Reed Act of 1924 went into effect, "marriage to a citizen no longer guaranteed Chinese women the right to enter the United States," but the Chinese continued to challenge exclusions, arguing "the natural right of a man to enjoy the companionship of his wife."[96] The district court for the Northern District of California interpreted the act in consolidated cases involving wives of both merchants and citizens. None of the individuals seeking to enter the United States had the consular visas prescribed by the act, basing their right of entry instead upon their familial status. The commissioner in San Francisco denied them entry on the grounds that they were ineligible for citizenship themselves and fit none of the other permitted categories.[97] The district court that first heard the case acknowledged that, with respect to merchants, "husbands and wives and their children have a natural right to be and reside with one another," but reasoned that this right was superseded by a sovereign state's right "to dictate as to what alien persons shall be permitted to come within its territorial boundaries," reading Congress's intervention as changing the rule that had prevailed since the late 1800s.[98] The court read the act as permitting citizens' wives entrance, but only if their husbands had procured special visas for them.

The Ninth Circuit certified the question regarding the exclusion of merchants' wives to the US Supreme Court for resolution. The Supreme

Court ruled that the congressional act had to be harmonized with the treaty, which allowed wives and children to accompany merchants. Writing for the Court, Justice James Clark McReynolds explained that the congressional statute did not abrogate the rights that these wives and children already possessed when the 1924 Johnson-Reed Act was passed.[99] In 1925, however, the Court ruled that the Chinese wives of citizens were barred from gaining citizenship themselves and could be legally excluded under the act.[100]

Thus, during the period from 1924 to 1930, the courts' interpretation of the Johnson-Reed Act allowed entry to wives of Chinese merchants but barred wives of birthright citizens, turning on its head any assumption that citizens had more rights than non-citizens.[101] One scholar attributes the anomaly to resentment over the *Wong Kim Ark* determination that Chinese born in the United States were birthright citizens.[102] In 1930, Congress amended the 1924 act to allow those married prior to 1924 to enter. While no wives of citizens had been admitted as legal immigrants in the interim, no women were returned to China.[103]

Still, as Todd Stevens argues, "the struggles of Chinese women to avoid deportation were a special case; they were ineligible for naturalization and remained immigrants no matter how long they lived and worked in the United States." Even as judges increasingly yielded to Congress after the Johnson-Reed Act, "the commissioners, when faced with a couple that gave a convincing performance as citizen and wife in the courtroom, found racial immigration restrictions more flexible than gender privileges."[104] And Chinese men with the most authority—those designated as desirable by treaty—proved better able to win recognition for their familial relationships than citizens.

Merchants' Wives and Their Minor Children in the Courts

Chinese claims of citizenship rested on a blend of constitutional and statutory law. Merchants' families, in contrast, looked to congressional legislation implementing the treaties that had identified small classes of desirable Chinese sojourners and residents: primarily merchants, but also diplomats, clergy, and students. Nonetheless, the basic principles of status and managed administrative deference also prevailed here. The Burlingame Treaty amendments of 1880 (Angell Treaty) permitted Chinese merchants to bring their "body and household servants" with them. Courts interpreted the phrase to include Chinese wives, reasoning that, although this treaty made no mention of merchant wives, "it assumed a wife belonged with her husband."[105] But even if in principle a merchant's wife was allowed to accompany her husband, entry could be problematic. Demands for evidence of identity and of the validity of a woman's relationship to her alleged husband, and questions about the husband's claim to merchant status posed significant barriers to wives and children of merchants seeking entry or reentry into the United States.[106]

The first questions involved the 1884 amendment to the Chinese Exclusion Act requiring a certificate of residence for reentry to the United States. Men were clearly subject to this requirement. But did a wife require a certificate from the Chinese government, just as her husband did? She was not a merchant and was not a member of an excluded class in her own right. The first Ninth Circuit ruling to address the status of a wife involved the habeas request of a woman detained when she sought entry with her husband, a laborer who had a certificate entitling him to entry. Sitting as a circuit judge in the 1884 case of *In re Ah Moy*, Justice Field acknowledged the "sacredness" of the marital relation but found that the couple's marital ties were "voluntarily assumed in the face of the law forbidding her coming to the United States without the required certificate. And they need not now be separated. He can return with and protect his child-wife in the celestial empire."[107] Rather than simply assume that her status followed that of her laborer-husband, Field deemed her status indeterminate, ruling that the statute implied her need to obtain her own certificate to secure entry. This same question would be raised, but ultimately settled differently, for merchants' wives.

The district courts considering the status of merchants' wives disagreed about the need for wives to obtain their own independent certificates to secure entry or prevent deportation. By 1900, five district courts and three circuit rulings had decided or touched on the question in opposite directions.[108] The Supreme Court stepped in to resolve the controversy in an appeal from Washington and found in favor of the wife, largely adopting the reasoning of Judge Deady's circuit ruling in an 1890 case.[109] Reading the amended Burlingame Treaty alongside the exclusionary statutory regime, the Court found that Congress could not have intended to establish impassable barriers to the wives and children of Chinese merchants. If certificates were required, "It is plain that in this case the woman could not obtain the certificate as a member of any of those specially enumerated classes. She is neither an official, a teacher, a student, a merchant nor a traveller for curiosity or pleasure. She is simply the wife of a merchant, who is himself a member of one of the classes mentioned in the treaty as entitled to admission."[110] Wives and children remained responsible only for proving their familial relationship to the merchant. The district court ruling preceding the Supreme Court's determination clarified that this principle supported and advanced commerce.[111]

Yet some lower courts continued to defer to customs officials who rejected certificates proffered by merchants' wives and children. And when such officials rejected evidence of a purported wife or child's relationship to a merchant, some courts accepted that decision without demur. Only a few months after the *Gue Lim* decision, an Oregon district court upheld an order excluding the wife and son of a merchant. The merchant had consulted with an attorney and secured certificates for them that he thought would entitle them to entry, but when the family attempted to enter the United States together, only the merchant was admitted. The court found that the collector of customs had exercised legitimate discretion in rejecting both the certificates and the wife and child's substantive claims to a right of entry based on their relationship to the merchant.[112]

Courts had grappled with what constituted a legitimate marriage for weddings conducted in China; the problem was the same in dealing with merchant spouses. Arranged marriages with limited contact between the parties, proxy ceremonies, and significant age differences between husband and wife often meant the parties could not satisfactorily answer immigration officials' questions about their alleged spouse. Immigration officials frequently rejected such marriages. In an 1894 case, an eighteen-year-old woman betrothed to an Oregon merchant at the age of two and married in a Chinese proxy ceremony arrived in the United States having never met her husband.[113] The merchant had taken careful measures to ensure her entry: he "consulted a firm of lawyers of high standing in the city, touching the right of his wife to land here . . . Acting on their advice, a certificate was prepared and forwarded to China, identifying the husband, and setting forth that the petitioner was his wife, and that such certificate was intended to evidence her right to land here, by virtue of such relation." Her solo arrival raised suspicion that she was a prostitute, but the district court judge found that she was not within any class of persons excluded by Congress. Consulting the law of contracts, the judge declared, "If the parties were married according to the laws of China, such marriage is valid here," but wondered if the merchant was actually married in China because he had not journeyed there for the ceremony. Still, the young woman "has made this journey in good faith" and to exclude her would be a "cruel injustice."[114]

The courts were not through with this young woman, known as Chung Shee. Having achieved entry through the habeas process, she was detained, identified as a laborer, and again ordered to be deported after she and her questionable husband moved to Los Angeles.[115] Despite the government's allegation of fraud in her original determination, the district court judge hearing her appeal ruled that the Oregon judgment should not be disturbed, and the Ninth Circuit upheld this ruling, finding that no new evidence supported the attempt to remove her from the country.[116]

Subsequent legal controversies turned on questions about whether the evidence presented had adequately supported a determination that a woman was not entitled to enter or remain. Appellate controversies addressed not only questions about the marriage's legitimacy but the merchant status of the man to whom a woman was married. In a few cases, the courts were dissatisfied with the weighing of the evidence or the procedural shortcuts taken. When the Bureau of Immigration doubted evidence about the marriage of one woman claiming to be the wife of a merchant, her entry was denied but she was permitted to remain on bail during appeal. During this time, Chan Shee resided with her merchant husband and remarried him under the laws of California. She sought reconsideration of her case on the grounds of her California marriage, but the bureau refused, arguing that she should have pursued an appeal of the original determination. The district court reversed that decision in 1916, noting that, practically, even if she were deported, the now unquestionably legitimate marriage would authorize her reentry.[117]

Around the same time, another young woman was languishing in detention at Angel Island after her claim of marriage to a merchant was rejected. Chew Hoy Quong had gone to China to find a bride, and when he returned with Quok Shee, immigration officials were convinced that the husband was merely "alleged" on the basis of discrepant responses "husband" and "wife" made to interrogators. Chew Hoy Quong appealed, and his effort to gain entry for his wife reached the Ninth Circuit twice. The first time, the court upheld the order denying admission, citing discrepancies in their testimony about their marriage

in China and travel to the United States and noting the large age dispar-
ity between them.[118] The husband persisted through nearly two years of
litigation, filing various additional appeals, including a writ of habeas
corpus. The Ninth Circuit was not insensitive to due process and fair
procedure complaints involving individual immigrants, and ultimately
held that the Department of Labor had engaged in unfair proceedings
in this case.[119] The young woman, detained throughout the proceedings, was freed to enter the United States.[120]

Sometimes, a man's status as a merchant came under scrutiny when
a wife—or wife and minor children—sought entry. In such cases, questionable claims of merchant status even for those who had resided in
the United States for some time could bar family members' entries. In
one case, the alleged merchant had originally entered the country as
the son of a merchant. Yee Won's self-identification as "a capitalist and
property owner" and the evidence he submitted of his financial holdings did not persuade the immigration inspector, who had received an
anonymous letter identifying him as a mere laundryman.[121] Because the
court could identify no unfairness in the proceedings and because the
wife and two minor children had failed to establish the husband's status
as a merchant, the denial of entry stood.[122] In another case, Chan Moy
had lived in the United States for more than thirty years as a laborer
with a certificate, but attempted to secure entry for his wife and child,
claiming that he was now a merchant. The immigration investigators
disagreed; while he appeared to be employed by a mercantile business,
he was working in an orchard at jobs that looked to them more like labor.[123] The Ninth Circuit upheld this judgment and explained that their
authority was limited: "We can only determine whether the Department
of Labor has exceeded its authority, or has misinterpreted the law . . . If
there is competent evidence of persuasive character to sustain its findings, its judgment is final and conclusive, and is not susceptible of review
or revision by the courts." Once Chan Moy was identified as a laborer, he
had no legal basis for maintaining a household in the United States, and
his son, Chan Gai Jan, and wife, Ng Shee, were not entitled to enter the
country.[124] This 1920 opinion was the last case during our time period
that produced a Ninth Circuit appellate opinion directly addressing the
status of a (purported) merchant's wife.

Under statutory language implementing the Burlingame Treaty and
its amendments, merchants' children could enter and reside in the
United States because of the principle of family unification. The policy

sought to ensure merchants' continued engagement in economically beneficial work by permitting them to maintain families in the United States.

For merchants' children who were still minors, the reasons inviting judicial oversight were similar to situations involving merchants' wives: courts might issue writs when dissatisfied with the process followed by administrators or lower courts, or when unconvinced by the evidence. Individuals claiming to be merchants' children filed for habeas relief when they were detained upon entry or caught in sweeps searching for illegitimate Chinese residents and ordered deported. As with the birthright cases, reversals of deportation orders were more frequent in the early 1900s; only significant misinterpretations of law or evidence prompting favorable rulings for Chinese in the 1920s.

The presumption that a legitimate minor son or daughter (or an adopted one) could enter and reside with their merchant father did not trump the Immigration Act of 1903 that barred entry to those with contagious diseases. In 1908, a California district court ruled that the 1903 act allowed administrators to deny a merchant son's admission.[125] The same district court issued a writ in a 1911 case where a young male was denied a full and fair hearing to establish that he was indeed the son of the merchant he claimed as his parent. A merchant's minor son who had been duly admitted to the United States in 1912 and arrested nearly two years later, charged with violating the US exclusion laws because he now worked as a laborer, received relief from the same court in 1914. The young man was discharged from custody.[126] In 1917, the Ninth Circuit ruled in favor of a merchant's son after previous fact finders had questioned both his identity and his age. Two years later, the Ninth Circuit supported another young man's petition seeking entry, holding that the lower court had erred in finding that his father, who was running a small store, was a laborer rather than a merchant.[127]

Most litigants, however, did not gain relief upon appeal in the 1910s and 1920s. *Lim Chan v. White* determined that the children of merchants, unlike individuals claiming to be the children of citizens, did not have access to the special board of hearing to present their claim for entry based on descent.[128] In 1924, the Ninth Circuit clarified that a Chinese official, governed by the same rules as those governing merchants, could then personally identify his servants and family members, "and upon such identification such persons are at once excluded from the general provisions of the act and shall be admitted without further evidence,"[129] but litigants challenging the process that had denied either the status of their fathers as merchants or their own status as children of merchants were repeatedly thwarted.[130]

Conclusion

To claim that "the Supreme Court had no difficulty in acquiescing to the exclusion of the federal courts from immigration decisions" oversimplifies a more complex relationship between courts (both the Supreme Court and the lower federal courts), Congress, and administrators.[131] While skirmishes continued around the boundary between state police powers and federal power, by 1875, immigration restriction had become a federal matter in terms of policy development by Congress, policy implementation and administration by the executive branch, and policy oversight by the federal courts. Immigration policy was a critical arena for shaping the national administrative state from the last quarter of the nineteenth century through at least the first quarter of the twentieth, but the courts, while legitimizing administrative determinations of rights, established the boundaries and parameters for administrative decision-making. This shift, while maintaining the courts' interpretive authority to manage familial relations, built more state capacity for managing the interface between family status determinations and immigration, an interface that remains crucially important.[132]

In the early years following the 1882 Chinese Exclusion Act, federal district courts on the West Coast considered so many habeas petitions that they complained of being overwhelmed. Local publics were so outraged at the courts' willingness to hear habeas appeals and admit some of those they felt the laws were meant to exclude that they pressed Congress to strip the courts of jurisdiction over these exclusion appeals. The courts only partly acquiesced, and the boundary contestation shaped the administrative state. Administrative rules and decision-making developed both in anticipation of and in relation to what immigration officials thought the Supreme Court would countenance. By taking the Court into account in formulating rules and procedures, administrative agencies sought to minimize interference, but their rulemaking occurred in the constant shadow of judicial oversight.

The courts' actions also shaped the relationship between race and citizenship, and the status of familial relationships for Chinese citizens and non-citizens. It carved out an anomalous status category for family members marked by their Chinese ancestry as ineligible for citizenship or civic membership, yet they were suffered to enter and remain in the United States based on their ties to men who fit more regularized statutory and constitutional categories.

The administrative apparatus primarily sought to exclude or remove all but a small number of economically useful Chinese merchants, diplomats and officials, and students, and this system was increasingly empowered to achieve this mission. However, the women and children who could claim some attachment either to a man with a legitimate right to be present or to the United States itself by birth presented boundary questions that both required judicial resolution and, because of their ambiguous status, continued to pose dilemmas for the courts throughout this period.

Peter Schuck suggests that the cases of *Nishimura Ekiu v. United States* and *Chae Chan Ping*, which had established Congress's plenary power to regulate aliens' entry into and residence in the United States, established a pattern of deference of judges to administrators that distinguished the trajectory of immigration law from other developing branches of administrative law. His account presents a kind of immigration law exceptionalism: "In a legal firmament transformed by revolutions in due process and equal protection doctrine and by a new conception of judicial role, immigration law remains the realm in which government authority is at the zenith, and individual entitlement is at the nadir."[133] Clearly, since immigration was related to the power to establish relations with other nations and conduct foreign affairs, the courts were deferential in many ways. And yet Daniel Ernst has suggested a broader pattern in relations between branches in the development of administrative law that resonates with our study. The relationship between federal courts and administrators during the late nineteenth and early twentieth centuries—and the ways in which immigration law maps onto these patterns of relationships—mattered for where room for challenge was found, and remains a rich area for investigation. Further, our investigation suggests that family was a critical site of complexity.

By around 1920, the Supreme Court in particular hinted at greater concern for procedural violations in appeals involving birthright citizenship. The Court had several important occasions to address claims that the secretary of labor overstepped his jurisdiction when he acted as final authority in deportation cases in which persons claimed American citizenship. Notably, during these years the Supreme Court increasingly engaged arguments about fundamental or foundational rights (speech, press), ruling both to expand the concept of liberty and to extend protection to some disfavored groups, such as religious minorities, under its rubric.[134] But this broader heightened judicial scrutiny of potential due process violations came just when the nation was further limiting immigration with literacy tests and quotas. The stakes were reduced when federal courts flexed their muscles against arbitrary and capricious executive officers on immigration matters. As support for immigration waned and drastic new immigration measures were instated, nascent rights principles from the Supreme Court received only uncertain support in the lower federal courts and did little for those of Chinese heritage. Not until Congress reworked the system in the 1960s would American immigration law cease to embed explicitly racialized categories, but even after this shift, the administrative capacity and authority built over the years has remained robust, and as Chapter 8 shows, this system continues to identify family status and rely upon family ties in its daily operations.

Nonetheless, the courts created and preserved cracks in the façade of exclusion that Congress constructed and enhanced. Treatment accorded to those seized within the United States often received more searching judicial scrutiny during the period of this study. Courts cautiously extended Fourteenth Amendment protections beyond citizens. Confiscation of property also tended to trigger procedural safeguards. Courts sometimes invoked the Fifth, Sixth, and Thirteenth Amendments when objecting to rights violations of non-citizens. Claims of US citizenship, especially for those residents facing deportation, often triggered at least minimal concern for due process. But amid the rising tide of anti-immigrant sentiment in the years leading up to the Johnson-Reed Act of 1924, neither the Supreme Court nor the Ninth Circuit's courts offered consistent and robust protection. While our study does not allow us to compare treatment of men and women, it is at least plausible that women, suspected of being prostitutes and not wives, were particularly hard-hit.

The dilemma of birthright citizenship for individuals of Chinese ancestry pitted the policy imperatives of advancing administrative discretion and limiting the Chinese presence in the United States directly against the courts' emergent role as the guarantors of rights under the Fourteenth Amendment. The Supreme Court, with interpretive assistance from the lower federal courts, articulated a clear commitment both to the Fourteenth Amendment's attribution of jus soli citizenship and the long-standing (and congressionally codified) common law principle of jus sanguinis citizenship. At the same time, however, the courts established parameters through which administrative agencies could make determinations about individuals' citizenship status that, if conducted properly, forestalled independent judicial review and foreclosed access to any robust rights held by citizens. While even this narrow open door proved too much for policy makers, who closed the door much more tightly in 1924, for a time it provided the avenue for an occasional Chinese victory over the machinery of exclusion and a means for the courts to regulate the basic functioning of administrative decision-making in the interest of procedural justice.

Appendix. Late-Nineteenth- and Early-Twentieth-Century US Immigration Measures

Act	Year	Purpose
Burlingame Treaty	1868	Aimed to ease immigration into the United States and represented a Chinese effort to limit American interference in internal Chinese affairs.
Page Act	1875	Required that any immigration from China, Japan, or any Asian country to the United States must be free and voluntary. Barred entry of prostitutes.
Angell Treaty of 1880 (Sino-American Treaty Revision)	1880	The Chinese government limited immigration of laborers to the United States in exchange for US protection of those here. Revision to Burlingame Treaty.
Chinese Exclusion Act	1882	Effectively halted Chinese immigration of skilled and unskilled laborers for ten years and prohibited Chinese from becoming US citizens.
Immigration Act	1882	Levied a 50-cent tax on all foreigners landing at US ports.
Treaty of Chemulpo	1882	Established diplomatic relations between the United States and Korea; allowed Korean immigration to the United States.

(continued on the next page)

Appendix. *Continued*

Act	Year	Purpose
Amendment, Exclusion Act	1884	Tightened provisions for all ethnic Chinese leaving and returning to United States; extended Exclusion Act provisions for ten years.
Contract Labor Law	1885	An act to prohibit the importation and migration of foreigners and aliens under contract or agreement to perform labor in the United States, its territories, and the District of Columbia.
Contract Labor Act Amendment	1887	Charged the secretary of the treasury with enforcing the Contract Labor Act and mandated that foreigners who arrive in violation of the act be immediately sent back.
Payson Act	1887	Restricted real estate ownership in the United States to citizens or those who have legally declared their intention to become citizens.
Act of October 19	1888	Required that immigrants who landed in violation of the Contract Labor Law of 1885 be sent back within one year of entry.
Scott Act	1888	Prohibited immigration of all Chinese laborers to the United States, including those who had gone back to China to visit. Ended certification (exit visa) process.
Immigration Act	1891	Amended various acts on immigration and importation of aliens under contract or agreement to perform labor; barred those likely to become public charges.
Geary Act	1892	Extended Scott Act for ten years, barring entry of most Chinese persons. Chinese residents in United States must acquire and carry certificates of residence or face deportation.
Act of March 3	1893	Added new reporting requirements for foreign arrivals into the United States, including information about occupation,

		marital status, ability to read or write, amount of money in possession, and information pertaining to physical and mental health.
Gresham-Yang Treaty	1894	China accepted the total prohibition of immigration to the United States in exchange for readmission of those back in China on a visit.
Scott Act Extension	1902	Extended Chinese exclusion laws indefinitely.
Immigration Act of March 3	1903	Further codified existing immigration laws, expanded the list of inadmissible immigrants to include anarchists and those involved in prostitution, and included provisions to deport prostitutes and those involved in prostitution.
Naturalization Act of June 29	1906	Combined the immigration and naturalization functions of the federal government. Retooled the naturalization process.
Immigration Act	1907	Added new restrictions to the classes of people barred from immigrating to the United States. Added new immigration procedures.
Expatriation Act	1907	Mandated that "any American woman who marries a foreigner shall take the nationality of her husband."
Mann White Slave Traffic Act	1910	Forbade the importation or interstate transportation of women for immoral purposes.
Act of March 4	1913	Divided the Department of Commerce and Labor into separate departments and transferred the Bureau of Immigration and Naturalization to the DOL.
Immigration Act	1917	An act to regulate the immigration of aliens to—and the residence of aliens in—the United States. Excluded immigration from South or Southeast Asia, including India. Also known as Asiatic Barred Zone Act.
Wartime Measure	1918	An act to prevent in time of war the departure from or entry into the United States contrary to public safety.

(*continued on the next page*)

Appendix. *Continued*

Act	Year	Purpose
Emergency Quota Law	1921	An act to limit the immigration of aliens into the United States.
Cable Act	1922	Repealed parts of the Expatriation Act, allowing women to marry non-US citizens without losing their citizenship.
Johnson-Reed Act	1924	An act to limit the immigration of aliens into the United States.
Cable Act Amendment 1	1930	Excluded prostitutes from the Cable Act. Eased repatriation requirements for marital expatriates.
Cable Act Amendment 2	1931	Repealed the provisions of the Cable Act that made women ineligible for repatriation because they were married to men from racially excluded categories (namely, Asian men).
Cable Act Amendment 3	1932	Made "a woman born in Hawaii prior to June 14, 1900," a citizen at birth, provided they resided in the United States on July 2, 1932.

Sources: Summary of Immigration Laws, 1875–1918, accessed at http://people
.sunyulster.edu/voughth/immlaws1875_1918.htm; Our Documents: Chinese
Exclusion Act, accessed at https://www.ourdocuments.gov/doc.php?flash=true
&doc=47; University of Wisconsin, US Immigration Legislation Online, accessed
at http://library.uwb.edu/static/USimmigration/USimmigrationlegislation.html;
US Department of Homeland Security, US Citizenship and Immigration Services,
Legislation from 1790–1900, accessed at http://www.nps.gov/elis/learn/
education/upload/Legislation-1790-1900.pdf; Illegal Immigrant Laws, accessed at
http://www.illegalimmigrants.org/laws
.html; Martha Gardner, *The Qualities of a Citizen: Women, Immigration, and Citizenship,
1870–1965* (Princeton, NJ: Princeton University Press, 2009); Meg Hacker, "When
Saying 'I Do' Meant Giving Up Your U.S. Citizenship," accessed at http://www
.archives.gov/publications/prologue/2014/spring/citizenship.pdf; Candice Lewis
Bredbenner, *A Nationality of Her Own: Women, Marriage, and the Law of Citizenship*
(Berkeley: University of California Press, 1998).

Notes

We thank Zoeth Flegenheimer, class of 2015, Allison Hrabar, 2016, Nathaniel Urban, 2018, and Navid Kiassat (all at Swarthmore College); and Heather Bennett (University at Albany, SUNY) for research assistance. Amy Rappole, JD, then a student at the University of Maryland's Francis King Carey School of Law, helped collect and classify some of our case law material.

1. See *Chy Lung v. Freeman*, 92 U.S. 275 (1876). See also *Henderson v. Mayor of City of New York*, 92 U.S. 259 (1875), on congressional power over immigration. Most of the Chinese who entered the United States came through West Coast ports, especially San Francisco, although some entered by land from Canada and Mexico. On the timing of increases/decreases in Chinese and Japanese farm work, see Carey McWilliams, *Factories in the Field* (Boston: Little, Brown, 1939), 66–72, 82–90. California passed its first Chinese immigration ban in 1858.

2. The 1882 act suspended the immigration of Chinese laborers; the 1880 revision of the Burlingame Treaty, known as the Angell Treaty, permitted restriction but not prohibition of Chinese immigration.

3. In an executive agreement signed by Theodore Roosevelt (the "Gentlemen's Agreement" of 1907–1908), Japan agreed to bar laborers intending to enter the United States; in exchange, San Francisco dropped plans to bar Asians from the public schools. The Immigration Act of 1924 barred entry of a number of other Asians.

4. California struck down its ban in the 1948 state court case *Perez v. Sharp*, 32 Cal. 2d 711. See Shira Morag-Levine, "A 'Vital Question of Self-Preservation': Chinese Wives, Merchants, and American Citizens Caught in the 1924 Immigration Act," *Stanford Journal of Civil Rights and Civil Liberties* 9, no. 1 (2013): 121–151, especially 134–137; and Irving G. Tragen, "Statutory Prohibitions against Interracial Marriage," *California Law Review* 32, no. 3 (1944): 269–280.

5. Morag-Levine, "A 'Vital Question,'" 134; some Chinese men married African American women, since these unions were permitted. In the Expatriation Act of 1907, Congress stripped citizenship from American women marrying foreign men. Although the Cable Act of 1922 rescinded some of these provisions, American women who married foreigners ineligible for naturalization still lost their citizenship. See Linda K. Kerber, *No Constitutional Right to Be Ladies: Women and the Obligation of Citizenship* (New York: Hill & Wang, 1998), 42–43. See also Candice Lewis Bredbrenner, *A Nationality of One's Own: Women, Marriage, and the Laws of Citizenship* (Berkeley: University of California Press, 1998).

6. See Julie Novkov, "Identity and Law in American Political Development," 662–681, especially 663–664, and Eileen McDonagh and Carol Nackenoff, "Gender and the American State,"112–131, especially 123–124, both in *The*

Oxford Handbook of American Political Development, ed. Richard Valelly, Suzanne Mettler, and Robert C. Lieberman (Oxford: Oxford University Press, 2016).

7. See Stephen Skowronek, *Building a New American State* (Cambridge: Cambridge University Press, 1982).

8. For instance, Daniel P. Carpenter, *The Forging of Bureaucratic Autonomy: Reputations, Networks, and Policy Innovation in Executive Agencies, 1862–1928* (Princeton, NJ: Princeton University Press, 2001), 6.

9. Daniel R. Ernst, *Tocqueville's Nightmare: The Administrative State Emerges in America, 1900–1940* (Oxford: Oxford University Press, 2014), 4.

10. Ernst, *Tocqueville's Nightmare*, 3.

11. Ernst, 2.

12. Anna O. Law, *The Immigration Battle in American Courts* (Cambridge: Cambridge University Press, 2010), 203.

13. This modest victory was tempered by the fact that natural-born citizens seeking to bring Chinese wives to the United States between passage of the Johnson-Reed Act of 1924 and 1930 were treated less favorably than merchants. Congress amended the law in 1930, allowing those married before 1924 to enter. See Todd Stevens, "Tender Ties: Husbands' Rights and Racial Exclusion in Chinese Marriage Cases, 1882–1924," *Law and Social Inquiry* 27, no. 2 (2002): 271–305, citing *Ex Parte Chan Shee* (1924), and *Chang Chan v. Nagle* (1925).

14. See Priscilla Yamin, *American Marriage: A Political Institution* (Philadelphia: University of Pennsylvania Press, 2012); and Patricia Strach, *All in the Family: The Private Roots of American Public Policy* (Palo Alto, CA: Stanford University Press, 2007).

15. See Lucy E. Salyer, *Laws Harsh as Tigers: Chinese Immigrants and the Shaping of Modern Immigration Law* (Chapel Hill: University of North Carolina Press, 1995).

16. Adrian Vermeule, "Portrait of an Equilibrium," *New Rambler* (March 4, 2015), reviewing Ernst, *Tocqueville's Nightmare*, http://newramblerreview.com/book-reviews/law/tocqueville-s-nightmare. Vermeule argues that the effort to keep the administrative state within the bounds of the law reflected a vision of a centralized administration trampling on legal rights.

17. San Francisco was the port of entry for the vast majority of Chinese arriving in the United States. The Pacific Mail Steamship Company terminal was replaced, after 1910, with the new processing and detention facility at Angel Island, removed from the mainland. Most of those denied entry were held on shipboard or, after 1910, at Angel Island. With intervention, some lucky detained women and children might be housed instead at Chinese home mission facilities run chiefly by women of various Protestant denominations.

18. Congressional Research Service, *History of the Immigration and Naturalization Service*, Report for the Select Commission on Immigration and Refugee Policy (Washington, DC: US Government Printing Office, 1980), 8–11. The

Bureau of Immigration shifted to the Department of Commerce and Labor in 1903 and to the new Department of Labor in 1913.

19. The Department of Commerce and Labor was separated into two Departments in 1913.

20. Reported opinions do not allow generalization about the success rate of petitions.

21. David C. Frederick, *Rugged Justice: The Ninth Circuit Court of Appeals and the American West, 1891–1941* (Berkeley: University of California Press, 1994), 52.

22. Gardner, *Qualities of a Citizen: Women, Immigration, and Citizenship, 1870–1965* (Princeton, NJ: Princeton University Press, 2005), 17. She notes that Japanese immigrants already in the United States could send for their wives under the Gentleman's Agreement of 1907.

23. *Fong Yue Ting v. United States*, 149 U.S. 698, 711, 712 (1893), a case originating in New York.

24. *Nishimura Ekiu v. United States*, 142 U.S. 651, 660 (January 1892).

25. *Fong Yue Ting*, 754, 759, and 761–762; *Yick Wo v. Hopkins* 118 U.S. 356 (1886). Anna Law points out that this is the first case where the majority "perpetuates the legal fiction that deportation does not constitute punishment"; *The Immigration Battle in American Courts*, 197.

26. *Fong Yue Ting*, 733–735, 738.

27. As but one example, see J. Thomas Scharf, "The Farce of the Chinese Exclusion Laws," *North American Review* 166 (1898): 85–97.

28. Scharf, "Farce of the Chinese Exclusion Laws," 93.

29. Sundry Civil Appropriations Act of August 18, 1894, chap. 301, quoted by Justice John Harlan in *Kaoru Yamataya v. Fisher*, 189 U.S. 86 (1903) at 96. Cited source: 28 Stat. at L. 372, 390 (U.S. Comp. Stat. 1901, p. 1303).

30. *Wong Wing v. United States*, 163 U.S. 228 (1896), a case from the Eastern District of Michigan. See Gerald L. Neuman, "*Wong Wing v. United States*: The Bill of Rights Protects Illegal Aliens," in *Immigration Law Stories*, ed. David Martin and Peter Schuck (St. Paul, MN: West Law/Foundation Press, 2005), 31–50. Neuman states that Frank Henry Canfield, who had considerable experience, represented Wong Wing, probably funded by the Chinese Six Companies. *Yick Wo v. Hopkins*, 118 U.S. 356 (1886), had extended equality rights to non-citizens, invalidating a San Francisco ordinance targeting Chinese laundry owners and operators.

31. Neuman, *Wong Wing v. United States*, 40.

32. Harlan, in *Yamataya v. Fisher*, 97.

33. *Yamataya v. Fisher*, 98–99, citing *Fok Yung Yo v. United States*, 185 U.S. 296, 305 (1902).

34. *Yamataya v. Fisher*, 101. These aliens had "become subject in all respects to [the nation's] jurisdiction." Justices Brewer and Peckham dissented.

35. A point emphasized by Salyer in *Laws Harsh as Tigers*, 98.

36. Salyer, 94, 100–102, 105, 107.

37. Immigration Act of 1917, §19; 64th Congress, Session II, Chapter 29; 39 Stat. 874, 890.

38. Kerber, *No Constitutional Right to Be Ladies*, 43.

39. 1855 Naturalization Act, Chapter 72, section one.

40. Kristin Collins, "Illegitimate Borders: *Jus Sanguinis* Citizenship and the Legal Construction of Family, Race, and Nation," *Yale Law Journal* 123 (2014): 2134, fn. 82.

41. Collins, "Illegitimate Borders."

42. The use of "Asian American" here is anachronistic but best captures the dilemma that policymakers felt.

43. Kerber, *No Constitutional Right to Be Ladies*, 43. Italics in original.

44. The Supreme Court upheld this principle to strip middle-class native-born Caucasian women of citizenship in *MacKenzie v. Hare*, 239 U.S. 299 (1915). The Cable Act of 1922 addressed some of the provisions most objectionable to these women, taking away an American man's former privilege of extending American citizenship to a wife through marriage; instead, she would have to become naturalized—unless she was racially ineligible for naturalization. See Nancy Cott, *Public Vows: A History of Marriage and the Nation* (Cambridge, MA: Harvard University Press, 2000), 165.

45. Collins, "Illegitimate Borders," 2158. This was effectively the Guyer rule, derived from *Guyer v. Smith*, 22 Md. 239 (1864); see Collins, 2154.

46. Collins, 2154, 2167.

47. Collins, 2168.

48. *White v. Wong Quen Luck*, 243 F. 547, 549 (9th Cir. 1917).

49. *Quan Hing Sun et al. v. White*, 54 F. 402 (9th Cir. 1918), 404–405.

50. See, e.g., *Ex parte Lee Dung Moo*, 230 F. 746 (N.D. Cal. 1916); *Ex parte Wong Foo*, 230 F. 534 (N.D. Cal. 1916); *Ex parte Tom Toy Tin*, 30 F. 747 (N.D. Cal. 1916).

51. *Quan Hing Sun*, 406.

52. *Quan Hing Sun*, 406–407; *Jeong Quey How v. White*, 258 F. 518 (9th Cir. 1919).

53. No seat turned over on the Ninth Circuit until 1923 (Frank Rudkin succeeded William Morrow); another turned over in 1925 (Wallace McCamant succeeded Erskine Ross).

54. Brandeis clarified that neither the Geary Act nor the Immigration Act of 1917 preserved an exceptional right to a *judicial* (as opposed to an executive) hearing in *Ng Fung Ho v. White*, 259 U.S. 276 (1922), 284.

55. *Ng Fung Ho*, 284.

56. *Ng Fung Ho*, 284. Ng Fung Ho and his son did not benefit from this decision since the Chinese Exclusion Act of May 5, 1892, as amended made it unlawful for a Chinese laborer not in possession of a certificate of residence to

remain in the United States. Regardless of the legality of Ng Fung Ho's entry, they were not birthright citizens and lost their appeal.

57. *Ng Fung Ho*, 284–285. Despite this ruling's limits on executive branch jurisdiction when citizenship was claimed, the Ninth Circuit later interpreted the fair hearing mandate narrowly in cases involving women.

58. *White v. Chan Wy Sheung*, 270 F. 764 (9th Cir. 1921).

59. *Chang Sim v. White*, 227 F. 765 (9th Cir. 1922); *Wong Fook Ngoey v. Nagle*, 300 F. 323 (9th Cir. 1924); *Fong Lim v. Nagle*, 2 F.2d 971 (9th Cir. 1925); *Young Fat v. Nagle*, 3 F.2d 439 (9th Cir. 1925).

60. *Soo Hoo Hung v. Nagle*, 3 F.2d 267 (9th Cir. 1925).

61. *In re Kwock Seu Lum*, 287 F. 363 (N.D. Cal. 1922).

62. Stevens, "Tender Ties," 297. This was in lieu of alleging discrimination based on Fourteenth Amendment protections afforded all persons.

63. Stevens, "Tender Ties," 297, 272, 298, 299. Adopted sons tried to bring their wives into the United States using family unification arguments, though these arguments did not as easily succeed.

64. Kathleen S. Sullivan, *Constitutional Context: Women's Rights Discourse in Nineteenth-Century America* (Baltimore, MD: Johns Hopkins University Press, 2007), 131.

65. See Sullivan, *Constitutional Context*, 132, for language used in debate in the Indiana Constitutional Convention of 1850.

66. See Nancy F. Cott, *Public Vows*, 136, about the writing of the Page Act.

67. Cott, 136. The effort to stamp out white slavery, prostitution, and vice intensified in the early years of the twentieth century, as bourgeois reformers (including many organized women) sought to regulate the behavior and amusements of young urban immigrants. See Chicago Vice Commission, *The Social Evil in Chicago* (Chicago: [Illinois] Vice Commission, 1911); Jane Addams, *A New Conscience and an Ancient Evil* (Chicago: University of Illinois Press, 2002 [1912]); Joanne J. Meyerowitz, *Women Adrift: Independent Wage Earners in Chicago, 1880s–1930s* (Chicago, IL: University of Chicago Press, 1988); Mary E. Odem, *Delinquent Daughters: Protecting and Policing Adolescent Female Sexuality in the United States, 1885–1920* (Chapel Hill: University of North Carolina Press, 1995).

68. Peggy Pascoe, "Gender Systems in Conflict: The Marriages of Mission-Educated Chinese American Women, 1874–1939," *Journal of Social History* 22 (1989): 631–652.

69. Gardner, *Qualities of a Citizen*, 20.

70. See Gardner, 18.

71. Candice Lewis Bredbenner, *A Nationality of Her Own: Women, Marriage, and the Law of Citizenship* (Berkeley: University of California Press, 1998); quoting Acting Secretary of Labor J. B. Densmore to the secretary of state, January 28, 1914.

72. Bredbenner, *A Nationality of Her Own*, 34, 35.

73. Bredbenner, 124, 125 (including both quotes).

74. Emergency Quota Law of 1921, 67th, Session I, Ch. 8, 5–7, accessed at http://library.uwb.edu/Static/USimmigration/42%20stat%205.pdf.

75. Gardner, *Qualities of a Citizen*, 125.

76. *Tsoi Sim v. United States*, 116 F. 920 (9th Cir. 1902); Gardner, *Qualities of a Citizen*, 18–19. Tsoi Sim had never left California since arriving in 1882.

77. *Tsoi Sim*, 923.

78. *Tsoi Sim*, 926.

79. *In re Tang Tun*, 168 F. 488 (9th Cir. 1909). In 1910, the Ninth Circuit further clarified that, as with citizens, a mere declaration that a plaintiff was married to a citizen did not entitle her to a more searching review of her challenge of a deportation order. *Hoo Choy v. North*, 183 F. 92 (9th Cir. 1910).

80. *Looe Shee v. North*, 170 F. 566, 567–570 (9th Cir. 1909).

81. The Immigration Act of February 20, 1907, not only excluded as a class of alien "prostitutes, or women or girls coming into the United States for the purpose of prostitution," but stipulated that "any alien woman or girl who shall be found an inmate of a house of prostitution or practicing prostitution at any time within three years after she shall have entered the United States, shall be deemed to be unlawfully within the United States and shall be deported." Those managing houses of prostitution were also deportable. See US Bureau of Immigration and Naturalization, "Immigration Laws and Regulations of July 1, 1907" (Washington, DC: Government Printing Office, 1910), accessed online at https://archive.org/stream/cu31924021131101#page/n9/mode/2up/search/prostitution.

82. *Looe Shee*, 571, quoting Justice Holmes in *Keller v. United States*, 213 U.S. 138 (1909).

83. *Wong Heung v. Elliott*, 179 F. 110 (9th Cir. 1910), 112. The court took a dim view of her husband, who "was himself a Chinese laborer, a laundryman, and he testified that sometimes he worked and sometimes he did not. It does not appear that he had any fixed place of abode; but it does appear that he had been in trouble, charged with breaches of the law."

84. *Ex parte Ung King Ieng*, 213 F. 119, 121 (DC N.D. Cal. 1914).

85. *Ex parte Tsuie Shee*, 218 F. 256 (N.D. Cal. 1914). After the administrative error was resolved, Tsuie Shee again faced a deportation order and again sought habeas relief. This time, although she claimed that the evidence used against her had been obtained by an illegal search of her husband's baggage, the Ninth Circuit refused to grant relief. *Tsuie Shee v. Backus*, 243 F. 551 (9th Cir. 1917).

86. *Low Kwai v. Backus*, 229 F. 481 (9th Cir. 1916).

87. *Mah Shee v. White*, 242 F. 868 (9th Cir. 1917).

88. See, e.g., *Choy Gum v. Backus*, 223 F. 487 (9th Cir. 1915).

89. *Jung Back Sing v. White*, 257 F. 416, 416–417 (9th Cir. 1919).

90. *Halsey v. Ho Ah Keau*, 295 F. 636, 639 (9th Cir. 1924). While his marriage to the second wife was possibly not solemnized according to Hawaiian law, he pleaded no contest to bigamy charges and paid a fine.

91. *Halsey v. Ho Ah Keau*, 638.

92. *Wong Wing Sing v. Nagle*, 299 F. 601, 601 (9th Cir. 1924).

93. *Wong Wing Sing.*

94. *Leong Shee v. White*, 295 F. 665 (9th Cir. 1924).

95. *Chun Shee v. Nagle*, 9 F.2d 342 (9th Cir. 1925).

96. Stevens, "Tender Ties," 299–300.

97. *Chun Shee v. Nagle.*

98. *Ex parte Cheung Sum Shee* and *ex parte Chan Shee*, 2 F.2d 995, 998, 999 (N.D. Cal. 1924).

99. *Cheung Sum Shee v. Nagle*, 268 U.S. 336, 345 (1924).

100. *Chang Chan, Wong Hung Kay, Yee Sin Jung et al. v. Nagle*, 268 U.S. 346 (1925).

101. Morag-Levine, "A 'Vital Question.'" The author focuses on two 1925 cases, *Chang Chan v. Nagle*, and *Cheung Sum Shee v. Nagle*, and a group of women arriving on the same ship.

102. Morag-Levine, "A 'Vital Question,'" 121.

103. According to Morag-Levine, 136, these women were allowed to remain awaiting indeterminate legislative action, with a $1,000 bond that was then renewed.

104. Stevens, "Tender Ties," 297, 301 (including both quotes).

105. Gardner, *Qualities of a Citizen*, 17–18.

106. Sucheng Chan, "The Exclusion of Chinese Women, 1870–1943," in *Entry Denied: Exclusion and the Chinese Community in America 1882–1943*, ed. Sucheng Chan (Philadelphia, PA: Temple University Press, 1991), 94–146 (on identity and establishing that she is a "valid wife").

107. *In re Ah Moy*, 21 F. 785, 786, 808 (CC D. Cal. 1884), also known as the Chinese Wife case. Shortly after, she requested to be released on bail while awaiting the ship that was to deport her. Field refused.

108. *United States v. Mrs. Gue Lim*, 176 U.S. 459, 464 (1900), cites district and circuit court cases holding a wife's right to enter without a certificate as *In re Chung Toy Ho* (1890), *In re Lee Yee Sing* (1898), and the precursor to this case, *United States v. Gue Lim* (1897). Cases averse to this doctrine included *In re Ah Quan* (1884), *In re Ah Moy* (1884), *In re Wo Tai Li* (1888), *In re Lum Lin Ying* (1894), and *In re Li Foon*, a case from New York (1897).

109. *In re Chung Toy Ho*, 42 F. 398 (C.C. D. Ore. 1890).

110. *United States v. Mrs. Gue Lim*, 466.

111. "The maintenance and extension of American commerce with the Oriental countries must redound to the benefit of the American people as a whole.

Chinese merchants in this country are doing an important part in fostering this important interest, and no benefit whatever can accrue to the people of this country by depriving them of liberty to dwell within our borders, with their families, under the protection of our laws." *United States v. Mrs. Gue Lim*, 83 F. 136, 140 (D. Wash. 1897).

112. *In re Lee Lung*, 102 F. 132 (D. Or. 1900).

113. *In re Lum Lin Ying*, 59 F. 682, 682 (D. Ore. 1894). She was also known as Chung Shee.

114. *In re Lum Lin Ying*, 683, 684.

115. *United States v. Chung Shee*, 76 F. 951, 952–953 (9th Cir. 1896).

116. Allegedly she had previously attempted to enter the United States in San Francisco, claiming marriage to a merchant residing there before attempting to enter in Portland as Lum Lin Ying, identifying a different spouse the following year. *United States v. Chung Shee*, 71 F. 277 (S.D. Cal. 1895); *United States v. Chung Shee*, 76 F. 951 (9th Cir. 1896).

117. *Ex parte Chan Shee*, 236 F. 579 (N.D. Cal. 1916).

118. *Chew Hoy Quong v. White*, 244 F. 749 (9th Cir. 1917). See also Robert Barde, "An Alleged Wife: One Immigrant in the Chinese Exclusion Era," *Prologue Magazine* 36, no. 1 (2004), accessed at https://www.archives.gov/publications/prologue/2004/spring/alleged-wife-1.html.

119. *Chew Hoy Quong v. White*, 249 F. 869 (9th Cir. 1918).

120. Barde, "An Alleged Wife," quoting the Circuit Court's April 1918 opinion in *Chew v. White, Immigration Com'r*, Case No. 3088.

121. *Yee Won v. White*, 258 F. 792, 794 (9th Cir. 1919).

122. *Yee Won*, 797–798.

123. *Chan Gai Jan v. White*, 266 F. 869, 870 (9th Cir. 1920). Chan Gai was the minor son, and the case was brought on behalf of him and his mother.

124. *Chan Gai Jan*, 871.

125. *Ex parte Lee Sher Wing*, 164 F. 506 (N.D. Cal. 1908). A new 1919 law exempted foreign government officials, their families, and their guests from this limitation, and in 1922, a Chinese official's son gained entry despite being diagnosed with clonorchiasis. *Ex parte Cheuk Gar Lim*, 285 F. 396 (S.D. Cal. 1922).

126. *Ex parte Chooey Dee Ying*, 214 F 873 (N.D. Cal. 1911); *Ex parte Lew Lin Shew*, 217 F. 317 (N.D. Cal. 1914).

127. *Woo Hoo v. White*, 243 F. 541 (9th Cir. 1917); *Ex parte Young Toy*, 262 F. 227 (N.D. Cal. 1919).

128. *Lim Chan v. White*, 262 F. 762 (9th Cir. 1920).

129. *Nagle v. Yang Yum*, 300 F. 799 (9th Cir. 1924).

130. See, e.g., *White v. Fong Gin Gee*, 265 F. 600 (9th Cir. 1920); *Fong You Tun v. Nagle*, 293 F. 900 (9th Cir. 1923); *Siu Say v. Nagle*, 95 F. 676 (9th Cir. 1924); *Chin Hong v. Nagle*, 7 F.2d 609 (9th Cir. 1925).

131. Salyer, *Laws Harsh as Tigers*, 28, referring to the period following the Scott Act and early congressional efforts to rein in the courts.

132. See Gash and Yamin, Chapter 8 in this volume.

133. Peter H. Schuck, *Citizens, Strangers, and In Betweens: Essays on Immigration and Citizenship* (Boulder, CO: Westview Press, 1998), 19.

134. See, for instance, the Court's rulings in *Meyer v. Nebraska*, 262 U.S. 390 (1923), and *Pierce v. Society of Sisters*, 268 U.S. 510 (1925).

8 | Deportability and (Dis)unification
Family Status and US Immigration Policy

Alison Gash and Priscilla Yamin

Introduction

On May 7, 2018, the Trump administration announced its intention to separate immigrant families crossing the border into the United States from Mexico. Within weeks of the announcement, thousands of children had been removed from parents who had crossed the border and been detained in Immigration and Customs Enforcement (ICE) facilities across the country. Although far from the first time that US officials had engaged in the practice of dismantling immigrant families (according to the Cato Institute, familial separation occasionally occurred at the border during the Obama and Bush administrations), Trump's directive marked the first time that a policy explicitly called for separating immigrant and refugee families upon their entrance into the United States and drew significant opposition and legal challenges.[1] The policy, known as "zero tolerance," had been implemented specifically to discourage families from seeking asylum: travel without permission and you risk losing your children; return home and you can be a family again.

There were two significant shortcomings in the policy's use as a deterrent to the influx of immigrants entering the United States. First, immigrant families had little knowledge that their families would be separated when they arrived at the border. Parents were shocked to learn the fate of their families upon arrival at the border, but news of the policy did not reach far enough to deter families from seeking entrance to the United States.[2] Second, according to court documents, federal staff had misplaced the children, sending them to detention centers without recording their whereabouts and leaving parents with little recourse to reunite with their loved ones even if they complied with the law.[3] The policy prompted an immediate and pronounced backlash. Activists called out reports of children being drugged.[4] Judges cited the impossible situation of children being forced to act as their own legal advocates.[5] Courts intervened and eventually the Trump administration stepped back from its policy. Yet, even after the policy had been suspended, immigration officials continued to use the promise of parent-child reunions—among those who were already detained—to compel immigrant parents to "abandon . . . their [asylum] claims."[6] Pundits wondered whether Trump's policy marked a turning point in US immigration policy—an abrupt departure from a bedrock respect for the sanctity of the family. Immigration activists, however, understood the Trump order as an extreme, but nevertheless consistent, version of US antagonism toward immigrant families.

We begin this chapter with the paradox that not only undergirds much of the outrage toward Trump's zero tolerance policy but also has long been a persistent tension in immigration policy: political officials frequently tout familial stability and family values as essential to democracy and society, while at the same time consistently dismantling and disturbing that very stability in certain families. Images of ICE agents commandeering crying children as they are removed from the arms of their parents are incongruent with the widely accepted belief that Americans value families over all else. This political and policy paradox of valuing families in theory but dismantling immigrant families in practice drives much of this outrage. In this chapter, we pose a different question: what work is family unity or (dis)unity doing for state actors and policy goals? We argue that zero tolerance is actually an example of long-standing (though contingent and varied) practices of leveraging immigrant familial commitments to control immigrant behavior and meet state policy interests. We posit that advocates, scholars, and the public misunderstand the role that state authorities play in defining family—particularly in the context of policy battles and political debates. Although the abstract rhetoric of "family values" assumes a basket of essential rights accorded to all families—or at least those that share biological or marital ties—in practice many biological families are separated at the will and with the authority of US policy actors. In other words, "what makes a family" is not only the decisions and actions of private individuals and relationships but the public policy determinations of state actors—at least when public benefits and legal protections are concerned. Historically and consistently, this clash is shaped by the interrelationship between the changing nature of the state, the evolution of family structures, and economic need.

We have argued elsewhere that family is not a sacred, private institution forged through citizen-initiated interdependencies that receive state protections.[7] Rather, family functions as a public, state-licensed status that is bestowed or denied by policy officials or legal actors in service of specific policy goals that are largely unrelated to protecting families. While state actors may not have deliberately claimed the authority of family licensure when they first offered legal and financial support to struggling families, over time the state has become a pivotal player in both establishing and enacting familial supports and determining which households can reap these benefits. The increase in family-centered state benefits, coupled with the demand for those benefits by a wide assortment of households claiming to meet the definition of "family," increases state actors' authority to grant some households the privileges of family—while leaving others to fend for themselves.[8]

We focus specifically on immigrant families and immigration policy in order to identify the state's power to destabilize and disassemble families.[9] The use of family in immigration policy shows how state actors have become even more deeply embedded in the functioning of this vital institution. We use our conception of "family status" to explore the disconnect between the belief in family unity and the practice of family dissolution in immigration policy.[10] This incongruity between principle and praxis is evident in past and current congressional immigration debates, as well as in scholarship on immigration policy. As we argue, one common but incomplete explanation for this contradiction is that the state has simply failed to live up to its commitments. We advance a more nuanced explanation, one that decouples state-provided family benefits from the social experience of family and links state-provided benefits and protections instead to state policy-making initiatives. These state supports are not meant to scaffold private relationships and rights, but are instead meant to serve public goals. The principle of family unity in immigration policy should be viewed as both contingent and as a privilege rather than a right, one that is provided only to those households who serve policy ends and whose characteristics (race, gender, sexuality, income status) render them eligible to receive state approval.

Seen through this lens, family unity—the capacity for interdependent family members to remain legally and socially tethered to one another—is a privilege of family status, and is granted or denied depending on the specific state interest. The state's ability to control different kinds of immigrant families by allowing family members to stay together or by creating barriers to keep them apart illustrates how family status and its concomitant benefits provide a platform for advancing a range of state purposes. By starting with the premise that family is a state-granted status rather than a guarantee, we see family-focused rhetoric in policy debates in immigration not as a commitment to family preservation but as an investment in family control; it is an assertion of state power. It also points to the dynamic and flexible nature of family as a political tool, shaped by state and economic priorities. Our focus on *disunity* highlights the problem of adopting an ahistorical or abstracted understanding of family, one that reads family as separate from rather than contingent upon state action.

Our argument is threefold. First, we assert that by understanding family as a status awarded by the state rather than a value that guides the state, we can begin to more accurately understand familial *dis*unification and reunification as two equally powerful tools in immigration policy. Second, and relatedly, in reading family as a status, we illuminate the way in which the very presumption of the state's commitment to family unity obfuscates the power of the state to actually declare which households, whether bound by love or law, can receive the benefits and protections of family, and the reasons for state action. Third, for immigrant families specifically, we argue that by understanding family as a state status, we can more clearly see the coercive potential of the state's use of family status. Even though historically or in other policy domains family unity may have benefited state interests, the specific case of immigration highlights how state threats to family unity, especially prominent since the 1980s, are meant to encourage immigrant families to leave the United States but can also paralyze them into a state of "deportability" or "illegality" that benefits economic interests.

Family Values or Family Status?

When we hear language from politicians and state officials that praises family as a cornerstone of society and the bedrock of citizenship, we assume that, as an institution, family offers its members rights, entitle-ments, and the automatic protection of law. In their efforts to articulate a legally permissive state interest in denying wedding licenses to LGBTQ couples, for example, state actors—members of Congress, state legislators, judges—highlighted the state's interest in preserving families headed by married heterosexual couples. Even with Supreme Court support for marriage equality, as Tamara Metz discusses in Chapter 2, state actors continue to destabilize same-sex families in order to meet policy goals or satiate political interests. In welfare reform debates, public officials frequently refer to the importance of marriage and family to legitimize their efforts to push welfare recipients to marry the fathers of their offspring. States have made legal commitments to traditional families by both statutorily and constitutionally reserving marriage for heterosexual dyadic couples and have earmarked fiscal resources to pressure single mothers on welfare into marriage and fathers into child support. In these examples, the state relies on the traditional nuclear family model as the core building block of society in order to justify legal and political investments. Read in isolation, these policies and actions seem to be gestures of the state's commitment to the family and indeed have been analyzed as such. Following such claims, we would expect to see the state extending these commitments to family stability in all policy domains and for all familial units—or at a minimum for those following the strictures of traditional biological families.

However, a closer look reveals what appears to be idiosyncratic investments in families by state actors and institutions. We can see that, at any one time, some households receive familial benefits while others do not. Same-sex couples and single mothers have been denied the benefits of family that white, heterosexual, married families take for granted. A more exacting evaluation, however, reveals that even those households that adhere to the central tenets of the traditional family—heterosexual, married, two-parent households with children—are vulnerable to denials of family benefits or, worse, to attacks that destabilize families to their core. In these instances, state actors have purposefully developed protocols to dismantle, rather than scaffold, mother-father-child relationships. And frequently in these cases, race or nationality is the only characteristic that differentiates these vulnerable households from the "traditional" family ideal that the state works so hard to protect.

Immigration provides one clear example of a policy arena in which the state actively works against its own stated commitments to the mother-father-child triad and instead promotes policies that destabilize or decimate familial cohesion. Mixed-status immigrant families (in particular non-white households), even those in which some members have green cards, cannot presume that they will be recognized as a family for the purposes of US immigration policy. While immigration policy has historically and theoretically prioritized family out of both moral sensibilities and a belief that familial stability facilitates assimilation and success, in practice immigrant families have also always been vulnerable to state intervention. Despite the institutionalization of family unity and reunification in immigration policy in 1965, immigrants have been either separated from their family members by deportation and travel restrictions or forced to live as "illegal" or "undocumented" because of lengthy residency and citizenship wait lists. We say more about this dynamic below.

Moreover, recent trends indicate a formal rejection of familial cohesion as a guiding principle—and a new explicit focus on family disunity—as a tool for immigration reform in general. President Trump's explosion of immigration-focused executive orders and initiatives are an example of how state policies can directly sideline familial cohesion and actively denounce the principle of family unity. In January 2017, Trump's first travel ban, barring even visa-carrying immigrants' and refugees' entry into the United States from seven largely Muslim countries, aroused panic and widespread media attention among US-based refugees, residents, and citizens whose immediate family members were prohibited from entering US airports and detained by airport security.[11] Two months later, Secretary of Homeland Security John Kelly indicated that he, too, held no allegiance to familial cohesion when it came to immigration policy. In an interview with Wolf Blitzer, Kelly confirmed early reports of the zero tolerance policy, explaining that it would prevent mothers and children from "manipulating the system . . . because they know up till this point we will keep the families together."[12]

These claims of manipulation are used to legitimize policies that target, destabilize, and "disunify" immigrant families in order to meet political demands to restrict immigration and to serve specific policy interests. In past instances, family disunification has fostered a deportable and, therefore, vulnerable workforce—especially useful for industries that require low-wage manual labor. Zero tolerance, conversely, imposes on immigrant parents a binary choice: remain united as a family in detention or consent to be separated while initiating legal proceedings.[13] This move marks a shift away from using family disunification to support economic interests and toward a focus on family disunity as a targeted tool for national security. Our family-status lens highlights the true significance of zero tolerance. Rather than indicating a new focus on family disunity as a policy tool, Trump's policy rejects the economic interests that structured past practices of family disunity in immigration policy.

That the state holds concomitant yet opposing positions on family, at once essentializing the mother-father-child triad while simultaneously dismantling it depending on the policy or political context, complicates both scholarly and political analyses of the politics of immigrant family welfare. In an era when immigrant families seem to be increasingly at risk and under attack by state action, we argue that a family-status lens helps to direct conversations about the state's commitments to family unity by inviting a different set of questions. What does the practice and principle of family disunity tell us about immigration policy, state power, and governance? What can we learn about state power by examining the interaction of family and immigration policy? In what ways does the state's power to define the family offer state actors an invaluable and unbeatable coercive tool?

Immigration scholars frequently look at family unification to better understand the politics and implications of immigration reform. We highlight family disunification to identify the capacity and authority of the state to control the boundaries and beneficiaries of family, specifically in its form as a status bestowed by the state. Why does this matter? Family is not merely an *effect* of politics but is an important *site* of politics.[14] We build on the insightful work of immigration scholars, especially work that highlights the intersections of race, state and family, in order to demonstrate how the state uses and wields family across a variety of domains to suit a range of political, economic, and state-building goals.

Family Unity in Immigration Policy

Since the mid-1800s, the notion of family and marriage has been a central theme in immigration policy.[15] As one scholar put it recently, "there is not a single politician on Capitol Hill that would say they are against family unity."[16] Advocates define "family unity" as a family's right to remain intact and the state's obligation to protect familial cohesion, especially in the context of deportation and visa allocation. "Family reunification" extends protections to families that have been forced to legally or geographically separate and wish to be reunited. The intention behind family reunification is to provide mechanisms to preserve or support family unity during or following migration.

In 1924, an intensified opposition to immigration led to the passage of the National Origins Act, which severely restricted entry into the United States by limiting immigration based on one's country of origin. However, as immigration scholar Catherine Lee argues, even within these new and increasing constraints, a commitment to family preservation existed. For instance, Progressive Era policymakers hailed the nuclear family as the panacea for what was widely perceived as a problem of failed immigrant assimilation, especially among single male immigrants.[17] By 1928, a commitment to family unity was formalized. Along with skilled immigrants, immediate family members of legal permanent immigrants gained preferred status.[18] At the same time, as Carol Nackenoff and Julie Novkov explain in Chapter 7 of this volume, this commitment to family unity by the courts directly contradicted the desire to exclude Chinese immigrants from entering the United States during the late nineteenth and early twentieth centuries.

The Hart-Celler Act, passed in 1965, and also known as the Immigration and Nationality Act, ended the national origins quota, making it easier for American citizens and resident aliens to sponsor family members.[19] Heralded by immigration scholars and historians as watershed legislation on par with the Civil Rights Act of 1964, Hart-Celler established a principle of equality in immigration by removing the national origins bar and formalized a new set of family-based preferences.[20] It put in place a preference system with a focus on immigrants' skills and family ties to US citizens or residents and gave no numerical limit for immediate relatives of US citizens. Immediate family members defined as children were given first preference, spouses were given second preference, and then came parents of US citizens.[21] Since this policy's implementation, many scholars and policymakers believe family unity to be "an important and perhaps the central pathway to legal immigration in the US."[22]

This focus on family rather than national origin remained in place through the early 1990s when Congress mandated the creation of the US Commission on Immigration Reform, dubbed the "Jordan Commission," after Senator Barbara Jordan, the commission's chair, to examine proposed reforms to create a more efficient system. Family reunification featured prominently in the Jordan Commission's reports, which highlighted the importance of nuclear family cohesion in attracting high-skilled immigrants to help energize the US economy. The commission advised the US government to "implement a prioritization of nuclear family relationships to determine who will be admitted through family-based immigration."[23] Prioritizing the nuclear family was the first step in limiting the reach of family unity policy, because in so stating, the commission recommended the elimination of other family-based admission categories such as adult children and siblings of US citizens.

With the passage of the Illegal Immigration Reform and Immigrant Responsibility Act of 1996 (IIRIRA), the notion of family unity continued to be complicated and undermined. Driven by pressures to reduce the overall number of immigrants, the commission established a tiered system to privilege some family members over others, constituting the first official limit on the principle of family unity. Family roles (mother, father, sister, for example) were ranked and sorted into different application processes. Under this framework the parents of adult citizen children, spouses of US citizens, and minor children of US citizens were considered "immediate family" and could access expedited and unlimited visas. "Preferred status" was given to adult or married minor children of US citizens, spouses and unmarried minor or adult children of permanent residents, and adult siblings of US citizens. The difference between "immediate" and "preferred" can mean years on a waiting list, in part due to caps on the number of visas allocated to "preference" applications and in part due to an applicant's preference rank.[24] For instance, "immediate relatives" compete for over 100,000 visas, while visas allocated to unmarried sons or daughters of US citizens (and their children) are capped at just over 23,000. These vacillating preferences point to an ambivalent relationship of supporting but also limiting access to the United States through family regulation and reveal the potential for policymakers to leverage immigrant commitments to their families in order to benefit the state.

Even with the implementation of this tiered family status, other concerns and so-called loopholes were raised in the 1990s in the push to reduce the influx of immigrants to the United States. One such argument was the claim that unauthorized immigrant parents use their American-born children as "anchors." According to this perspective, immigrant parents "exploit" their children's status as American citizens by birth and use it as a way to gain access to the United States. In another policy venue or political battle, the desire of a mother or father to remain with their children would be encouraged and praised, but in the context of immigration policy immigrant parents' steadfast commitment to their children is framed as a subversive act against US interests. This imagery paints immigrant households as predatory—as attempting to take advantage of US actors operating in good faith—and the rhetoric of "anchor babies" bolsters long-standing practices of dismantling families of color.

State adherence to the principle of family unity was meant to support the state in its desires to assimilate immigrant workers and to reduce the risks they posed to white families. But since its inception, it has been referenced to support the rights of immigrant workers to stay tethered to their families and of immigrant parents to remain with their citizen-children. Whether the principle of family unity has supported immigrant families is up for debate. Some advocates argue that state policy and immigration officials have failed to live up to the principle of family unity, using it in name only and allowing it to fall by the wayside when other considerations arise. Anti-immigration activists and political actors complain that family unity encourages immigration and believe, as John Kelly does, that the United States must dispel any notions of family unity in order to stem the tide of asylum seekers. We argue that both of these positions provide only an incomplete understanding of the work that family status is performing in immigration policy and encourage scholars to examine state preferences for familial disunity in some policy contexts. Below we examine a subset of immigration scholarship in order to explore how scholars understand and interact with state commitments to family unity. We find that immigration scholars and policy makers frequently press the state to live up to the family unity claims, but miss the ways in which state actors are using family as a status and family separation as a stick to control immigrant family decisions.

Immigration Scholarship

The tension between the expected treatment of family and the practice of family is present in the scholarship on immigration policy, specifically on immigrant families.[25] In general, this scholarship sets out to highlight the profound effect that immigration reform efforts, particularly the Clinton-era reforms, have had on the status and well-being of immigrant families. On the whole, though, scholars begin with the presumption that family unity is currently an organizing principle of immigration policy. Scholars highlight the ways in which immigration policy and practice fail to live up to the principles of family unity, which is referenced as a long-standing goal of US immigration law. Starting from the perspective that the state supports family unity, scholars question why the state is deviating from its strongly held commitments to family stability and offer recommendations as to how state actors and institutions can better perform their responsibilities. Scholars do not read threats to family unity as a deliberate element of state family policy or as a political tool deployed by state actors to maximize political and economic goals.

The most frequent charge that the scholars we analyzed level against the state is its failure to acknowledge and incorporate, in the tiered system referenced above, the various familial forms that immigrant families adopt.[26] These scholars argue that immigrant families take on a variety of configurations and reflect a range of different values that include an extended family model. In many instances, scholars explain, immigrant familial configurations reflect caregiving relationships, or functional elements rather than marital or biological ties, that are not scaffolded by family unity measures in immigration policy. Scholars and advocates stress the idea that familial arrangements are the product of shared intimacies and interdependencies, and often extend more broadly than the nuclear model permits. For example, Vivian Garrison and Carol Weiss describe Dominican immigrant families as "stem kindred," which operates as "corporately functioning self-perpetuating kindred united by consolidated socioeconomic interests."[27] Garrison and Weiss claim that in designating some family members as "immediate" and others as "preferred," the state fragments families that emotionally and economically rely on the support of those "preferred" (and therefore downgraded) relatives.[28] We view this fragmentation as serving three important purposes: (1) to maintain the state's primacy in questions regarding familial benefits and autonomy, (2) to emphasize the use of family status as a viable regulatory mechanism, and (3) to respond to the economic interests of industries that rely on high-skilled or low-wage workers.

The idea of "deliberate disunity" shadows other elements of immigration policy referenced by scholars. For instance, "of age" requirements that stipulate that a US citizen must be twenty-one or older in order to petition an immediate relative are especially devastating to immigrant families that mirror the traditional ideal. This directive incapacitates families comprised of minor US citizen-children and non-citizen parents by imposing extreme hardships on their parents. For instance, although a parent could theoretically apply for citizenship once their child is old enough to petition the state, if a parent is in the United States without legal documentation for more than 180 days, they risk being classified as "inadmissible" for up to ten years. This leaves little opportunity for undocumented parents who stay in the United States with their dependent citizen-children to gain citizenship.[29] Once dissolved, these families become even more politicized because citizen-children are perceived as a drain on limited state resources and a problematic symptom of a too-generous system of family unification. These children are cast as a burden on the state rather than victims of state action.

Scholars focus on the contradictions, inequalities, and unintended consequences in legislation and regulatory language and the resulting difficulties that are imposed on immigrant families. When Congress passed IIRIRA in 1996, Fernando Colon-Novarro notes, the intent was to constrain immigrant families further from seeking refuge in the United States.[30] However, instead, undocumented or status-unstable immigrants (especially those in mixed-status families) were compelled to remain within US borders, fearing that if they left the United States at any time they would not be permitted to return. Mixed-status families, most frequently households comprised of unauthorized immigrant parents and their citizen-children, are particularly vulnerable to state control and family separations.[31] For instance, workplace raids frequently leave the citizen-children of unauthorized parents, a significant population within the immigrant community, in constant fear of losing their parents and having to leave their homes.

Scholars highlight how these obstacles leave immigrant families with little recourse but to operate at the outskirts of the law. Immigrants must either depart the United States and leave their family members behind, ask their family members to leave the United States even if they are authorized to remain in the country and risk exposing their family members to economic or political turmoil, or remain in the US illegally but safeguard their family's stability.[32] Families who remain in the United States whose children are otherwise eligible to receive state benefits frequently forgo these important resources in order to remain invisible to policy agents.[33]

In order to address the policy-induced constraints placed on immigrant families, some scholars urge the state to address this false choice and ask state actors to address and rectify the policy shortfalls that keep families in a long-term but taxing state of legal uncertainty. According to many scholars, policy officials could explore several options that would help recalibrate immigration regulations to complement rather than subvert family values. We argue, however, that these recommendations do not account for the ways in which immigration policy explicitly deploys family unification in order to further specific state goals. The state relies on its power to grant status to some families but not others—framed in this instance within family unification and family-based citizenship procedures—to negotiate, incentivize, coerce, and threaten immigrant families into making decisions that align with US (rather than their own) interests.

Implied in these recommendations is the assumption that the state has an interest in and commitment to working on behalf of families, particularly those that conform to the nuclear family model. These recommendations thus do not capture the notion that policy and economic actors may benefit from and have an interest in maintaining immigrant familial struggles. In our sample, few scholars actually question whether the state has an interest in employing these inefficiencies and inconsistencies, a question that we take up below. Catherine Lee is one notable outlier in this group. Her work *Fictive Kinship* explores how family is used by the state to produce and shape a national identity that is based on racial and gendered biases. In so doing, she similarly dispels notions that the state is working on behalf of the family.[34]

Our status argument focuses a different lens on the fact of state-imposed familial disunity. State actors have the authority to make decisions that affect the fate of many immigrant families under ambiguous policy directives. Since their inception in 1965, when the family unity provisions were codified into law, conceptions of family derived from immigration policy allow the state to advance family unity discourse while also limiting the ability of some immigrant families to live as a family. Family-based immigration regulations also authorize state actors to entice certain immigrant populations with the benefits of family unity while paralyzing other immigrant communities with the threat of disunity, each approach feeding specific economic and policy aims. We aim to highlight this tension and to explore why and how the state uses the family to undercut immigrant familial cohesion for certain immigrant families. A family-status frame intimates a more dynamic and contingent relationship between family and the state, where family emanates not only from biological ties or interdependent relationships, but also from state political and policy interests.

Valuations of Family Status in Immigration Rhetoric

One specific dynamic we see among the state, the family, and the economy is the differential treatment of high-skilled and low-wage worker families. We argue that in the case of immigration, the state uses its authority to entice high-skilled immigrants and exploit low-wage immigrants in order to cultivate economic strength. Pleas to state actors for immigrant family unity or for a more navigable pathway to citizenship for spouses and family members are evaluated based on economic value. State actors are open to claims made by so-called high-skilled immigrants. However, they also create the conditions for family *dis*unity by delaying extension of family status to low-wage immigrant households, placing immigrants into, as both Nicholas De Genova and Jill Harrison and Sarah Lloyd describe, an ongoing and "palpable sense of deportability."[35] Increases in enforcement, Harrison and Lloyd argue, coupled with shifting "migration practices," influence the capacity of "the state to serve two of its key 'productive' functions: protecting capital accumulation within industry and ensuring the state's own political legitimacy in the eyes of the public." Their research on Latino dairy farm workers in Wisconsin highlights how undocumented workers experience deportability and are forced live as outlaws.[36] We argue that by threatening immigrant familial commitments, immigration policy produces both the condition of deportability and the compunction for immigrant families to remain tethered to the US workforce—as vulnerable low-wage laborers.

Family (Dis)Unity through Economic Value

In 2013, Congress attempted to initiate another round of immigration reform, conducting a series of hearings to explore, among other things, family-based regulations. Among the varied factions of immigration supporters, opponents, and policy officials who testified, many referenced the incoherencies of family unification measures. In her opening remarks, Representative Zoe Lofgren described the system as "dysfunctional in many ways" because it "keep[s] families apart for decades" while "hindering economic growth and American global competitiveness." Instead of continuing the current system that has been "keeping families apart for decades," Lofgren called for "a moral and humane system," an "immigration system that works so that workers and families who want to come here are able to go through that system rather than around it . . . a system to help keep families together."[37]

Those who testified during hearings stressed the weaknesses in the family-based system, paying particular attention to the backlog of family members and spouses who have little hope of gaining legal status, and noting the challenges that confront undocumented workers and their families. During the hearing, state actors expressed more sympathy for the claims of familial instability from immigrants who are perceived as having high economic value, and far less when appeals for family stability were issued on behalf of low-wage immigrant workers. State actors appear to privilege high-skilled worker families in their discussion of family unity. More importantly, family unity appears to be something that is *earned* through economic value rather than granted to support interdependent relationships. In other words, the economy drives the discussion of family unification in immigration debates.

Of course, many who participated in the debates, particularly those advocating on behalf of immigrants who were not admitted under skilled workforce programs, referenced the moral imperative of family stability. Witnesses highlighted the sociological benefits of family: conveying values, nurturing children and dependents, raising a stable citizenry. In his testimony, for instance, San Antonio mayor Julián Castro argued, "Families make each individual stronger. That is the basis, I think, of much of the strength of our communities, the economic progress, the moral progress that we have made."[38]

Multiple members of Congress described the ways in which immigrant families are disunified, while also pressing for family unity as paramount to "the national interest." As one member explained, we have yet to "provide a system that will actually meet our needs, both in the economy . . . and that also respects the needs for . . . families to be united." [39] Participants bemoaned the increase in the number of "mixed status" families consisting of "newly legalized" immigrants and their unauthorized spouses or children, which had increased in part because of the judicial "stranglehold" that makes it impossible for family members of authorized immigrants or citizens to fight deportation. Here, one member of Congress called for policy officials to think about the children of immigrants who are separated from their parents. "How do we reunite [parents] with their children?" she asked. Describing a tour of "a residential facility for foster youth," she recalled a "group of children that were arriving . . . from California, who were being sent to live in Miami. So not only are they completely disconnected from their parents but any environment that they might have known." She asked, "What is to happen to those kids?"[40]

Yet, despite these considerations of family unity and concerns for the families with pending applications, economic value (rather than familial need) drives the majority of the debate. As one representative articulated about high-value immigrants: "You get to come from the very first day with your wife. You get to come from the very first day with your children. Because we believe we should welcome you and your talent."[41] This quote highlights the benefits that familial status provides as a reward for meritorious work. Committee members and witnesses also underscored the inextricable link between innovation and immigration. Google, Intel, Twitter, "advances in education," and computer-based EKGs, argued a Duke researcher, are "the sort of Earth-changing things that are happening" because of "skilled immigrants. People like me, engineers, scientists . . . a whole assortment of people [who] are driving these changes."[42] More than one expert raised the specter of "brain drain," the possibility that stingy recognition of and benefits for the relatives of authorized immigrant workers would hinder US economic growth.[43]

Throughout the hearings, as in this exchange below between a witness and Judiciary Committee member Jerry Nadler, familial stability is characterized as a zero-sum choice that rests on economic value.

Nadler: There are some who support the idea of increasing the number of green cards in the employment-based system, we have heard that, but only if a commensurate number of green cards are eliminated from the family-based system: Do you buy into this zero-sum approach, and can we be a Nation that supports both business groups and keeping families together?

Castro: This is not a zero-sum game. There is no reason that we need to choose between these. I believe that we should have both employment-based and continue our family-based allocation as well as, of course, addressing the issue of high-skilled immigrants and other skilled immigrants. I would also, frankly, suggest that being able to pick crops in the sun, under the hot sun, for 12, 14 hours a day, to do back-breaking work, is a kind of skill; maybe not one we would call a high skill, but certainly a skill that many, many folks either do not or cannot do. And so to answer your question, I believe that that is a false dichotomy.

These kinds of debates characterize how central being "deserving" is—in this case through economic value—in the battle for family status and, for immigrant families, family unity.

Hearing testimony highlights the reality that ideological claims for family unity are not enough to maintain a policy or principle of family preservation. Questions of economic efficiency outweigh more moralistic broad-based family values arguments and force us to revisit our assumptions about how the state perceives the importance of family. Rather than understanding stable families as essential to a productive or healthy society, state actors operate as if family stability is earned or awarded in exchange for specific economic provisions—in this case, high-skilled labor for the innovation economy. Exploring family as a status reveals important, yet less studied, dynamics among the state, the family and the economy.

Deportability and Disunification through Family Status

Understanding family as a state-bestowed status better captures the complicated relationship among state action, economic pressures, and the politics of immigrant family cohesion. As we have stated above, family status explains why state actors can apply different standards for different households seeking the benefits of family. Although state actors frequently praise the ideals of family or call for increased protections for the family in public debate, they have historically been quick to qualify or waive these commitments when doing so would serve a set of specific policy interests. This is true regardless of ideology or party. The hearing testimony discussed above highlights how familial stability hinges on both state perceptions of economic value and the characteristics of labor populations. Family unity is used to reward high-skilled workers (those in limited supply and high demand)—to "sweeten the deal" for their high-skilled labor. Low-wage workers, who face a vastly more limited set of employment options, are threatened with familial *dis*unification, leaving them legally vulnerable and economically constrained.

By understanding family as a state-granted status, we can see how family (dis)unity serves as a critical pillar of immigration policy and how family unification is used to entice or coerce immigrant families. We identify two prominent ways in which the threat of family disunification, coupled with the hope of reunification, is used to entrap immigrant families into a state of permanent illegality or enduring fear. When public officials delay family status to households of low-skilled immigrant workers—by excluding important familial relationships from the class of priority applicants, by limiting the capacity for child-citizens to sponsor their parents, by neglecting backlogs of eligible applicants—they force these immigrant families into an impossible position. Their choices: leave the country and obey the law but place family members at risk by either abandoning them in the United States or returning them to the upheaval of their country of origin, or remain in the United States but risk being deported and permanently losing the chance of becoming a citizen. Immigrant households are placed in a holding pattern. To get at this dynamic, we borrow from recent Latino studies scholarship on deportability. Deportability captures the "experience of living and working in the USA without legal authorization" and the ongoing exploitation that keeps unauthorized workers "in entry-level positions for years, [where they] earn entry-level pay, work very long hours, and take few days off from work."[44] Being in a "state of deportability" means living with the fear that at any moment you could be deported and separated from your loved ones without them knowing what happened to you. The term also explicates the role of the state in creating this liminal space in which unauthorized workers and their loved ones confront the daily possibility of being removed from state, community, and family.

We argue that the legally ambiguous status created by family-member rankings and mixed-status regulations places some immigrant families in this legally precarious position. This hope for, but lack of, family status creates an uncertainty in an immigrant's citizenship status. "Preferred" family members have the potential for citizenship but are placed on interminable waitlists. Undocumented parents of citizen-children are permitted to apply for citizenship, but only once their children reach adulthood. In both cases, their ongoing "pending" status places families in a legal quagmire: either leave your family while awaiting a decision and remain legally viable, or stay with your family and lose your legal status. In both cases, undocumented workers and their families are left unstable and unprotected. Undocumented workers who choose to remain with their citizen–family members are potentially "deportable" and vulnerable.[45]

For what purpose? We argue that just as the promise of family unity is used to entice high-skilled workers, the threat of disunity is used to keep low-wage labor chained to US economic interests. By threatening immigrant commitments to familial stability—the very motivation that frequently prompts immigration to the United States—and by offering a plausible pathway to family-based citizenship, the state encourages immigrants to remain in the US illegally while providing a captive source of low-wage labor. By rendering these pathways virtually unattainable and then criminalizing those who necessarily ignore regulatory obstacles in order to follow their familial commitments, state actors create a class of workers that are deportable and, therefore, limited in their potential to seek out higher-wage employment. This population of workers comprises over half of US farm labor, according to recent US Department of Agriculture statistics, and significant percentages of workers in other manual labor positions such as construction, housekeeping, and transportation. In significant ways, unauthorized workers are essential to these industries. One study estimated that if the supply of immigrant workers were reduced by 50 percent, "more than 3,500 dairy farms would close, leading to a big drop in milk production and a spike in prices of about 30 percent."[46] Policies calling for the complete exclusion of immigrant workers could "increase milk prices by 90 percent."[47] Without an increase in the legal pathways for immigrant workers to enter these positions, the pool of deportable immigrants provides a stable and steady supply of employees willing to take on jobs that few Americans will take in industries that are mainstays of the US economy. This may be why, at the same time that US officials have implemented a zero tolerance policy arguing, as President Trump has, that "our country's full," they have also moved forward with H-2B programs designed to issue temporary visas to immigrant workers willing to work in industries in low demand among American workers.[48] As Trump's zero tolerance policies threaten to deplete a critical source of labor—unauthorized immigrants—federal officials have considered other methods for securing low-wage manual labor.

But state actors benefit from and prey upon immigrant desires for family unity in a second way. Immigrant family commitments provide state actors with valuable leverage to control their behaviors. State actors can use family unity as a carrot and a stick to compel individuals seeking asylum to rethink their decision to seek refuge in the United States. The most recent and salient example is zero tolerance. Once separated and detained, parents are told that they can have their children back if they waive their due process rights to an asylum proceeding. Family cohesion is used to both deter families from entering the United States and then, once families are separated, to bribe asylum seekers into withdrawing their appeals even when their claims have merit. Confronted with the worst-case scenario, immigrant families are left with little option but to accept the terms offered by state actors. They must choose between returning to the violence that prompted their initial application for asylum and regaining custody of their children, or continuing to pursue asylum, risking having their children removed and detained. Understood in this way, zero tolerance does not mark a deviation from the principles of family unity but a departure from the use of family unity (and disunity) as a way of leveraging economic interests. Here Trump is rejecting economic motivations and using family specifically and exclusively for national security interests. As one White House official explained, "He just wants to separate families."[49]

Understanding family as a status also illuminates how race and class work together to create many of the inequalities inherent in immigration policy implementation. Nationality and ethnicity play an important role in determining which immigrant populations may serve as the "special favorites" of immigration policy, and which will be labeled as not deserving of access. Past regulations on Chinese immigrants, as described in Chapter 7, or Jewish children fleeing Nazi Germany, or recent attempts to block immigrants from Mexico or Muslim countries, are just a few of the many examples in which nationality and ethnicity are central to immigration policy. When we compare the experiences of immigrants crossing the border in Mexico to those who are admitted through targeted high-skilled initiatives, we can see how race and class intersect in ways that downgrade the value of certain immigrants of color while upgrading others. It is in the context of considerations of family-status benefits (in this case family unity), that debates and decisions regarding the valuation of certain immigrant communities, in particular communities of color, are made.

The Benefits of the Family-Status Framework

We use immigration policy and its scholarly analysis to highlight how family can be understood as a status licensed by the state. In so doing, we are motivated by two important goals. First, we want to encourage research and advocacy on behalf of immigrant families that sees state commitments to family unity as serving policy rather than familial ends.

Scholars have offered critical insights into the ways in which state policy has run afoul of its rhetorical commitments to family values. We argue that, through discussions of family status, the state holds significant authority in a range of policy arenas to determine which households may receive the benefits associated with family, benefits that are often critical for assuring the safety and welfare of family dependents. We argue that, rather than asking why state actors have deviated from their commitments to family, scholars and advocates should see family as historically operating as a mechanism of state building and policy advancement. This orientation toward the role of family in immigration might open up other avenues of scholarship and activism.

As we have seen, through the implementation of immigration policy, state actors determine whether a household can persist as a family and whether its interdependencies can remain intact without fear of further state intrusion. State actors have the authority to determine (1) which relationships constitute a family, (2) whether these relationships can meaningfully endure, (3) and whether families must plan for the possibility of policy-authorized upheaval. By defining the legal space for individuals to carry out their roles as dependents and caregivers and determining who has access to that space, state actors and agents can force families' members to operate as legal strangers in service of specific state goals.

The state does not do this with a particular family type in mind, despite its rhetorical allegiance to the nuclear family. Rather, state actors wield particular conceptions and predilections for family forms conditioned by the policy context within which the debates are taking place. As we have shown above, disunified families have been important in immigration policy. In the context of immigration, state actors are driven by political pressure to limit the number of immigrants—particularly those from specific regions who are perceived as either threatening or low-skilled. The practice of maintaining family disunity and denying families family status has been one powerful tool through which the state manages citizens and immigrants. When advocates demand that Congress "amend current immigration law to protect this right" to family unity or family reunification, they ignore the possibility that (1) family unity is not a right and (2) that the state has an interest in employing case-by-case, rather than universal and consistent, designations and definitions of family.

In addition, our family-status lens highlights how state actors create a class of "law-rejecting" immigrant communities by forcing them into a condition of "deportability." These immigrant families are castigated as outlaws because they are perceived as rejecting laws. Yet the very laws they are breaking are those that would force them to disavow the commitments to family unity that sit at the center of debates over marriage equality and welfare reform. If unauthorized immigrants follow the law and leave their children in the United States, they reject these family values. But if they prioritize family values and stay without explicit legal authorization, they are violating the law and considered criminals. Family status thus unearths the false choice that many immigrant families are required to make. State policy requires deportable parents to raise their children outside the confines of law and without the benefit of state investment. By forcing families into this position, state policy paradoxically creates the "fragile families" (the economically, legally and socially unstable families) that it frequently vilifies. Then the state can hold families captive, forcing them to operate as legally, economically, and socially vulnerable workers.

In this way, our family-status lens yields several critical implications. First, it offers a more accurate portrait of the ways in which the state interacts with immigrant families. Where family values rhetoric would have us assume that family stability should occupy an almost untouchable standing in immigration reform debates relative to appeals to economic value, a family-status account better explains the state's seemingly erratic and contradictory pursuits of family disunity in the context of immigration. The state entices those who promote economic innovation and entraps those who provide essential, yet devalued labor by offering up the protections of family unification in one instance and the threat of family disruption in the other. At the same time, family status functions to maintain compliance with certain requests of citizens and non-citizens. Lacking but needing the benefits of family status makes immigrant protest risky in a very specific and significant ways.

Second, this approach connects the growing scholarship on deportability with the important scholarship on the family as an institution. Where deportability scholars trace the economic and legally vulnerable status of unauthorized immigrants to state policies and economic interests, they may not focus on the family-based mechanisms employed by the state to indenture immigrant labor. Family scholars offer a similar focus on the effects of state policy on immigrant family conditions but may limit their exploration to the ways in which immigration policy influences immigrant families. Our family-status lens provides a framework for highlighting how state-determined family benefits are used to further economic and national security interests. This marriage of family, security, and economy can help advocates make more targeted demands of state actors and private interests. Rather than appealing to the rhetorical commitments made by state actors, immigrant family advocates can call attention to the potentially coercive leveraging of family benefits to create classes of economically valuable yet vulnerable workers. Family status allows us not only to identify the right questions in the context of immigration politics, but also to explain these deeply troubling consequences.

Notes

1. Marshall Cohen, "Fact-Checking Trump's Family Separation Claims," CNN, November 26, 2018, last viewed at www.cnn.com on April 15, 2019. Of course, the numbers of US-born children separated from immigrant parents through deportation is significantly higher and has been a consistent feature of modern US immigration policy.

2. Rick Jervis, "'He's All I Have Left': Immigrants Crossing into US Unaware, Stunned by Family Separations," *USA Today*, June 20, 2018, last viewed on www.usatoday.com on April 15, 2019.

3. Julia Jacobs, "U.S. Says It Could Take 2 Years to Identify Up to Thousands of Separated Immigrant Families," *New York Times*, April 6, 2019, last viewed at www.nytimes.com on April 15, 2019.

4. "U.S. Centers Force Migrant Children to Take Drugs: Lawsuit," Reuters, June 20, 2018, last viewed on www.reuters.com on April 15, 2019.

5. Christina Jewett and Shefali Luthra, "Immigrant Toddlers Ordered to Appear in Court Alone," *USA Today*, June 27, 2018, last viewed on www.usatoday.com on April 15, 2019.

6. Quote from Dree Collopy from the American Immigration Lawyers Association. Emma Platoff, Alexa Ura, Jolie McCullough and Darla Cameron, "While Migrant Families Seek Shelter from Violence, Trump Administration Narrows Path to Asylum," *Texas Tribune*, July 10, 2018, last viewed on texastribune.org on May 14, 2019.

7. Alison Gash and Priscilla Yamin, "State, Status and the American Family," *Polity* 48, no. 2 (2016): 146–164.

8. Gash and Yamin, "State, Status and the American Family."

9. We also address the role of immigration policy in destabilizing immigrant families in an earlier article. Alison Gash and Priscilla Yamin, "'Illegalizing'

Families: State, Status, and Deportability," *New Political Science* 41, no. 1 (2019): 1–16.

10. Catherine Lee, *Fictive Kinship: Family Reunification and the Meaning of Race and Nation in American Immigration* (New York: Russell Sage Foundation, 2013).

11. On January 29, 2017, the *New York Times* showcased a photograph of Haider Sameer Abdulkhaleq Alshawi hugging his wife and young child in Houston as they were reunited after Alshawi's detainment at Kennedy Airport. Andy Newman, "Highlights: Reaction to Trump's Travel Ban," *New York Times.*

12. Ian Gordon, "Inside Trump's Border Crackdown on Women and Kids," *Mother Jones*, March 19, 2017, last viewed at www.motherjones.com on April 15, 2019.

13. "Trump Pushed to Close El Paso Border, Reinstate Family Separation Policy," CNN, April 8, 2019, updated April 9, 2019, http://www.wtvm.com/2019/04/09/trump-pushed-close-el-paso-border-reinstate-family-separation-policy-sources-say/.

14. This is also true for the institution of marriage. See Priscilla Yamin, *American Marriage: A Political Institution* (Philadelphia: University of Pennsylvania Press, 2012).

15. Maria E. Enchautegui and Cecilia Menjivar, "Paradoxes of Family Immigration Policy: Separation, Reorganization and Reunification of Families under Current Immigration Laws," *Law and Policy* 37, nos. 1–2 (2015): 1–29; Catherine Lee, *Fictive Kinship*, 2.

16. Monique Lee Hawthorne, "Family Unity in Immigration Law: Broadening the Scope of 'Family,'" *Lewis & Clark Law Review* 11 (2007): 810.

17. Desmond King, *Making Americans: Immigration, Race and the Origins of the Diverse Democracy* (Cambridge, MA: Harvard University Press, 2002), 64.

18. Lee, *Fictive Kinship*.

19. Lee, 3.

20. Maria Cecila Hwang and Rhacel Salazar Parrenas, "Not Every Family: Selective Reunification of Contemporary US Immigration Law," *International Labor and Working-Class History* 78, no. 1 (2010): 100–109.

21. Immigration and Nationality Act of 1965, or Hart-Celler Act, H.R. 2580, Pub. L. 89–236, 79 Stat. 911, 89th Congress, October 3, 1965.

22. Lee, *Fictive Kinship*, 3.

23. Jordan Commission, "Becoming an American: Immigration and Immigrant Policy," September 1997, https://www.numbersusa.com/content/learn/illegal-immigration/us-commission-immigration-reform-barbara-jordan-commission.html, accessed April 24, 2017.

24. Shani King, "U.S. Immigration Law and the Traditional Nuclear Family Conception of Family: Toward a Functional Definition of Family That Protects Children's Fundamental Human Rights," *Columbia Human Rights Law Review* 21 (2009–2010): 509–567.

25. We compiled a sample of thirty articles on immigration family reunification, compiled from topical searches on suggestions from immigration scholars.

26. Enchautegui and Menjivar, "Paradoxes of Family Immigration Policy"; and Victoria Degtyarova, "Defining Family in Immigration Law: Accounting for Nontraditional Families in Citizenship by Descent," *Yale Law Journal* 120, no. 4 (2001): 862–908.

27. Garrison and Weiss, "Dominican Family Networks and United States Immigration Policy: A Case Study," *International Migration Review* 13, no. 2 (1979): 264–283.

28. Enchautegui and Menjivar, "Paradoxes of Family Immigration Policy."

29. Fernando Colon-Navarro, "Familia E Immigración: What Happened to Family Unity?" *Florida Journal of International Law* 19 (2007): 481–510.

30. Colon-Navarro, "Familia E Immigración."

31. Deborah A. Boehm, "For My Children: Constructing Family and Navigating the State in the U.S.-Mexico Transnation," *Anthropological Quarterly* 81, no. 4 (2008): 777–802. Mixed-status families are also a function of the state's rejection of immigrant familial configurations. See Enchautegui and Menjivar, "Paradoxes of Family Immigration Policy"; and Victoria Degtyareva, "Defining Family in Immigration Law."

32. Garrison and Weiss, "Dominican Family Networks"; Colon-Navarro, "Familia E Immigración"; Hawthorne, "Family Unity in Immigration Law"; Lori Nessel, "Forced to Choose: Torture, Family, Reunification, and United States Immigration Policy," *Temple Law Review* 78 (2005): 897–948; David B. Thronson, "Creating Crisis: Immigration Raids and the Destabilization of Immigration Families," *Wake Forest Law Review* 43, no. 2 (2008): 391–418.

33. Michael Fix and Wendy Zimmerman," All Under One Roof: Mixed Status Families in an Era of Reform," *International Migration Review* 35, no. 2 (2001): 397–419.

34. Lee, *Fictive Kinship*.

35. Nicholas De Genova, "The Legal Production of Mexican/Migrant 'Illegality,'" *Latino Studies* 4, no. 2 (2004): 161.

36. Jill Harrison and Sarah Lloyd, "Illegality at Work: Deportability and the Productive New Era of Immigration Enforcement," *Antipode* 44, no. 2 (March 2012): 365.

37. Testimony of Lofgren, US House of Representatives, Committee on the Judiciary (February 5, 2013), "America's Immigration System: Opportunities for Legal Immigration and Enforcement of Laws Against Illegal Immigration," https://www.govinfo.gov/content/pkg/CHRG-113hhrg78633/html/CHRG-113hhrg78633.htm, accessed on April 15, 2019.

38. Testimony of Castro, House Committee on the Judiciary, "America's Immigration System," 6.

39. Testimony of Lofgren, House Committee on the Judiciary, 226.

40. Testimony of Bass, House Committee on the Judiciary, 238.

41. Testimony of Gutierrez, House Committee on the Judiciary, 246.

42. Testimony of Vivek Wadhwa, House Committee on the Judiciary, 14.

43. Both Julián Castro and Vivek Wadhwa of Duke University referenced "brain drain" and "brainpower" in the context of their comments on family reunification.

44. Harrison and Lloyd, "Illegality at Work," 380.

45. De Genova, "The Legal Production of Mexican/Migrant 'Illegality,'" 165. De Genova explains, "Preferring the undocumented workers, employers could evade the bond and contracting fees, minimum employment periods, fixed wages and other safeguards."

46. Mary Jo Dudley, "These U.S. Industries Can't Work without Illegal Immigrants," CBS News, January 10, 2019, last viewed at www.cbsnews.com on April 15, 2019.

47. Dudley, "These U.S. Industries."

48. San Diego Union-Tribune Editorial Board, "Doubling of Worker Visas Shows Trump Double-Talk on Immigration," Editorial (syndicated), *Baltimore Sun*, April 9, 2019, last viewed at www.baltimoresun.com on April 15, 2019.

49. Jake Tapper, "Trump Pushed to Close El Paso Border," April 9, 2019, https://www.cnn.com/2019/04/08/politics/trump-family-separation-el-paso-kirstjen-nielsen/index.html.

Conclusion

Julie Novkov and Carol Nackenoff

This volume challenges the dominant paradigm by demystifying an institution that, far too often, confronts scholars—but especially privileged male ones—as natural and undeserving of political analysis. The chapters in *Stating the Family* present perspectives on critical questions about the family's role in the political sphere—as both a target and a means of development, and as a site where state building and state transformations take place. They also illustrate some of the unintended political consequences that can occur when family roles become activated. The authors place the family at the center of political and legal analysis, not just as a subject of regulation, but rather as an agent of development and change, and ultimately as a space that advocates for neoliberal agendas have been able to mobilize, transforming the way that care takes place and how responsibility for care is allocated.

A full critique of neoliberal transformation must necessarily incorporate an analysis of family and family policy, both in the current era and by tracing the roots of the transformation back by considering institutional development and change. As this book suggests, privatization encompasses more than the mere removal of state support for effective civic membership. Privatization removes the background guarantee of support that family is presumed to provide as a silent institutional partner with the state. To understand privatization and the contemporary relationship between politics and late capitalism, we cannot continue to ignore the family and family policy, as they serve as critical undergirders. A direct analysis of family and its increasingly significant involvement in replacing or implementing work formerly managed or supported by the state has another side. It can prompt clearer understandings of how shifting responsibilities to fragile families damages the interests of democracy, paving the way for re-envisioning this relationship.

Understanding family as a mobilized space, however, has implications beyond a consideration of neoliberalism. It raises the possibility of reclaiming and transforming politics by thinking critically through the work that family does, should do, and could do with more support and recognition. This insight lays important groundwork for grappling with present and future problems of care in the wake of the collapse of the New Deal bargain that bound both coverage of health expenses and retirement care to wage labor.

Incorporating the family into the analysis of law, regulation, and policy expands our explanatory capacities by making invisible or obscured things visible. Family relations and the ideological frames around particular family roles define and carry out much important work that shapes state development, the allocation of resources, and individuals' civic statuses. Yet as the contributors to *Stating the Family* illustrate, without looking specifically at family and the work it does, we can neither see how these things happen, nor how they change over time. The chapters consider the rhetorical, ideological, and institutional uses of family in policy making and the significance of particular familial roles in political action by policy makers, advocates for change, and family members themselves. They also explore the effects, intended and unintended, of policy making around the family and its members. We hope this volume will spur good scholars who have heretofore neglected the role of the family and family policies in shaping the American state to bring the family into theoretical and empirical scholarship about law, development, and politics. The family is interwoven with every major institution in the American state, and each relationship between the family and American institutions raises possibilities of new critiques and new transformative visions.

The collected chapters help to expand how we understand development by focusing attention on how changes in the family itself can affect how state policy works and provide incentives for visible policy change to accommodate what is happening with families. When policy makers seek to use the family more aggressively to manage care work, rather than serving as a bottom-line caregiver, we may observe changes in marriage promotion policy or differential state investments in marital versus non-marital families. Through the lens of the family, we believe we can better understand political development. Policy makers' conceptions of successful and unsuccessful families and the means they use to address unsuccessful families change over time in response to the work they hope to get families to do—though these changes may or may not achieve the ends desired. And while family values remains a constant rhetorical tool to secure political advantage, the content shifts over time, encouraging policy-based reinforcement of different normative elements of the family's function in civil society and for the state's purposes. The political construction of families must become a more central object of investigation. Appeals to "family values" require interrogation and should not be taken as a commitment at face value to concrete state support for families. We must consider what ideological work appeals to family values perform, and how particular configurations and articulations of family values resonate with particular political agendas.

While liberal political theory understands family as pre-political, this volume makes a compelling case that family is political, and that it is crucial to understanding how politics works. *Stating the Family* also illustrates why we must think of family as encompassing political frameworks beyond liberalism and its traditional division of public and private. While some elements of family and familial relations exist comfortably within individualistic liberal frameworks, family brings to the fore competing frameworks of status, community, vulnerability and responsibility, and affective bonds. These elements, only partially captured and formalized in law and policy, render family a unique and powerful space in the political lives of humans and human communities.

The chapters gathered here provide only a few examples of how illuminating the core intersections of family, policy, and politics expands and changes our understanding of how politics works and how and where political development occurs. We hope, through this volume, to advance a conversation with ample room for more voices.

About the Contributors

Gwendoline Alphonso is associate professor of political science at Fairfield University in Connecticut. She received her PhD and JSD from Cornell University and is the author of *Polarized Families, Polarized Parties: Contesting Values and Economics in American Politics* (University of Pennsylvania Press, 2018).

Ellen Ann Andersen is associate professor of political science at the University of Vermont. She is the author of *Out of the Closets and into the Courts: Legal Opportunity Structure and Gay Rights Litigation* (University of Michigan Press, 2005; paperback, updated, 2006) and has published work in various edited volumes and journals, including the *American Sociological Review*, the *American Journal of Political Science, PS*, and *Political Behavior*. She holds a PhD from the University of Michigan.

Richard Bensel is the Gary S. Davis Professor of Government at Cornell University. He is the author of many books, including *Yankee Leviathan: The Origins of Central State Authority in America, 1859–1877* (Cambridge University Press, 1991) and, most recently, *Passion and Preferences: William Jennings Bryan and the 1896 Democratic National Convention* (Cambridge University Press, 2008). He won the J. David Greenstone Prize for best book from the Politics and History Section of the American Political Science Association for *The Political Economy of American Industrialization, 1877–1900* (Cambridge University Press, 2000).

Naomi Cahn is Harold H. Greene Professor of Law at George Washington University School of Law. She is the author of a number of books; with June Carbone, she has written *Marriage Markets: How Inequality Is Remaking the American Family* (Oxford University Press, 2014) and *Red Families v. Blue Families* (Oxford University Press, 2010). She holds a JD from Columbia University and an LLM from Georgetown University.

June Carbone is Robina Professor in Law, Science, and Technology at the University of Minnesota Law School. She received her JD from Yale

Law School. Among her publications are *Marriage Markets: How Inequality Is Remaking the American Family* (Oxford University Press, 2014) and *Red Families v. Blue Families* (Oxford University Press, 2010), both with Naomi Cahn.

Alison Gash is associate professor of political science at the University of Oregon. She received her PhD from the University of California at Berkeley. She is the author of *Below the Radar: How Silence Can Save Civil Rights* (Oxford University Press, 2015). Her research on family and identity has been featured in *Law and Social Inquiry, Polity, New Political Science,* and *Politics, Groups and Identities* as well as media outlets such as *Politico, Washington Monthly, Fortune,* and *Slate.* She is the co-recipient of the Christian Bay Award for the best paper presented in *New Political Science* for her co-authored article "Illegalizing Families: State, Status and Deportability."

Eileen McDonagh is professor of political science at Northeastern University in Massachusetts. She received her PhD from Harvard University and is the author of several books, including *The Motherless State: Women's Political Leadership and American Democracy* (University of Chicago Press, 2009), which won the J. David Greenstone Prize for best book from the Politics and History Section of the American Political Science Association, and of *Breaking the Abortion Deadlock: From Choice to Consent* (Oxford University Press, 1996).

Tamara Metz is associate professor of political science and humanities and the director of the Center for Teaching and Learning at Reed College. She is the author of *Untying the Knot: Marriage, the State, and the Case for Their Divorce* (Princeton University Press, 2010); co-editor of *Justice, Politics, and the Family* (Paradigm Press, 2014), and has published work in various edited volumes and journals, including *Contemporary Political Theory, Politics & Gender, Social Theory and Practice, Journal of Politics, The Encyclopedia of Political Thought,* and *The Nation.* She received her PhD in government from Harvard University.

Carol Nackenoff is Richter Professor of Political Science at Swarthmore College in Pennsylvania. She received her PhD from the University of Chicago. She is author of *The Fictional Republic: Horatio Alger and American Political Discourse* (Oxford University Press, 1994) and co-edited *State-*

building from the Margins with Julie Novkov (University of Pennsylvania Press, 2014) and *Jane Addams and the Practice of Democracy* with Marilyn Fischer and Wendy Chmielewski (University of Illinois Press, 2009). She is the author of a number of articles, book chapters, encyclopedia entries, and the Oxford Bibliographies Online entry on the US Supreme Court.

Julie Novkov is professor of political science and of women's, gender, and sexuality studies at the University at Albany, SUNY. Her book, *Racial Union: Law, Intimacy, and the White State in Alabama, 1865–1954* (Michigan, 2008) was co-recipient of the APSA Ralph Bunch Award, and she is the author of *The Supreme Court and the Presidency* (CQ Press, 2013) and *Constituting Workers, Protecting Women* (University of Michigan Press, 2001). She has co-edited three volumes: *Statebuilding from the Margins* with Carol Nackenoff (University of Pennsylvania Press, 2014), *Race and American Political Development* with Joseph Lowndes and Dorian Warren (Routledge Press, 2008), and *Security Disarmed* with Barbara Sutton and Sandra Morgen (Rutgers University Press, 2008). She is the author of numerous other peer-reviewed articles and book chapters.

Elizabeth (Libby) Sharrow is assistant professor of political science and history at the University of Massachusetts at Amherst. She writes on the history of public policy and the politics of sex and gender in the United States. Her current research focuses on Title IX of the Education Amendments of 1972 and its application to sports, and she is completing a book manuscript tentatively titled *Allowed to Play, but Not to Win: Title IX and the Political Constructions of Sex and Gender in Public Policy.* Libby holds a MPP and a PhD from the University of Minnesota.

Joan C. Tronto is professor emerita of political science at the University of Minnesota and the City University of New York. She received her PhD from Princeton University. She is the author of *Democratic Caring: Markets, Justice and Equality* (New York University Press, 2013) and *Moral Boundaries: A Political Argument for an Ethic of Care* (Routledge, 1993).

Priscilla Yamin is associate professor of political science and department head of women's, gender and sexuality studies at the University of Oregon. She received her PhD from the New School for Social Research. She is the author of *American Marriage: A Political Institution* (University of Pennsylvania Press, 2012). Her work on family, marriage, and intersectionality has appeared in journals such as *New Political Science, Polity,* and *Politics, Groups and Identities.* She is the co-recipient of the Christian Bay Award for the best paper presented in *New Political Science* at the American Political Science Association annual meeting for her co-authored article "Illegalizing Families: State, Status and Deportability."

Case Index

Subject Index